MEDIA CONTROL
IN IRELAND
1923–1983

KIERAN WOODMAN

SOUTHERN ILLINOIS UNIVERSITY PRESS
CARBONDALE AND EDWARDSVILLE

Library of Congress Cataloging in Publication Data

Woodman, Kieran.
 Media control in Ireland 1923–1983.

 Includes index.
  1. Mass media–Censorship–Ireland. 2. Mass media–Law and legislation–Ireland. 3. Freedom of speech–Ireland–History–20th century. I. Title. p96.C42I738
1985 302.2'34'09415 84–27672 ISBN 0–8093–1240–9

CONTENTS

FOREWORD

Revolutionary ideology makes few plans for the stable peace on which its activity is predicated. The Irish in the 1920s were alone responsible for the conditions that would determine the quality of life that political freedom now made possible. Social control was, and continued to be, the dominant consideration. In exercising the rights of free citizens it became the policy of church and state to curtail their enjoyment on the fearful grounds that their exploitation might lead to abuse. First, for moral reasons, then for political purposes, freedom of expression was restricted by a form of censorship that was, with the passage of time, to grow progressively indefensible as understanding deepened of the nature of man and the functioning of his institutions.

This work examines the moral, political and intellectual climate in which occurred the changing conditions that governed communications over the period. It portrays the statutory and societal measures that sought to control literary output and contemporary media performance. It presents an outline of the history of government intervention in the conduct of the national broadcasting service's handling of news and features in general, and the reporting of events in Northern Ireland in particular. It considers the implications of the redefinition of individual responsibility for moral actions as a result of new directions in theology taken by the Catholic church. It reviews the problems of reporting terrorist activities which arise when government policy is at variance with the professional obligations of the journalist to provide for an informed electorate.

In writing this book I have contracted many debts inside and outside the university, both in the United States and in Ireland. To Dean Sharon Murphy of Marquette and her late husband, Jim, without whose encouragement this venture would never have even been initiated never mind brought to conclusion, I wish to express a profound and sincere thanks. To President Somit of SIU who continued the auspicious tradition of generously supporting Irish scholars working in the Mid-West, I affirm a sincere appreciation. Alan Cohen, of the Humanities Library of that University, has been a long-enduring friend and a resourceful scholar who has pointed out paths when even the direction was not altogether clear. Outside the University, Joyce Barbiere, Don and Francis MacDonald, Dan Riffe and many others provided an environment that encouraged ideas to develop and facilitated the means for testing hypotheses. Finally to someone who has always befriended Irish workers in communication, Emeritus Professor H. R. Long, no words can adequately pay tribute for a lifetime of dedication to high standards of professional behaviour, commitment to the art of enlarging the awareness of those who need and want to know, and the whole, seasoned with a wit and kindliness of which I was only one of the many beneficiaries.

In Ireland, working in a university, I derived considerable advantage from the fact that colleagues in History, Law, Philosophy, Politics and Theology from the National University of Ireland (Galway) read all or part of the manuscript to its obvious enhancement. I am indebted also to Alf Mac Lochlainn, Librarian, and all the staff of the college library in Galway for their help. Outside the University, both print and electronic media executives and consultants were most generous in providing information, data and responses to surveys.

Finally I would wish to acknowledge my debt to Seán MacBride who encouraged the venture in the first place and then did much to enlarge my awareness of the developments that have taken place in the elaboration of the concepts relating to human rights.

CHAPTER I

THE MEDIA IN IRELAND – AN OVERVIEW

The Republic of Ireland is a state of 3.4 million people with a surface area of 26,000 square miles. It is served by three national dailies, *The Irish Times, The Irish Press* and the *Irish Independent*, and one regional daily, *The Cork Examiner*. Total average daily circulation for all four newspapers is 424,937. There are two national evening newspapers, the *Evening Herald* and the *Evening Press*, and one regional evening, the *Evening Echo*, whose aggregate circulation amounts to 318,455. Four national Sunday newspapers, *The Sunday Independent, The Sunday Press, The Sunday Tribune* and the *Sunday World* have a combined sale of 1,055,378. There are over 50 weekly newspapers whose total circulation is in excess of 900,000. To these figures must be added the average daily sale of 210,000 British newspapers. Market surveys in Ireland have revealed that six out of ten people read a national daily or evening newspaper, and the same statistic holds for local newspapers. For Sunday newspapers the figure has been calculated at eight people out of every ten. In addition to the Irish newspapers at least 40% of the population regularly read a British Sunday newspaper.

To understand the communication situation in Ireland it is necessary to recall that the country has the lowest population density of any member of the European Economic Community. As a result of economic changes, the country is rapidly becoming industrialized, less than 25% of the employed workers being now found in agriculture. Over half the population is urban, 30% of whom live in and around Dublin. Education is compulsory up to the age of fifteen. About 51% of the relevant age cohort complete the second level cycle, and 14% of the population are to be found in third level at age twenty. The voting age is eighteen for national and local elections. Currently (1984) unemployment is running at around 16% with approximately 217,000 drawing unemployment benefit.

Irish daily newspapers originally reflected a particular ideology but competition for a shrinking market has resulted in a gradual homogeniza-tion. *The Irish Times* is certainly more liberal, *The Irish Press* more re-publican, and the *Irish Independent* is more conservative, but these labels are growing progressively less meaningful. While *The Irish Times* with the smallest circulation (80,000 approx.) is admired, none of the others is pre-pared to yield it permanent pride of place in any of the more influential sectors of journalism, such as business reports, political analysis or fea-tures reflecting national and international culture. Ashdown's appraisal would be hard to fault:

Irish morning newspapers pay more attention to political, social, economic and foreign news than their British counterparts, but considerably less than some other European newspapers. Criticism of the government and the church is vigor-ous, but the use of salacious materials, and coverage of crime and violence, is cir-cumspect.[1]

On a continuum between tabloid and quality, the three national dailies and the regional daily would lie towards, if not within, the latter category. Since *The Irish Times* appears in these pages as a reference source more frequently than do the others, it is worth pointing out that it is the paper of record, though, as has been said, that title will continue to be disputed. Since 1974 it has been a newspaper trust. Independent, liberal, and hav-ing now overcome it identification with the Protestant unionist minority of pre-independence, it devotes more of its columns to social, political and economic news than do the others and to that end maintains reporters in Belfast, London, Brussels and New York. Its appeal is mainly confined to the capital and large provincial cities. Analysis of its contents, in addi-tion to the above, would suggest that its policy is to cater for the better educated sector of the public. The Sunday and evening newspapers are aimed at a popular audience. The *Sunday World*, the only tabloid, is un-ique in being frankly sensational, gossipy and titillating, though here again it would be considered mild by British standards. Probably the most exciting event to happen in newspapers was the advent of the *Sunday Tribune*, which manages to combine radicalism with a derring-do inves-tigative journalism that does not eschew headlines more likely to be found among the tabloids.

Provincial newspapers have a circulation ranging between the 5,000 and 40,000 mark. They satisfy the need for local identity. Usually uncom-mitted politically, they have been known to take stands over issues which could have been neither profitable nor fashionable. Editors share with editors of the nationals complete freedom as to policy-formation. Range of contents and quality of treatment vary, but there is generally a high level of seriousness and a commendable accuracy in the treatment of af-

[1] Paul G. Ashdown, 'Irish Press Profiled', *Grassroots Editor*, Spring 1981, p. 3.

fairs within their circulation area. Subject-matter and language which the provincial newspaper-reader will accept in the national dailies would not be acceptable in the local paper. There is an unsubstantiated, but nonetheless prevalent, notion that the emigrant would prefer to receive the local rather than the national newspaper.

Major concentrations of newspaper holdings are always possible but have not happened to an extent that has caused any public outcry. There are groupings of newspapers around Dublin, the *Irish Independent* alone controlling three of them. On the other hand, local loyalties are strong enough to make take-overs less of a danger to local newspapers than is the projected local radio franchise. One distinction the newspaper industry in Ireland would gladly surrender is the rate of value added tax, imposed on both advertising and paper sales, which is the highest in Europe. Owners, media analysts and journalists make common cause in denouncing this short-sighted policy of placing a levy on this traditionally most reliable of arenas for the elaboration of the democratic process. In common with other countries, each oil crisis has seen newsprint costs soar so that financial difficulties, given the current recession which has reduced advertising by up to 40%, may not be too far away for many papers that would in different circumstances be commercially viable. In the midst of these problems it is surprising that there does not appear to have been any recrudescence of a demand by vested interests for the exclusion or additional taxing of British newspapers. This tolerance has been to the benefit of the reader in that standards are maintained as to production, layout, editorial content and innovation. Informal on-the-job training on a provincial newspaper where the journalist learned to cope with the wide variety of news that occurred in the communities he or she served is usually followed by promition to one of the nationals, where facilities are available for staff to specialize in such areas as industrial relations, economics, education, health and hygiene, women's affairs and in other matters. Postgraduate and non-degree courses in journalism have been on offer in technical institutes, and it is likely that future recruitment will draw more and more from this source, at least in the metropolitan area.

The Easter Week Rising in 1916 was the first anti-colonial struggle ever waged by a territory or nation which was part of the British Empire. It was also, at least in the patriotic hagiography of the time, the occasion for the world's first broadcast when the insurgents used a ship's transmitter to broadcast their communiques about the insurrection in Morse code to any one who was listening. 'It seems to have had an extremely low TAM-rating.'[1] Regular broadcasting began in 1926, and today for all its small-

---

[1] Mícheál Ó hUanacháin, 'The Broadcasting Dilemma', *Administration*, 28:1 (1980) p. 33.

ness by comparison with its British neighbour, its management has to contend with all the problems facing the latter and a few local difficulties as well. The Broadcasting Anthority Act of 1960 was, and is, the parent act governing the control and operation of what is now a public broadcasting service, renamed Radio Telefís Éireann (RTÉ) in 1965. It is responsible for two television channels with approximately 70 hours weekly viewing each, two radio services providing 18–20 hours of daily programmes each, and an Irish-language MF and VHF programme which is on the air each day for five to eight hours. The Authority is made up of seven to nine members appointed by the Government and entrusted with the responsibility of determining through a Director-General the policy and strategy of what is in effect a semi-state body. Financing of broadcasting has been dictated by the economic situation of the country which could not support a non-commercial public system like the BBC and by its cultural policies which could not tolerate a totally commercial one as found in the United States. What has been decided in fact is that resources are to be found both from licensing fees (the amount of which must receive the approval of the government) and from advertising revenue which in itself is limited by the National Prices Commission's role in determining changes, by the Minister's say in fixing the maximum amount of advertising permitted, and, to a certain extent, by its intrinsic obligations as a public service. Since its establishment RTÉ has had to contend with certain factors, some unique, others of a kind facing any broadcasting service in a country with limited moneys at its disposal. There is the obligation to be impartial, to eschew editorializing and to refrain from having views identified as those of the Authority or its employees. There is Section 31 of the Broadcasting Authority Act of 1960 which empowers the responsible Minister for Posts and Telegraphs to issue a directive instructing RTÉ to refrain from broadcasting material that could conceivably promote the aims of a subversive organization. RTÉ also suffers from its apparent monopoly position as a broadcasting service in that there is no other broadcasting service answerable inside the State which might share with it the difficult task of defining how far democratically-elected politicians should be prepared to go on the air in accepting the criticism they have no option but to endure from the newspapers. While the ambiguity of covering subversive organizations was to be reduced by the drawing up of guidelines after the 1976 Act, there remains a sense of uncertainty so that self-censorship is always possible in the presentation of controversial issues. It will be argued here that the availability of British television, initially, to all of urban Ireland in 1984, will make the maintenance of restraints no longer good sense even on the narrow grounds of political self-interest.

Broadcasting in Ireland suffers from a scarcity of resources and a scarcity of talent commensurate with the appetite of its consumers. Its programmes are very much influenced by print norms which the paucity of training sources does little to correct. Organization problems and union problems are probably not unique to RTÉ but there have been comments and criticism that weaknesses in command structure, coupled with an alleged industrial relations militancy among rank-and-file members, have not allowed the service to realize its maximum potential.[1]

In addition to personnel problems, the service has been hindered by an inadequate communications infrastructure which can impede the coverage of local stories. As long as RTÉ is 'statutorily bound to find both current and capital expenditure from current revenue,'[2] which it is unable to control, problems will continue. While this situation is being improved, there does not appear to be total consensus as to the parameters of the station's remit. For many years, for example, Northern Ireland was ignored. Then, in the mid-sixties, that situation was rectified and, prior to the issuing of the directive in the early seventies, the service was superior to that which the British broadcasting authorities were offering. Only now does it appear to be appropriate and possible to conceive of broadcasting to Northern Ireland as a contribution to the reduction of tension. However, given the relatively short life-span of the Authority, the fact that technology, in this field as in others, has outstripped man's power to harness it to his will, the one permanently debilitating factor in the operation of the system has been, and continues to be, the reserve powers of government which contribute an additional dimension to the uncertainties of planning in an industry where forward planning is esential.

The defining characteristic of a national television service is its home production. The economics of television are, on the other hand, for a small country such that it is always less expensive to import than to produce. Costs are related to size of viewing audience and in Ireland this consideration means that they can be reduced by as much as fifty percent and upwards. Whatever about cultural items, however, news broadcasting and current affairs are almost exclusively the concern of the national station. Admittedly the view may be narrower and even insular, but a neutral republic must discover what it is thinking and about what it should be thinking. In presenting the agenda and relevant documents, Irish television must compete, in sophistication and in depth of treatment, with its more powerful external competitors if its message is to be accorded the desired attention. The days of 'talking heads' are over; the audience seeks to be reassured on the basis of its own judgment, and, to that end, authentic, immediate and intelligible evidence must be forthcoming. RTÉ has endeavoured to live up to these standards but there have been constraints, official-financial and unofficial-political. Like their print colleagues the authority has to worry about the Censorship of Publications

---

[1] Peter B. Orlick, 'Systemic Limitations to Irish Broadcast Journalism', *Journal of Broadcasting*, 20:4 (1976) pp. 471ff.
[2] Desmond Fisher, *Broadcasting In Ireland* (London: Routledge, 1978) p. 79.

Act, the Offenses Against the State Act, the laws of libel, trade unions, advertisers, and other management problems. Nowhere has it been suggested that collectively these constituted a greater problem than a television-conscious Minister whose fear of its impact is matched only by his desire to harness it for his own, and his party's, advantage. In the last analysis, newspapers can say what they choose about the government of the day, this side of libel and defamation. In RTÉ, everything can be broadcast most of the time, and most can be broadcast every time, but not everything every time.

In Ireland there is no Freedom of Information Act; indeed with the Official Secrets Act and the internal regulations (often abused for administrative and political convenience) that govern what civil servants may divulge, there is a very definite barrier placed on making information available. While restrictive practices exist everywhere, their prevalence is more common – or believed to be more common – in Ireland. People, therefore, on account of the smallness of size and population, have long been accustomed to turning to other sources. Market research surveys show that family and church affiliations have played a major role in the formation of views held on moral questions for every three out of four persons interviewed. On other matters, the media do play a role but principally in providing background information and updating data useful for forming opinions. Television has not been found to change political opinions. What the viewer takes from a programme either confirms his original view, reinforces existing beliefs or stabilizes his attitudes. Further surveys have shown that people get about 17% of their information from the print media, over 50% from television and 20% from radio. The remainder regarded family and friends as their main sources of information. Six out of ten people hear the news on radio each day. Nine out of ten households have a television set, and of these six will view the main new bulletin of the day and the 40-minutes current affairs programme that folows. But the public service position of RTÉ should not in consequence be equated with being the dominant influence in shaping people's opinions. The increasing availability of British programmes provides alternative analyses of events and different aspects of contemporary culture. Discrepancies reinforce a national distrust of official sources and confirm a dispersed community in the conviction that it is not safe to allow anyone to do the thinking that one should do oneself. While recognizing the responsible position print and electronic media adopt, too many election results have been too ineptly forecast to suggest that they were doing the elector's thinking for them.

By and large, whether television or radio, national or provincial newspaper, the functions of the media are usually discharged to the satisfaction of the public, the proof of which is their readiness to pay for them.

The experience of seeing each day how press, radio and television discharge the role of public watchdog inspires confidence that the supervision and scrutiny of legislation, the safeguarding of citizens' rights and the ventilation of their grievances are all being undertaken in the service of democracy. The media are evolving a complementarity which will·enhance the quality of the individual's participation in shaping his own life. What has marred this process which permits, through knowledge, the enlargement of the human spirit is a censorship that loses sight of its purpose, or fails to redefine its aim in a changing environment.

CHAPTER 2

CENSORSHIP AND IRISH LAW

Control of freedom of expression has over the period been determined by constitutional and statutory measures. Their purpose reflects the moral and political temper of the times. This chapter seeks to trace their development as Irish society grew more self-confident in the efficacy of its institutions and more reliant on its own legal solutions to the problems created by a society growing progressively more media-dependent. It examines the differential approach to natural law in general and the conditions governing freedom of expression in particular. It outlines the establishment of a broadcasting system and foreshadows some of the difficulties that arise when the enjoyment of internationally approved rights is seen by governments to be at variance with the public interest.

Ireland has had in its sixty years of independence two Constitutions. The first, in 1922, was, for its period, liberal and democratic. Religious freedom and equality were guaranteed, as were freedom of speech, freedom of association, freedom from arbitrary arrest and the right to elementary education. The second Constitution, in 1937, retained these same basic rights but there are differences in emphasis. First is the fact that the document is an Irish production and not part of the negotiated outcome of the cessation of hostilities with the British. Second, its content reflects Catholic thinking in the guarantees given to the family, in its rejection of divorce, in the affirmation of man's right to ownership and in according a special position (deleted in 1972 by the Fifth Amendment) to the Catholic Church. This Constitution would generally be regarded by historians as the articulation of a political consensus about the nature of the social contract, as understood by pragmatists in a difficult economic period, who were yet conscious of the values of parliamentary democracy, of the teaching of the papal encyclicals, and of the need to create a solid national identity that would justify and reinforce the independence that had been won. The Catholic ethos was in the ascendant.

The Irish State appeared wholly committed to the maintenance of Catholic values, and it was difficult to see what further evolution in Church-State relations was possible. If further development did take place after 1937, this was because the concept of what was involved in a State being committed to Catholic values was changing. It was coming to comprise a particular attitude not only to moral issues but to social issues as well.[1]

How this attitude was to evolve in relation to the freedom of speech may be seen from an examination of the development of thinking about the Constitution itself and that body of law that impacted, directly or indirectly, on its enjoyment. The departure point will therefore be in a confessional Constitution, reflecting the wishes of a people 92% Catholic, the autonomously defined rights of whose Church it goes almost but not quite the whole way in conceding.

In charting the course of Irish democracy, certain historical events and judicial decisions must be registered in plotting the graph of political control by the government in the life of its citizens. A few years after independence had been won and the State established, the power of the electorate to influence policy was modified by the abolition of the Initiative and the Referendum from the 1922 Constitution. The power of the Senate to hold up a Bill was further reduced by the 1937 Constitution to a maximum of 90 days, and this period nowadays may be further reduced if the Taoiseach certifies that the Bill is urgent. Parliamentary institutions have been altered so as to enhance the importance of party discipline and control by the Executive. The independence of action of the individual has been progressively eroded as loyalty and conformity have come more and more to be recognized as the price the individual member must pay for organizational support.

In common with other European countries, and particularly since the end of World War II, successive Irish governments have been concerned to relieve want, encourage economic development, improve facilities, equalize opportunities, better living conditions and succour the infirm, the weak and the needy. As the complexity of resulting social welfare legislation is in direct ratio to its volume, Dáil Éireann has had to surrender the creation of subordinate legislation to the process of Ministerial Orders. This delegation by the Oireachtas has allowed the Executive to acquire considerable power in interpreting and implementing matters of principle as well as of detail arising from the administration of these laws. Granted that the regulations on which such powers are based must lie on the table of the Dáil, the fact that little or no provision has been made for consultation prior to their drafting has meant that little or no check has been kept on the assumption of the powers already mentioned. The for-

---

[1] J.H. Whyte, *Church and State in Modern Ireland 1923–70* (Dublin: Gill and Macmillan, 1971), p. 61.

mula that is part of all Irish Acts – whereby 'the Minister may by order make regulations prescribing all or any of the following matters and things' – has been aptly characterized as 'unconfined and vagrant' whereas such delegations of legislative authority should be 'canalized with banks that keep it from overflowing.'[1]

Another aspect to be borne in mind in gauging the measure of the citizen's control is the delimitation of the authority of the courts as more and more administrative bodies are set up to exercise functions of a judicial nature. Many of these bodies are not obliged to give an oral hearing, furnish reasons for decisions, disclose evidence or indicate persons consulted. Provided the matter has been dealt with in accordance with the Act, it is not always possible for the courts to review the Minister's decision, giving grounds for the contention that legalism transcends justice. While the Constitution (Article 40.4.1) does guarantee that 'No person shall be deprived of his personal liberty save in accordance with the law,' the Supreme Court has ruled that this guarantee may not be invoked to invalidate any Act, and hence any action taken under the Act which impairs the personal liberty of the individual (but see Chapters 8 and 9). In a similar manner access to the courts may be barred if the order objected to is adjudged to be an administrative decision taken by a statutorily competent body rather than a judicial decision. It is arguable that in Ireland (as in the U.K.) the optimal tension that should exist among the Executive, Legislature and Judiciary has been replaced by Government dominance. Nor is this new. Cabinet governments to succeed have, since 1937, depended on political parties, on government within a government, on collective Cabinet responsibility, and on powers vested in the Taoiseach to bring about the dissolution of the Dáil which can act either as carrot or stick. Operating at any tolerable level of efficiency,

the system gives the government control over Parliament. When a government has attained a position of such strength and supremacy, it is very difficult to curb it and no Constitution is worth much to the people.[2]

The question must therefore be asked, 'Are the rights accruing to citizens being eroded by the cumulative impact of positive laws in the social domain?'

The preamble to the Irish Constitution of 1937 begins with the words:

In the name of the most Holy Trinity, from Whom is all authority and to Whom, as our final end, all actions of both men and States must be referred.

We, the people of Éire,

Humbly acknowledging all our obligations to our Divine Lord, Jesus Christ...

It will be apparent in thus recognizing God as the source of all law, natural

---

[1] Judgement of Mr. Justice Cardozo in *Schlecter Poultry Corporation* vs *United States* (295 U.S. a/351).
[2] F. C. King, 'Our Constitution and Our Freedom', *Christus Rex* 7 (1953), p. 508.

law from which constitutional rights derive was understood as the expression of the Eternal Law. In this view rights are not created, they are acknowledged, and as such do not rest upon the Constitution itself. They are designated by Article 40.3 as personal rights in contrast to those legal rights which are created by legislation. One of these is the right to express oneself, 'subject to public order and morality.' Others inhere in the family, in education, in the practice of religion and in private ownership. What is the nature and extent of these rights?

Chief Justice Kennedy in a minority decision[1] said that since all lawful authority derived from God, any legislative or judicial act repugnant to the natural law would of necessity be unconstitutional and invalid. This view stands in sharp contrast to the positivist notion of parliamentary sovereignty implicit in Article 40 of the Constitution which by the addition of the words 'save in accordance with the law' would appear to qualify rights, held through their derivation to be absolute. Sir William Blackstone, two hundred years previously, had written,

Man, considered as a creature must necessarily be subject to the laws of his Creator, for he is entirely a dependent being... This Will of his Maker is called the Law of Nature... This law of nature being coeval with mankind, and dictated by God himself is of course superior in obligation to any other. It is binding over all the globe, in all countries, and at all times: no human laws are of any validity, if contrary to this: and such of them as are valid derive all their force and all their authority, mediately or immediately from this origin.[2]

As far as natural rights are concerned therefore, in Blackstone's view, not only do they not require any sanction by human law but no human legislation has the 'power to abridge or destroy them.' In principle, the Irish people do not need a constitution to ensure that their natural rights are not subordinated to positive laws. Parliament in the Irish Constitution is not the supreme law giver. The Irish people gave themselves the present Constitution which they understood to be the outcome of, and which they interpreted according to, the philosophy implicit in the Preamble. Granted just as a Constitution is man-made, the product and servant of its times, so too will its interpretation in relation to statutory law be the outcome of pressures, fashions of thinking and political imperatives. However, the fact remains that it is upon the basis of the principles enshrined in the Preamble that the nature and extent of the powers exercised by the Oireachtas are to be evaluated. Certainly the particular application of the Constitution requires the philosophical consensus of its time, as well as judicial experience, to discover the significance of natural law in each manifestation of contemporary human conduct. To counteract any pas-

[1] *The State* v *Lennon* (1935). I.R. 170, 183.
[2] Gareth Jones (ed), *The Sovereignty of the Law – Selection from Blackstone's Commentaries on the Laws of England* (London: Macmillan, 1978) vol. I, section II, p. 28.

sing waywardness of interpretation, it must be remembered that Ireland is a signatory to the *Universal Declaration of Human Rights* (1948) and to the *Convention for the Protection of Human Rights and Fundamental Freedoms* (1950). It also, as has been seen, recognizes the truth of the Christian religion. How its citizens enjoy the rights that derive from these statements, which aggregatively continue to articulate the natural law, can bear examination.

Natural law is to be understood as that prescriptive behavior appropriate to the nature of man living as a rational human being in society. It confers rights and imposes obligations on him as an individual and as a member of society. To discharge these obligations, the rights with which Man is endowed are inviolable. Those rights, deemed to embody the quality of life which its citizens demand, are written into the country's constitution. The expression of these rights has brought about certain consequences:

Constitutions always have to strike a balance between safeguarding the individual's rights and permitting parliament to regulate them for the common good. It has become manifest that the Constitution by using different phraseology has in respect of certain of these rights weighted the balance in favor of Parliament. And, secondly, where the language implies or affirms a theory of natural law based on St. Thomas, the balance is more strongly tilted towards the guarantee of the individual's rights. No reason is to be found in the Constitution as to why these guarantees should be so differently expressed. But they are: and the effect has been to create a sort of hierarchy of rights in which some have more effective guarantees than others.[1]

As a comparative perusal will substantiate, language varies relative to the Christian, as opposed to the juridical, stress found in the Irish Constitution.

Articles 40 to 44 deal with human rights. Article 40 is concerned with rights dealing with the person, the right to personal liberty, the inviolability of the dwelling, the right to free expression of opinion, to peaceful assembly, and to form associations. All citizens are deemed to be equal before the law and the State undertakes to guarantee and vindicate their rights. Article 41 deals with family rights, Article 42 with educational rights, Article 43 with property rights and Article 44 with religion.

In Article 40, a distinction of some significance is drawn between, on the one hand, the enjoyment of the right to personal liberty and to inviolability of the dwelling which can only be restricted 'in accordance with the law,' and, on the other hand, the right to freedom of expression and to freedom of association which are 'subject to public order and morality.'

[1] Declan Costello, 'The Natural Law and the Irish Constitution', *Studies* 45(1956) pp. 404–405.

The first phrase, 'in accordance with the law' is analogous to the American 'due process.' When, however, legislation was introduced that was intended to provide for the arrest and detention at the State's pleasure of those engaged in activities judged to be prejudicial to the preservation of public peace (Offenses Against the State (Amendment) Bill, 1940) the suppression of the safeguarding 'in accordance with the law' was declared to be constitutional, on the grounds, that while the natural right to personal freedom still existed,

There is nothing in this Clause of the preamble which could be invoked to necessitate the sacrifice of the common good in the interests of the freedom of the individual.[1]

As for the State's guarantee enshrined in the Constitution 'by its laws to defend and vindicate the personal rights of the citizen,' the Supreme Court added that this guarantee applied just as much to all the citizens as it did to the particular,

and the duty of determining the extent to which the rights of any particular citizen or class of citizen can properly be harmonized with the right of the citizen as a whole seems to us to be a matter which is peculiarly within the province of the Oireachtas and any attempt by the Court to control the Oireachtas in the exercise of their function, would, in our opinion, be an usurpation of its authority.

By this decision, the Irish Courts declined to play a constructionist role in the formulation of the contemporary meaning of the natural rights of the individual, which the Supreme Court in the United States had for example assumed, and handed back to the Oireachtas the charge of determining their absoluteness in the light of what legislators considered necessary for the public needs. In effect 'in accordance with the law' meant in accordance with whatever law a political party enjoying a majority in parliament chose to introduce as long as it was determined to be in the interest of the common good. The rights of the citizen to his personal liberty and to the inviolability of his dwelling could now be infringed by ministerial order, and just so long as the action was done in accordance with a law passed by the Oireachtas, the Supreme Court would not interfere.

It will be remembered that the right to free expression of opinion, together with the right to freedom of assembly and to freedom of association were described as being 'subject to public order and morality.' This qualification has been interpreted by the courts to mean that the legislature has power to regulate and control the exercise of the right. Each Act, or order made under the administration of an Act, can in theory be investigated by the courts to determine whether executive action was an infringement of a right guaranteed by the Constitution, or whether it sought only to regulate or control its exercise. By contrast with the previous per-

[1] 1940. I.R. p. 479.

sonal rights of personal liberty and inviolability of dwelling, which can be infringed 'in accordance with the law,' such observances will not inhibit the courts from declaring a law to be unconstitutional if the enjoyment of these latter rights is denied. In summary it would appear that habeas corpus can be suspended and the inviolability of the dwelling disregarded if the Oireachtas passes a law that is in the interests of the common good, while any alleged infringement or impairment of the right to freedom of speech or to freedom of assembly must be tested against what enjoyment of the right entails in the spirit of the Preamble.

This distinction between 'in accordance with the law' and 'subject to public order and morality' that characterizes the Personal Rights of Article 40 is not as significant, however, as that which exists between it and the other Articles dealing with fundamental rights.

This Article 40 had declared the existence of certain personal rights which the State had undertaken to defend and vindicate. There is no statement of the nature of these rights or that they are inalienable or superior to positive law. But when the rights in the following Articles (i.e. Articles 41, 42, 43 and 44) are set out it is of interest to note with how much greater force they are stressed and how much more absolutely they are guaranteed; and also that for the first time in this set of Articles, the concept of natural law and of rights superior to positive law appears.[1] The Family is recognized 'as a moral institution possessing inalienable and imprescriptible rights, antecedent and superior to all positive law.' The State 'guarantees to respect the inalienable right' of parents to provide for the eductation of their children. Again in Article 43 on private property, 'The State acknowledges that man, in virtue of his rational being, has the natural right, antecedent to positive law, to the private ownership of external goods,' and it is only with the Article guaranteeing 'freedom of conscience and the free profession and practice of religion' that the proviso of 'subject to public order and morality' reappears. It is an interesting commentary on Irish values that it was in a case concerning the disposition of property that the courts made the most emphatic declaration of the right of the individual against that of the common good and declared that the determination of the circumstances was a matter for the courts to decide and not for the legislature.

It is sufficient for us to say that this State by its Constitution, acknowledges that the right to private property is such a right [i.e. a natural right] and that this right is antecedent to all positive law. This, in our opinion, means that man by virtue and as an attribute of his human personality, is so entitled to such a right that no positive law is competent to deprive him of it...[2]

Enough has been written here to underscore the difference of approach to

---

[1] Costello, 'The Natural Law and the Irish Constitution', p. 409.
[2] *Buckley and Others* v. *Attorney General and Another* 1950, I.R. p. 67.

this matter of property and to personal rights of which freedom of expression is obviously in a democratic society, dedicated to the notion of parliamentary government, one of undoubted significance. In the court's judgment certain rights had to be harmonized with the rights of citizens as a whole, and the measure of harmonization was a matter for the government. By contrast, the courts appear to have higher regard for those fundamental rights whose relationships to the Christian view of the natural law had been propagated in Ireland by a scholasticism that had for generations pre-empted the philosophical foreground. Not so fortunate were the others whose language revealed their secular and rationalist antecedents. At the same time it does appear somewhat odd that the inalienable and imprescriptible rights accorded to the family should not in equal measure be available to the individual. It is difficult to accept that a country which would reject the accusation of a juridical positivism does indeed decide cases on their merits rather than on the basis of the principles implicit in the natural law.[1] Whether the courts have been active and determined enough, not only in presenting the dignity of the individual as an essential basis of the social structure which unites all men, but also in preserving their own area of competence, is a matter for conjecture. Article 34 of the Constitution lays down that 'Justice shall be administered in courts established by law by judges appointed in the manner provided by this Constitution.' The behavior of a Minister who unilaterally interns a citizen on suspicion or who arbitrarily denies him access to the media because of his associations does not offer much reassurance. Thus the reality of an omnipotent parliament after the British model grows apace in defiance of the division of powers laid out in the Constitution. And as it grows, the risks to openness, fairness and impartiality as the basis for administering the national polity increase.

Reference has already been made to the guarantee of the liberty of discussion in passing, but because of its significance for the development of this exposition, it is appropriate to quote the relevant section in full. Article 40.6.1.i affirms:

The State guarantees liberty for the exercise of the following rights, subject to public order and morality:

i. The right of the citizens to express freely their convictions and opinions.

The education of public opinion being, however, a matter of such grave import to the common good, the State shall endeavour to ensure that organs of public opinion, such as the radio, the press, the cinema, while preserving their rightful liberty of expression, including criticisms of Government policy, shall not be used to undermine public order or morality or the authority of the State. The publication or

---

[1] C. Gavan Duffy, 'The Irish Constitution and Current Problems', *Christus Rex* 12 (1958) p. 110 and passim.

utterance of blasphemous, seditious, or indecent matter is an offense which shall be punishable in accordance with the law.

Kelly[1] points out problems in the wording of the sub-section, the first arising from the semantic inadequacy of 'organs of public opinion.' The press, in Ireland as elsewhere, expresses the outlook of its owners, and while public opinion may be represented, that representation carries no further than the measure by which it agrees with their policy, or is susceptible of interpretation by their fallible servants. It may seek to form public opinion: rarely will it confine itself to acting as its vehicle. Again, does the State intend to 'ensure' that the Press, which is privately owned, will conform to the public interest in the same way as it would with an organ of opinion that was publicly owned? The second problem will of course lie in exercising the 'rightful liberty of expression, including criticism of Government policy' without, at the same time, incurring the charge of undermining 'public order or morality or the authority of the State.' When does such criticism slip over the edge of fair comment and descend into the abyss of subversion?

This indeterminate and ambivalent language, at once cautionary and at the same time purporting to promote the common good, a dual characteristic which indeed attends all the fundamental constitutional guarantees except those relating to property and family, is a departure from the tradition of accepting English norms as guidelines in the shaping of Irish jurisprudence. Prior restraint was to be Ireland's own contribution to the communicative process.

Taking the last paragraph of the quoted section of the Constitution first, as making least impact on the communicative process, spoken blasphemy is an offense at common law. Written blasphemy is covered by the Defamation Act 1961, section 13(1), which lays down penalties to be applied. No prosecutions have taken place in the life of the State.

As regards the publication of obscene and indecent matter the solution which has been arrived at in Ireland in relation to printed material and films will be considered in due course. Insofar as theatrical performances are concerned, the Dublin producer of Tennessee Williams's *Rose Tattoo* was charged in 1957 with 'showing for gain an indecent and profane performance.' The case went no further than the District Court where it was dismissed.

As for sedition, it is in Irish law an indictable misdemeanor, and, as in England, takes within its purview, as will be seen, any word or writing calculated to disturb the peace of the State or to incite others in such an attempt. Again, as in England, it is enough that the sedition be uttered. It is not necessary that the public peace be disturbed, since it is the intent, and not the consequences, which constitutes the offense. Further, it is not per-

[1] J.M. Kelly, 'The constitutional position of RTÉ', *Administration* 15:3 (1967) pp. 204 ff.

missible to argue justification on the grounds that the published material has been copied from foreign newspapers and indeed the importation of foreign newspapers and periodicals may be banned if it is considered that they contain seditious or other unlawful matter. As a matter of record, no action has ever been taken under the headings of seditious libel and seditious conspiracy since prosecutions are more feasible by various statutory Acts, most of which have been passed since the adoption of the Constitution of 1937. What these Acts are, how they impinge on freedom of expression and how they justify intervention to ensure that citizens' 'rightful liberty of expression ... shall not be used to undermine public order or morality or the authority of the State' will repay investigation.

Military censorship of publications operated during the Civil War, 1922–1923. The murder of the Minister for Justice, Kevin O'Higgins, in 1927 was the occasion for the Public Safety Act of 1927 that prohibited publication of any statement from, or on behalf of, an unlawful association. Four years later, when, on the occasion of further political violence, the 1922 Constitution was amended to make any such publications an infraction of the Basic Law, a successful prosecution was brought by the Cosgrave government against the editor of *The Irish Press* for seditious libel. The Offenses against the State Act of 1939 made it unlawful to publish 'any letter, article or communication which is sent or contributed or purports to be sent or contributed by or on behalf of an unlawful organisation.' The Offenses against the State (Amendment) Act 1972 supplements this provision by section 4(1) which states that:

(a) Any public statement made orally, in writing or otherwise ... that constitutes an interference with the course of justice shall be unlawful.

(b) A statement ... shall be deemed to constitute an interference with the course of justice if it is intended ... directly or indirectly to influence any court, person or authority concerned with the institution, conduct or defense of any civil or criminal proceedings.

The Emergency Powers Act (1939) authorized and provided for the censorship and control of newspapers as well as placing restrictions on the electronic media and on the free movement of the mails. This measure was normal for a country seeking to maintain a neutrality in the presence of a worldwide conflict. Its provisions in relation to communications ceased to be in force with the expiry of the Act in 1945, but its influence was to continue for many years afterwards. During the war, however, the Irish, if they did not withdraw from the realities of comtemporary history, were prepared, in the interests of a 'sacred egoism' and 'the nightmarish satisfaction of looking on in comparative safety at horrors we can do nothing to prevent,'[1] to forego some of the basic rights accorded to them by

---

[1] Michael Tierney, 'Ireland and the Anglo-Saxon heresy', *Studies* 30 (1940) p. 2.

the Constitution. Unfortunately, the experience was to be renewed thirty years later when their island isolation was no longer sufficient to afford protection. As regards the divulging of information considered vital to the preservation of the State, the Official Secrets Acts, 1963, building on the British Acts of 1911 and 1920, and on the Emergency Powers Act cited above, makes it an offense to communicate any official information relating to the Defense Forces, the police, fortifications, contracts, or 'any other matter whatsoever which would or might be prejudicial to the safety or preservation of the State.' While interference with a letter or postal packet is deemed to be an offense under the Post Office Act of 1908, powers are available to the responsible Minister to open, detain, or delay any such communication under warrant from his hand. Telephone tapping appears to rest on the same basis.

As regards specific press legislation, Ireland took over existing English law in this regard as in so many others. The first important statute is the Libel Act of 1843 which permitted a defense plea that the publication was without malice or gross negligence provided that a full apology had been tendered in appropriate circumstances. The Law of Libel (Amendment) Act, 1888, protected fair and accurate reports published in newspapers unless it could be shown that they had been published maliciously. As will be seen, reports of court proceedings are further limited by the nature of the alleged offense. Reports of parliamentary debates were privileged even if defamatory statements were included, since it was assumed that the advantage to the general public outweighed any personal injury, and that the fact of publication was understood as permitting a rebuttal. The Defamation Act of 1961 has codified the law 'relating to absolute and qualified privilege, together with privilege subject to explanation, in the case of publication by the press or over the radio and television, of matters which are alleged to be defamatory.'[1]

One limitation on the freedom of expression in any country is of course the concept of contempt of court. Criticism of the courts is permissible, provided it remain within the bounds of reasonableness and good faith. Lord Arkin, in a judgment cited with approval by the Irish Bench, stated that 'Justice is not a cloistered virtue: she must be allowed to suffer the scrutiny, and respectful, even though outspoken, comments of ordinary men.'[2] The history of comment on the conduct of legal proceedings in Ireland does not persuade that this approach has been everywhere adopted. What is probably more disturbing to the media is the fact that it is never quite clear what is permissible and what is unacceptable since the circumstances which prompt each utterance are so varied, and the prece-

[1] Gerard A. Lee, 'Fundamental Rights in the Irish Constitution', *Christus Rex* 23:2 (1969) p. 146.
[2] *Arabard* v. *Attorney General for Trinidad and Tobago* (1936).

dents so few and dispersed over time, as to make it impossible to predict with certainty what will be the outcome. An example of this dilemma is to be found in contrasting cases twenty years apart. On the one hand, Hanna J. in *Attorney-General* v. *O'Kelly*, citing Pallas C.J., stated:

The court acts ... not out of regard to the particular judge. What it looks at is the dignity of the administration of justice, and it acts ... against that which is aimed against the administration of justice, and against what amounts to a defamation of the court which is engaged in the administration of justice. Within these main limitations the law permits, to the advantage of the public, free, full, severe but respectful criticism.[1]

A contrast to this reaction is that of Gavan Duffy in *Attorney-General* v. *Connolly* where the defendant had written an editorial in a magazine named *Resurgence* in December, 1946, in which there appeared the following:

Henry White: Another soldier of Ireland has fallen into the hands of the Republic's enemies and is fast approaching his martyrdom. This much is certain, if the present course of Fianna Fáil [the majority political party] justice is allowed its way. Henry White has been handed over by the black police of the North to their equally shaded brothers of the South. And now he awaits his death, which sentence will inevitably be passed on him after his mockery of a trial before the Special Criminal Court is over.[2]

White had been charged with the murder of a policeman, Garda George Mordant. He was found guilty and sentenced to death five days *after* the editorial complained of had been seized. The Judge on finding Connolly guilty of criminal contempt and on requiring of him that he enter into recognizance of the sum of £50 to be of good behavior for twelve months, stated:

The defendant asserts his right of free speech, but the right of free speech is not a license to undermine public order... This Court will always, I trust, be vigilant to protect the constitutional right of fair criticism ... but a political opponent cannot be allowed, under cover of an attack on the Executive, to present a Court to public obloquy as a mischievous and wicked sham.[3]

Two punishable contempts, one for the publication of insulting comments on a judge's conduct of a trial, the other for imputing predictability of conviction, but both uttered before a verdict was announced, are not without a measure of consistency through there is a difference (probably justified) in the learned judge's comments on how the freedom of expression is to be enjoyed.

A third case in the same year (1946) provides an additional yardstick of comparison. Michael O'Ryan was a Waterford County Councillor who

---

[1] 1928. I.R. 308 pp. 329–330.
[2] Ross Connolly, Editorial. *Resurgence*, December, 1946, p. 2.
[3] 1947. I.R. p. 213.

sent an abusive letter to a Circuit Court Judge subsequent to the termination of proceedings relating to a disturbance of the peace. The comments included:

You, Sir, were foisted on the judicial bench at a time when legal ability was not the best qualification best fitted to lead it. You are as poor at marshalling your facts as you were mediocre at law.

I wonder if indeed ... the letter came from the local lodge of the Grand Orient and embossed with the square and compass, how would it be treated by your Lordship?

Your ilk and breed in this country are the inheritors of lands, castle and wealths secured by the brute laws of robbery, spoliage and confiscation of the property of Catholic Ireland.

Mr. O'Ryan's letter was read out at a meeting of the County Council and was duly reported in the *Waterford Standard* whose editor was David Boyd. Before the case came to court both O'Ryan and Boyd apologized and O'Ryan withdrew all the allegations and the contents of the letter. He was fined £50, and £25 towards the costs of the case. No order was made against Boyd at all. In fact, Gavan Duffy J. said that he had 'rendered a public service to the administration of justice by publishing it.' The President of the same Court said:

Judges and others in authority are open to criticism. Fair and free criticism is allowable and should be welcomed. We must safeguard the rights of the citizen and the rights of newspaper editors. The last thing I would wish is that citizens should feel that the Courts are too ready to use against legitimate criticism the powerful weapon of attachment for comtempt of court. I would rather err on the other side.[1]

These three cases are adduced not to question the validity of the findings but to underline the problems confronting the communicator who feels encouraged on the one hand by the fact that 'justice is not a cloistered virtue,' is ready with 'his severe but respectful criticism' but is fearful that the exercise of his free speech may be found to be 'a license to undermine public order.' These three judgments were to remain the major relevant citations for thirty years in that area of contempt of court in which the media were involved. As one legalist said:

The lesson to be learned from the reported decisions may afford the would-be critic only cold comfort. Since the judiciary does not have a common threshold of tolerance, it is to be expected that judges's reaction to criticism will not be uniform, and the resilience of the judicial epidermis will vary from court to court. Other areas of our law may be codified by statute or rationalized by a zealous Supreme Court or House of Lords, but in this field the subjective judgment seems destined to remain unchallenged: it is unlikely that we shall ever find a judge on the Clapham omnibus.[2]

[1] 1946. I.R. p. 70.
[2] Matthew Russell, 'Contempt of Court', *Irish Jurist* 3 (1968), p. 3.

The accuracy of this assessment will be tested in the 70s when the cases of a daily newspaper, a Sunday newspaper and a periodical which had been accused of criminal contempt arising from abusive criticism of judges and judgements, are examined in relation to the measure of control under which freedom of the press operates.

One further case in relation to contempt of court insofar as it affected freedom of expression arises from the sense of duty that obliges reporters to respect the confidentiality of their sources. A journalist had interviewed and taped a member of the IRA. Subsequently he refused to identify the person concerned or to give evidence about the circumstance of their interview. The Special Criminal Court sentenced him to three months imprisonment, later reduced to a fine by the Court of Criminal Appeal. Walsh J. said in his summary that within the restriction laid down by Article 40.6.1 journalists have the right to publish news, and as a corollary the right to gather it, without seeking government approval or consent. It was obvious, however, that not all newsgathering entails a relationship of confidentiality.

But even when it does, journalists or reporters are not any more constitutionally or illegally immune than other citizens from disclosing information received in confidence ... So far as the administration of justice is concerned the public has a right to every man's evidence except for those persons protected by a constitutional or other established and recognized privilege... It would be impossible for the judicial power to permit any other body or power to decide for it whether or not certain evidence would be disclosed or produced.

In Irish courts, press resports are restricted where the publication of proceedings might prejudice the accused's right to a fair trial. The Criminal Procedure Act of 1967, section 17, merely allows 'statement of the fact that such examination in relation to a named person on a specified charge has been held and of the decision thereon.' Similar safeguards protect the privacy of individuals' lives and affairs from invasion by the media. Financial matters, matrimonial causes, matters involving minors, disclosure of secret manufacturing processes, and other cognate actions may be heard *in camera* under section 45(1) of the Courts (Supplemental Provisions) Act 1961. However, as Kelly, to whom this review of constitutional and statutory law is indebted, points out,

Inasmuch as these provisions envisage the absence of reporters from such proceedings, they represent limitations on freedom of expression or reportage only to the extent that a breach of the Court's privacy may be a contempt.[1]

How far provocative words and messages should be considered as coming within the definition of freedom of expression in the sense intended by the Constitution is not always too clear. The Criminal Law Act of 1976 states

---

[1] J. M. Kelly, *The Irish Constitution* (Dublin: Jurist Publishing Co. Ltd., 1980), p. 448.

that a person is guilty of an offense if he knowingly makes a false report that might cause apprehension for the safety of persons or property, or knowingly furnishes the Garda Síochána (the police) with false information.

So far, consideration has been directed to a review of the workings of the Constitution and to the impact of various statutory instruments on the dimensions of meaningfulness for freedom of expression as found in Ireland since gaining independence. It is now appropriate to examine in detail specific legislation that has been enacted by the Oireachtas with the intention of controlling the output of the media in that interval of time preceding the present decade.

The first measure of control introduced by the Government which had been elected in 1923 was the Censorship of Films Act, 1923 by which were established the office of Official Censor of Films and a Censorship of Films Appeal Board. The Act requires the Censor to certify that the 'picture' (film) submitted to him is fit for public showing:

unless he is of opinion that such picture or some part thereof is unfit for general exhibition in public by reason of its being indecent, obscene or blasphemous or because the exhibition thereof in public would tend to inculcate principles contrary to public morality or would be subversive to public morality. (Section 7, (2).)

Any person aggrieved by a decision of the Official Censor may appeal to the Appeal Board to whom the Censor must furnish in writing the reasons for the related decision. The Appeal Board then communicates its opinion to the Censor who grants or withholds a certificate in accordance with their judgement. The Censorship of Films (Amendment) Acts of 1925 and 1930 brought trailers, advertisements and soundtrack under the control of the Censor. The Act of 1970 is plainly a liberating Act in that it permits fresh application to be made in respect of films about which adverse judgements have previously been entered.

Reference will be made in depth to the circumstances and climate in which that most contentious form of Irish censorhip evolved, namely, the Censorship of Publications Acts, 1929 to 1967. Of the first of these Acts one of its two provisions still remaining in force deals with restrictions on publication of reports of judicial proceedings, about which it was made unlawful to print:

(a) any indecent matter the publication of which would be calculated to injure public morals, or

(b) any indecent medical, surgical or physiological details the publication of which would be calculated to injure public morals. (Part III, Section 14(1).)

The proceedings referred to dealt with 'divorce, nullity of marriage, judicial separation or restitution of conjugal rights' and obviously envisaged

English as well as Irish newspapers. Reports were allowed to contain names of the parties involved, a statement of charges and countercharges, particulars of points of law raised, the summing-up of the judge and the findings of the jury. The other provision forbade the printing, sale and distribution of

Any book or periodical publication (whether appearing on the register of prohibited publications or not) which advocates or which might reasonably be supposed to advocate the unnatural prevention of conception or the procurement of abortion or miscarriage or any method, treatment, or appliance to be used for the purpose of such prevention or procurement. (Part IV, Section 16.)

The Censorship of Publications Act of 1946 repealed Part II of the Act of 1929 which dealt with censorship of publications, properly so called. Section 2 appointed a Censorship Board of five persons named by the Minister for Justice; Section 3 appointed a Censorship of Publications Appeal Board, whose chairman had to be a judge or practicing lawyer. Section 6 required the Board to

examine every book duly referred to them by an officer of customs and excise and every book in respect of which a complaint is made to them in the prescribed manner by any other person and ... any other book on their own initiative.

When the Board came to examine a book, it was to have regard to

(a) the literary, artistic, scientific or historic merit or importance, and the general tenor of, the book;

(b) the language in which it is written;

(c) the nature and extent of the circulation which, in their opinion, it is likely to have;

(d) the class of reader which, in their opinion, may reasonably be expected to read it;

(e) any other matter relating to the book which appears to them to be relevant. (Section 6(2).)

The major difference between the two Acts in relation to the criteria determining the character of a book lay in the fact that in the 1929 Act, the Board was to have regard to 'its general tendency' whereas in the 1946 Act the Board need only satisfy themselves that it was 'indecent or obscene' on the basis of whatever amount they had read of it. In both Acts the Board could if it wished communicate with the author, editor or publisher of the edition of the book which was the subject of the complaint and could 'take into account any representation made by him in relation thereto.' This sub-section was to have particular significance when a ruling of the Board was later challenged as a denial of the constitutional right to freedom of expression.

Having duly examined the book and judged it to be either indecent ('the word 'indecent' shall be construed as including suggestive of, or inciting to sexual immorality or unnatural vice or likely in any other similar way to corrupt or deprave')[1] or obscene (no definition offered) or advocating the unnatural prevention of conception, then the Board must prohibit its sale and publication. Section 9 of the Act deals with periodicals of which, if the Board are of the opinion that recently published issues complained of

(a) have usually or frequently been indecent or obscene, or

(b) have advocated the unnatural prevention of conception or the procurement of abortion or miscarriage or the use of any method, treatment or appliance for the purpose of such prevention or procurement, or

(c) have devoted an unduly large proportion of space to the publication of matter relating to crime (Section 9(1).),

the Board must prohibit the sale and distribution of further issues. Sections 8 and 10 provided for an Appeal Board which was empowered to review decisions about books and periodicals taken by the Censorship Board. Section 14 in making the sale and distribution of prohibited books or periodicals an offense laid down a fine of fifty pounds or 'at the discretion of the court, ... imprisonment with or without hard labor for a term not exceeding six months or ... both such fine and imprisonment.' Section 16 required the Board to keep a Register of Prohibited Publications and Section 17 provided for the issue of a search warrant where there were reasonable grounds for 'suspecting that in any specified building, land, premises or other place there are kept for sale or distribution any prohibited book or prohibited periodical publications.'

As will be seen, these two Acts proved to be very controversial. In 1967 a new Censorship of Publications Act, reflecting the changed intellectual and moral climate, was introduced that successfully mitigated their severity by legislating that

a prohibition order made on the grounds that a book is indecent or obscene shall cease to have effect on the 31st day of December following the expiration of the period of twelve years beginning on the date on which the order takes effect unless it is sooner revoked by the Appeal Board under section 8 of the Act of 1946.

This limitation on the life of a prohibition order released thousands of titles, and created in their wake a new scale of values by which books that were patently not pornographic might be assessed. A further epilogue remained to be written, but to all intents and purposes the extremes of what had sadly marred Irish cultural history had disappeared.

Broadcasting appears first in Irish legislation in a quite brief Part II of the Wireless Telegraphy Act of 1926. By Section 2 of the Act,

the expression 'wireless telegraphy' means and includes any system of communicating messages, spoken words, music, images, pictures, prints or other communications, sounds, signs, or signals...

[1] Censorship of Publications Act 1929. Part I, Preliminary Section 2.

the prescience of which is almost as remarkable as the unintended humor[1] contained further on in the same section

the expression 'broadcast matter' means and includes any lectures, speeches, news, reports, advertisements, recitations, dramatic entertainments, and other spoken words and any music (whether vocal or instrumental) and other sounds approved by the Minister ... .

The Act empowered the Minister to acquire and establish such and so many broadcasting station as he deemed fit. Only the State was to be vested with this power, a prerogative that was not challenged despite the fact that no exclusionary statement appears in this, or in subsequent Acts. Section 11 (1) of the Act prohibits wireless operators either on land, on the sea or in the air from sending messages that are 'of an indecent, obscene or offensive character' or are 'subversive of public order.' Section 19 (1) requires the Minister to establish 'an advisory committee to advise and assist him in the conduct of the broadcasting stations maintained by him under this Act.' Until 1960, the broadcasting system was run directly by the minister named in the Act, the Minister for Post and Telegraphs, who was responsible to Dáil Éireann.

The Broadcasting Authority Act of 1960 established, in place of this arrangement, an authority to be known as Radio Éireann later changed to Radio Telefís Éireann (RTÉ) by an Amending Act of 1966. The members of this Authority were to be nominated by the Government and could at any time be removed from office. This Authority was to appoint a Director-General, and additional officers and servants by means of a public competition, save where such a mode of selection was not to apply under the Act. The Authority was enjoined to bear constantly in mind the restoration of the Irish language and the promotion of the national culture. As regards the specific activity of broadcasting, by Section 18,

(1) It shall be the duty of the Authority to secure that when it broadcasts any information, news or feature which relates to matters of public controversy or is the subject of current public debate, the information, news or feature is presented objectively and impartially and without any expression of the Authority's own views.

In the light of subsequent events the interpretation of this sub-section became crucial, particularly when it is taken with Section 31:

(1) The Minister may direct the Authority in writing to refrain from broadcasting any particular matter or matter of any particular class, and the Authority shall comply with the direction,

(2) The Minister may direct the Authority in writing to allocate broadcasting time for any announcements by or on behalf of any Minister of State in connection with

---

[1] Maurice Gorham, *Forty Years of Irish Broadcasting* (Dublin: Talbot Press, 1967), p. 34.

the function of that Minister of State, and the Authority shall comply with the direction.

Reviewing this legislation in the light of Article 40.6.1 guaranteeing freedom of expression, one is immediately seized of the possible dangers that inhere in a monopoly situation. It was not contemplated of course that the Government would have control over the day-to-day running of the broadcasting service in a way that would enable it to edit and organize information, enlightment and entertainment to suit its political needs. However, its unspoken presumption of being the sole proprietor of broadcasting facilities coupled with its statutorily conferred right to nominate the members of the Authority that was responsible for the maintenance of such a service left it with residual powers to use, or to leave in the air as a threat to use, if ever the occasion required. Again, if a monopoly is to be justified in order to copperfasten the protection of citizens from sedition, blasphemy, obscenity and libel, as implied in the Constitution, why was not a monopoly sought for 'other organs of opinion' under Article 43.2.2?

The next area of doubt surrounds that section of the Act which deals with the manner in which RTÉ is expected to fulfil the duty of impartiality imposed by the Act. How does one reconcile this obligation with the obligation to promote the Irish language and culture unless its opponents are to be excluded on the grounds that they are using public facilities to 'undermine public order or morality or the authority of the State?' Again, Kelly[1] points out that outside the narrow range of 'controversy' and 'debate' which are to be 'presented objectively and impartially' there are, for example, social functions too numerous to catalogue at which the tacit presence of a politician speaks with greater volume and deeper resonance than any ministerial broadcast under the Act.

Finally, Ireland, as has been said, is a signatory to the *European Convention on Human Rights and Fundamental Freedoms*, Article 10 of which provides:

Everybody has the right of freedom of expression. This right shall include freedom to hold opinions and to receive and impart information and ideas without interference by public authority and regardless of frontiers. This Article shall not prevent States from requiring the licensing of broadcasting, television or cinema enterprises.

It is difficult to believe that the right referred to is really being enjoyed when the major principal vehicle for its expression is controlled by the State and there is no alternative in existence. Limitations on the freedom designated in the article must be necessary limitations which are applied only to protect the democracy of which it is one of the attributes. Since all

---

[1] Kelly, 'The Constitutional Position of RTÉ', p. 207.

democracies are pluralist, diversity of opinion is their outcome. Such diversity must be granted an outlet until there is persuasive evidence that the consequences are not compatible with public order and morality. By this Act, a ministerial written communication is enough to ensure that democracy need not be put to the test of discovering whether the exercise of freedom of expression is a better safeguard than its denial. As will appear, there were and always had been incidents, both before and after the Act, to justify grave misgiving as to whether the operation of the electronic media served political interest first, and then the public weal.

This examination of the Constitution and statutory legislation in so far as they relate to freedom of expression has been intended to provide an outline of the formal instruments that impair its enjoyment. It will be the purpose of subsequent chapters to provide the backcloth against which their enactment and interpretation may be the better understood, and these in turn will make intelligible the actuality of censorship during the period to be studied. Between 1922 and 1969 there were two Constitutions whose provisions for freedom of expression remained unchallenged. There were during this time four Censorship of Films Acts, three Censorship of Publications Acts, and two Acts setting up and controlling the broadcasting media. In addition there were passed at least nine substantive acts that inhibited communications, the constitutionality of which was not tested. The courts, for their part, imposed their own limitations on the freedom of expression in the interests of preventing the administration of justice being brought into disrepute, while at the same time demolishing the reporter's claim to remain silent. In all this, it is interesting to note that the legislators themselves were over this period remarkably free from the compulsion to take retributive action against (and hence censor) any attempt to diminish their collective image or misrepresent their corporate action. The *Report of the Committee on the Constitution* states:

Free expression of opinion is a vital part of democracy and in proceeding to deal with what it considers to be abuses arising therefrom, Parliament generally finds itself in embarrassment and difficulty. Particularly is this so when the offending matter has a political content so that the views of individual Members in relation to it are far from unanimous. A further difficulty is that attacks on Parliament and abuse of the Members often come from persons of no special responsibility and a Parliamentary reaction then gives them wider publicity and greater significance than they otherwise would have. If action is taken on them the accusation most commonly heard is that Parliament is judge and jury in its own cause.[1]

The proof of these tolerant sentiments lies in the fact that in the forty-five

[1] *Report of the Committee on the Constitution*. 1967. (Dublin: Stationery Office, 1967), p. 64.

years of parliamentary democracy, the members have taken action only on three occasions to interfere with freedom of expression. Two of these involved statements made outside Parliament by their own members and the third, it was decided, was best treated by being ignored. The wisdom of their masterly inaction was not however to be carried and applied beyond the precincts of the Oireachtas.

CHAPTER 3

THE BEGINNINGS OF CENSORSHIP

Media control does not operate in a vacuum. It responds to the interacting influences that are themselves the product of religious, political, social and economic forces that characterize a rural, conservative Ireland in the first decade of independence. The war against the British had been followed by a civil war, and when an uneasy peace had been established there was a need for, and a desire for, a return to enough of the old certainties that would allow society to function in conformity with generally accepted norms. The Catholic church in Ireland was to take upon itself the drawing up of a moral charter. Its fears of the moral instability and anti-social tendencies of its flock as an aftermath to the armed struggle were to lead it to sponsor legislation that came more and more to be repressive and inhibiting to the emergence of individual responsibility. The country as a whole appeared to regress.

The Ireland which gained its independence in 1922 was primarily committed to the achievement of an identity. The architects of the new state had in mind the reversal of tendencies to accept as absolutes external views as to what should constitute their way of thinking and living. They had not, however, identified sufficiently clearly the constituents of the distinctive culture nor elaborated in adequate detail the social and economic policies which would serve to nourish and strengthen it. To ensure that the state would continue to function it was necessary to maintain, at least in the short term, existing administrative and legal institutions. This decision entailed the continuation of the existing machinery of government and, as has been seen, the corpus of statutory and common law.

Economically the country was stagnant. Industries were few and depended largely on the British market. Unemployment was widespread. In the first decade of independence, free trade and fiscal rectitude were the main lodestars by which the government determined its budget objectives. Social problems as manifested in a high infant mortality rate, rampant unemployment, slum tenements, poor medical provision, limited education facilities and general insufficient welfare provision were, if not unique to the new Irish Free State in the post-war depression of the 1920s, none the less debilitating. The situation, however, was not desperate. The population as a whole was probably more literate than most (Tussing[1] gives a figure of 88% literacy for the year 1911, 15 years before education was made compulsory); an infrastructure of railways and canals had been developed to a point beyond which the limited industrialization extant could sustain it; and partially as a result of these advances which in themselves facilitated the process, the Irish people had for a hundred years' history registered a political awareness that had few counterparts in its pervasiveness of all of society.

However the mental energy released by independence had not been directed to any radical evaluation of the superimposed policies to which the country now stood an involuntary legatee. The reasons for this omission were to be found in the character of pre-independence Irish society. The 1926 Census revealed a predominantly rural society, 61% of the people living outside towns or villages, 53% of those registered as employed worked in agriculture, and slightly less than half of all farmers depended for their livelihood on farms of less than 30 acres.[2] This occupational pattern was in turn to influence the thinking and outlook of the urban dwellers. The struggle to obtain possession of the land had bred an individualism in its exploitation.

Economic endeavor, both upon the individual farms and in the form of cooperation between farms, (was) controlled through the operation of social forces springing from the family.[3]

Those who sought employment in the towns brought with them these same values and perspectives. Too many years under what they had come to understand to be the dominance of an alien and usurping power had limited their frame of reference so that considerations which were not personal in their import were, more frequently than not, excluded. The result was that the emergence of an entrepreneurial class with its concomitant concentration of capital, its recognition of the need for planning, and the formation of an intellectual-technocrat cadre (there were in 1901 less than 1600 university students in a 32-county Ireland) was delayed for over forty years. The homogeneity that characterized Irish society in the post-independence years was due in no small measure to the identity of outlook which permeated rural Ireland – an outlook that was economically

[1] A. Dale Tussing, *Irish Educational Expenditures – Past Present and Future* (Dublin: ESRI, 1978) p. 53.
[2] Figures given in Terence Brown, *Ireland – A Social and Cultural History, 1922–79* (London: Fontana, 1981), p. 18–19.
[3] Conrad M. Arensberg and S. T. Kimball, *Family and Community in Ireland* (Cambridge, Mass.: Harvard U. P.), p. 75.

prudential, formally puritanical and socially conservative.

To understand this independent Irish state in the 1920s it is incumbent to appreciate the role of the Roman Catholic Church in shaping the minds and attitudes of the population. Prior to independence and following it, whether the source be Catholic or non-Catholic, sympathetic or hostile, overwhelmingly the evidence[1] indicates that attendance at religious services ranged from 90% in the cities to 100% in small towns and rural areas. Even a notoriously hostile critic admitted that Ireland was 'the world's most devoutly Catholic country.'[2] Obviously in Ireland such participation in church services tended to confirm the people in their traditional conservatism.

This adherence to orthodoxy, however, was neither unqualified nor unreserved. Church-going could very often be merely a function of the desire not to break community taboos rather than the outcome of an intellectual conviction.[3] Condemnations from the ecclesiastical bench have often remained unheeded in Irish history and such widely distanced political activists in time and method as Parnell and the IRA have managed to defy episcopal denunciations and survive. What is particular in the Irish context is the political sophistication that in the first place tacitly and spontaneously sets aside Church competence in areas not deemed to lie within its purview, and, in the second place, expresses or articulates an alternative point of view, vigorously and trenchantly, without feeling the need to institutionalize itself as a permanent anti-clerical opposition, as happened frequently in continental Europe.

Perhaps the paradoxicality of this situation becomes more intelligible if it is recalled that the written constitution of the State has since its inception been ostensibly neutral in relation to the affairs of religious foundations. Article 8 of the 1922 Constitution – the year independence was won – reads like an elaboration of one phrase of the First Amendment to the U.S. Constitution:

Freedom of conscience and the free practice of religion are, subject to public order and morality, guaranteed to every citizen, and no law may be made either directly or indirectly to endow any religion, or prohibit or restrict the free exercise thereof or give any preference, or impose any disability on account of religious belief or religious status... .

On the surface, then, the neutrality of the state in matters of religion seemed clear and evident. The Church in Ireland had never known establishment in the form enjoyed by the Church of England. It did not seek to copperfasten a special relationship for itself which would have guaranteed its endowments and extended its spiritual governance as had other

[1] C. K. Ward, 'Social-religious research in Ireland', *Social Compass* 11 (1964) p. 26.

[2] Paul Blanshard, *The Irish and Catholic Power* (London: Cape, 1954) p. 29.

[3] J. H. Whyte, *Church and State in Modern Ireland 1923–70*, p. 7.

countries like Italy, Spain and Portugal. Indeed the attitude shared by Government and Church alike appeared to have been that the fewer the formal contacts the better. Informal communications were another matter. Sermons at confirmations, speeches to Total Abstinence Societies, addresses to the Catholic Young Men's Society, oblique statements to the press, these and other occasions presented endless opportunities for sending messages. The Government listened as it should to the strongest non-elective body in the country. The latter's organizational strength, the rigid conformity it required of its members to a central policy, their deployment throughout every activity in society, recreational, cultural, educational, health, and many others, the stability of its constituency, the almost unquestioning acceptance of its moral values, its identification with a personalist God and with Christ's Vicar on earth, its associations with the emergence of the Irish image, all made its inclusion at one remove from discussions concerning the future evolution and development of the State an absolute imperative.

As has been noted, the exchange of views was indirect. Committees were set up or conferences were held. Views emerged, opinions filtered, soundings were taken, and background material was collected. Deputations were received. Pastoral letters were an annual communiqué, where the strength of any conviction was measured by the extent of its concurrence in what the bishops wrote. These were reprinted in the daily newspapers and constituted the gravamen of sermons on succeeding Sundays. The Church was not going to default on any opportunity to call attention to its function as the politically non-partisan institutional voice of Ireland discharging its responsibilities to provide guidance on the indeterminate fields of faith and morals. If, in consequence, it were to sway opinion against beliefs and practice which were part of the minority's way of life and to claim for itself implicitly a special position as the majority faith, that was the price the Irish nation must pay to be free of grievous error. In return for the concession the Government, of whatever party, derived authentication, support, a value system and a not inconsiderable force for internal peace and civic control.

Whenever the Church in Ireland did modify this stance and seek to intrude into spheres that had not been agreed as belonging to its legitimate interests it could not always be sure of the outcome. Attempts, for example, to impose social and political norms associated with the out-dated teaching of the Encyclicals encountered an abrasive rejection that signalled limits had been reached. There were in addition other participants whose views began to compete with the bishops' for a hearing. Progressive exposure to the media provided contrasts to domestic points of view at the same time as increases in educational opportunity in Ireland, as in the rest of Europe, enabled more and more people to contribute to thinking on issues that revealed wider parameters than those offered by faith and fatherland. Even though the rate of change was not to gather momentum for some time, consensus about attitudes to the Church was to become a reducing reality.

However, for all the blemishes attributable to the Roman Catholic Church in Ireland, membership in it was not taken lightly. It provided a tiny population with a sense of identity which derived from their belonging to the largest denomination in the Christian faith, or as belonging to 'the Irish race,' that multi-million diaspora which was regarded as synonymous with its religion. The average Irishman had no illusions as to the significance of his country's power role in the Weltpolitik of the period. Where he conceived his country's importance to lie was in reaffirming those spiritual values which had, in truth, won her renown a millennium earlier. In February, 1932, on the occasion of the opening of Ireland's first high-power broadcasting station, the understandable triumphalism chose to express itself in reiterating this mission of helping to save Western Civilization from the materialism on which she claimed by her rebellion she had turned her back:

In this day, if Ireland is faithful to her mission – and please God she will be, if as of old she recalls men to forgotten truths, if she places before them the ideals of justice, of order, of freedom rightly used, or Christian brotherhood – then indeed she can do the world a service as great as that which she rendered in the time of Columcille and Columbanus, because the need of our time is no whit less. You sometimes hear Ireland charged with a narrow and intolerant nationalism, but Ireland today has no dearer hope than this: that, true to her holiest traditions, she should humbly serve the truth, and help by truth to save the world.[1]

This religious expansionism was however destined to draw its ideological inspiration from the narrow confines of an unquestioning ultramontanism assimilated by a clergy with no great intellectual ambitions to explore the meaning their faith might have in developing national contexts. To carry out this task of spiritual witness in the world of the twentieth century, Ireland needed in the words of one sympathetic observer of ecclesiastical life 'the services of a priesthood, learned, zealous and disciplined into the solidarity of aim and principle.'[2] Where in continental Europe, after the World War I holocaust, the Christian religions were drawing closer to one another in their attempt to redefine a common rational basis for the religious experience, in Ireland the bishops continued to identify the source of the spiritual and social malaise as

The evil one (who) is ever setting his snares for unwary feet. At the moment, his traps for the innocent are chiefly the dance hall, the bad book, the indecent paper,

[1] Eamon de Valera, reported in *Catholic Bulletin*, 23 (1933), p. 243.
[2] Herman J. Heuser, *Canon Sheehan of Doneraile* (London: Longman 1917) p. 41.

the motion picture, the immodest fashion in female dress – all of which tend to destroy the virtuous characteristics of our race.[1]

To economic stagnancy, an inadequate social welfare provision, a conservative nationalism and a religious formalism, must also be added by way of an explanation of the cultural outlook of Irish society in the second quarter of the century, the influence of the Rising of 1916, the sufferings brought about by the activities of British para-militaries, the legacy of a Civil War that claimed more lives than did the Rebellion and its aftermath, and finally the partitioning of the country resulting in the traumatic loss of six of its counties, foreseeable perhaps, but which was to ensure that recourse to arms, then and now, was an ever-present threat to the establishment and consolidation of generally agreed norms of political conduct. Whichever was the dominant force,

the fact remains that Irish repressiveness, ... was extreme in those first crucial decades, and that it severely stunted the cultural and social development of a country which a protracted colonial mismanagement had left in desperate need of revival in both spheres.[2]

Any such development would depend on the free and unfettered exchange of ideas. What were the conditions obtaining in Ireland at that time which would make for open discussion?

The two major statutes governing the amount of latitude conceded to the expression of opinion were the British Obscene Publications Act of 1857 and the Customs Consolidation Act of 1876, both of which, as has been noted, subsequently became part of Irish law. As regards the former, a police stipendiary magistrate was empowered to issue a warrant of seizure for the articles complained of and a summons to the vendor to show why these goods should not be destroyed. Obscenity was not defined by the Act, but British courts had followed Lord Justice Cockburn's judgement:

I think that the test of obscenity is this, whether the tendency of the matter charged as obscenity is to deprave and corrupt those whose minds are open to such immoral influences, and into whose hands a publication of this sort may fall.[3]

While the initiative to institute proceedings was not confined to the state, it was unusual, but not unheard of, for a private individual to set the law in motion at his own expense. Incorporating the Act into Irish law did not however provide Irish courts with the same powers, since most publications to which exception would be taken lay outside their jurisdiction, and action therefore was possible only through the prosecution of distributors.

[1] Acta et Decreta Concilii Plenarii Episcoporum Hiberniae, Maynooth, 1927, p. 142.
[2] Brown, ibid, p. 41.
[3] *Regina* v. *Hicklin*, L.R. 3Q.B. 1868, p. 371.

The Customs Consolidation Act of 1876 which prohibits the importation of indecent or obscene articles and their carriage through the post is on the other hand still vigorous Irish law. Even after the Censorship Acts had been introduced, the Customs Authorities continued by virtue of section 42 of the Act to impound publications sent as merchandise (personal importation under license was not prohibited), and hand over to successive Censorship Boards the decision as to whether there was a prima facie case for exclusion. The general practice, then as now, is for a joint department of Customs and Postal officials to examine books coming into the country, to forward those about which they have reservations to the Revenue Commissioners accompanied by an explanatory note, and then for these latter to decide whether to forward these publications to the Censorship Board or simply permit their importation. As regards periodicals, this same section of the Act provides for the seizure and loss of 'indecent or obscene prints, paintings, photographs, books, cards, lithographic or other engravings or any other indecent or obscene articles' by the Commissioners of Customs acting on the authority granted to them by this legislation. Adams, to whose analysis of the censorship process in relation to printed matter prior to 1968 all subsequent scholarship must remain indebted, says:

It would appear that this power has seldom been used, for the Customs authorities are very wary and are anxious to avoid mistakes which could lead to a public outcry, or to representations on the part of those financially concerned in the sale of these periodicals. The outcry occasioned by the non-distribution of the issue of the *Observer* for 1st April, 1956 (it contained a pre-advertised article on family planning) easily justifies their caution in the exercise of these powers: in fact, according to the Reports of the Censorship Board, all complaints regarding periodicals are formal complaints (i.e. from members of the public).[1]

These then were the two major Acts dealing with the freedom of expression which the new state received as part of its colonial legacy. That they failed to answer an articulated need for the exercise of greater social control is apparent from the activities of vigilance committees and from the fulminations in Lenten Pastorals of a type already referred to. Dissatisfaction was further heightened by the identification of suspect subject-matter with an alien British source and was eventually to lead to English Sunday newspapers being taken from trains and burnt in public.[2] The country was now the victim of a post-war syndrome experienced in many countries as the necessity to firm up moral codes that had become less rigorous. The majority of Irish people had been conditioned to accept some form of control. What many were to find disturbing was that the

[1] Michael Adams, *Censorship: The Irish experience*, p. 175.
[2] Editorial 'Censorship by the Gun,' *The Irish Times*. 15/9/1928.

propagandists of censorship were not exclusively concerned with reports of court proceedings concerning sexual offenses and divorce actions. Cardinal Logue was accused in 1908 of attempting to suppress a periodical called the *Irish Peasant* because 'it had advocated some sort of popular control of primary education in Ireland.'[1] Labor papers were attacked because they advocated better conditions and higher wages for the working class. The Most Rev. Dr. Clancy, Bishop of Elphin is reported as having written in December, 1911, to the Chairman of the Local Vigilance Committee for the Suppression of Immoral Literature in Sligo that

Indeed, the great danger of the future will not be a revolt against Faith so much as a revolt against the established order of social and commercial life. In a word, the Christian war cry for the future should be, 'Le socialisme, voilà l'ennemi.'[2]

Before independence had been won, the battlelines had indeed been drawn. On the one hand, D. P. Moran, the founder in 1900 and editor of *The Leader*, a Dublin review of current affairs, had always argued for press control on nationalist as well as moral grounds; on the other, Yeats and the other main figures of the Anglo-Irish efflorescence continued to argue that 'A nation that would submit to have its reading prescribed for it by self-elected committees of ignorant busybodies ... would have surrendered a definite and vital safeguard of its moral and political health.'[3] One safeguard for the robustness of this moral and physical health would lie in the quality of its communications. What thinking had been done as to their function in an independent State? How were the press, the radio and film intended to reflect the national will? What was to be the extent of their contribution?

British press reporting had made the Irish newspaper reading public conscious of the difference between reality and what was printed. Moreover, they realized that, whereas they were able to check for misrepresentation on their own doorstep, they had no guarantee of the accuracy or veracity of foreign news which an Irish publisher would buy from an international agency, as much for economic reasons as for dependability. Cleary was, therefore, expressing a conviction born of experience when he argued that the bitter struggle the new State had just undergone ought to convince the Irish of the need to pass a law making it illegal to tamper with the truth, to adulterate its ingredients, and to distort its emphasis. Press freedom ought to be extended to protect honest criticism of wrongdoers. A newspaper should not have to consider all the time whether it had the resources to justify in a court of law what it had said in its columns. The individual's reputation must be protected, certainly, But as against this, people in the mass have rights even greater than the indi-

---

[1] Frederick Ryan, 'The Latest Crusade,' *The Irish Review* I (1912) p. 523.

[2] ibid, p. 525.

[3] ibid, p. 526.

vidual: the wrong done by the neglect of these rights is much graver: yet the right not to be deceived is scarcely recognized for people in the mass, unless the character of the individual is at stake. The freedom of the people is more important than the freedom of the press: and the wholesale truth adulteration of modern times has beyond doubt gone further to impair the freedom of the people than anything attempted in despotic ages. The traditional tyrant of history could coerce you to act as he wanted, but not to think as he wanted.[1]

The writer was an academic of some standing and could therefore be supposed to be arguing for open and informed discussion in the marketplace where truth could be relied upon to prevail. But his words may be read as foreshadowing the moral dilemma many others would experience for the next thirty of forty years. Could the people be free if the press were not? Adulteration of truth will always impair freedom, but does one man's truth constitute another man's refusal to accept his own reality? How is the control of thought to be distinguished from limiting the range of the mind's endeavors?

For Barry the influence for good might all too easily be surrendered on the altar of sensationalism. The press in a new, free Ireland had a duty to decide what news it might purvey to the people. Journalists could not justify the reporting of sex cases, for example, on the grounds that they served as a warning to the unwary. On the contrary,

The publication of every crime is, no doubt, more or less likely to lead those who are weak to its commission by familiarizing their minds with it, lessening their abhorrence of it, and showing that the perpetration of it is not unthinkable.[2]

This shielding of the Irish mind from indecencies carried the implication that such reporting served only the material interests of the non-Irish publisher, and, in consequence, that foreign items of news (apart from those emanating from the Vatican) were more than likely not only to be untrue but also suspect in their intentions. By eliminating them as influences hostile to the true Irish ethos, the Irish people would, it followed, turn to their own national newspapers where 'the possibilities of effective influences upon the public authorities are much greater than in the most highly organized countries.'[3] Since the national press did not have to meet the high costs of production, of distribution, and of competing for a fixed national advertising budget, their journalistic success did not entail the sacrifice of standards. By and large, the argument has been shown to be true.

However, there was no turning back the tide of English newspapers that kept coming in to satisfy the Irish demand. Two weekly papers alone, the *News of the World* and the *Sporting Times*, were selling a quarter of a

[1] Arthur E. Cleary, 'Truth Adulteration,' *Studies* 13 (1924), p. 594.
[2] David Barry, 'The Ethics of Journalism,' *Irish Ecclesiastical Record* 5th ser. 19 (1922), p. 524.
[3] Denis Gwynn, 'The Modern Newspaper,' *Studies* 15 (1926), p. 380.

million copies between them in 1926. The consequences as seen by the *Irish Rosary* were calamitous. It editorialized that the Catholic mind could no longer 'soar above all earthly things' as long as it continued to be beset by 'the preponderating mass of printed filth' which one person in nine persisted in buying. It also appealed to race-consciousness, to the reasons that had made Irishmen ten years previously take on the might of the British Empire, and to the threat that such newspapers might constitute for that Christian consciousness which had prompted their forefathers to make the same sacrifice of their lives for the faith as had the first martyrs in the Roman arenas. There was a need for a Literature Commission, but that was not the solution the leader-writer felt to be appropriate. 'The real effective remedy and censorship is to keep all offending journals out of the country, once and for all.'[1] The *Irish Rosary* was to repeat this theme, inveighing against 'the tainted Press' (May 1926), 'a weekly gutter-organ' (April 1928), 'lessons of sanctity of crime' (August 1928), and 'the incubus of a foreign and often polluted Press' (September 1928).

During this decade Ireland saw the incorporation of one newspaper and the establishment of another, both identifying with opposing political parties but, within the limits of traditional invective, behaving responsibly. The third paper, *The Irish Times*, was caught between the desire to sustain its image as a paper of record and its obligation to stand for principles whose worth was often occluded by their identification with British thinking. The paper had not accepted in full the new state as a permanent and viable entity. Until it would do so, its contribution to maintaining civil rights would be regarded with suspicion.

For the second of the media, this problem did not arise. Political thought in the hierarchy of needs comes a long time after survival has been assured. Radio broadcasting in Ireland began in 1926 with a shoestring budget, a lack of expertise, a Department of Finance stranglehold on initiative, expansion and imagination, and a determination to succeed that was explicable only as the outcome of a commitment and a conviction that the quality of the enterprise required it be matched by patience and dedication.[1] The first director was a Health Insurance Inspector who like all other permanent employees for the next 34 years was to be appointed as a civil servant and therefore subject to all the restraints that characterized government employment. Given the nature of bureaucracy under a conservative government, it was inevitable that rigid control would be exercised over every aspect of running the station, from the employment of a charwoman through the purchase of a piano to the engagement of an orchestra.

[1] Michael Walsh, 'Enemies in Our Midst,' p. 298.
[2] Maurice Gorham, *Forty Years of Irish Broadcasting*, pp. 27ff.

As has been seen, the Wireless Telegraphy Act of 1926 made broad-casting a legitimate government activity, the most significant implication probably being that the forces of law could be immediately invoked to compel the payment of license fees which were supposed to make the ser-vice self-sufficient. In view of the recruitment policy, it was unlikely that any activity would impinge on sensitive areas to an extent that would oc-casion official reaction. What was broadcast was still the least important aspect about broadcasting. One lady was banned because of political opinions expressed outside broadcasting but neither the Deputy who raised the matter nor the Minister responsible seemed to know anything of the circumstances. Her crime in fact was that she had protested about the publication of a letter in *The Irish Times* which might prejudice a fair trial for men accused of the aforementioned assassination of Kevin O'Higgins. She was not to be re-employed until a change of government took place five years later. In the meantime assessment of station perfor-mance was limited to points of view expressed by deputies when discus-sing the Estimates. Comment on what was broadcast then as now re-flected the range of people's interests and wishes. The debates further re-vealed that all news bulletins were pirated, an item of information that, far from arousing some sense of shame at least among opposition de-puties, only incited them to hurl accusations of peddling British prop-aganda at the responsible Minister. During the period under review, sur-vival was the main objective. No one would dream of prejudicing an al-ready precarious existence by articulating adverse comment on the politi-cal situation that had brought it about. The service was squarely and un-questionably the minimum that any self-respecting government must pro-vide if it were at all serious about protecting Irish culture from alien influ-ences. Beyond that obligation it was to be kept on a short leash and sus-tained irregularly.

The Censorship of Films Act was one of the first acts passed by the Irish Parliament. It established the office of Official Censor of Films and en-joined the holder to refrain from granting a certificate permitting the showing of a film which he deemed to be 'indecent, obscene or blasphem-ous... .'[1] The *Catholic Bulletin* was pleased. It was convinced that the Catholic public of all Ireland found the material shown freely in Dublin entirely repugnant. With the Bill passed into law,

The interlaced 'business' interests engaged in this unwholesome and degrading traffic ... so cunningly masked that even the worthy efforts of the Vigilance Com-mittees... have not been entirely able to expose their devices.[2]

would no longer be a corruptive force in Irish society. Apart from such

---

[1] Censorship of Films Act 7(2). Dublin, The Stationery Office, 1923, p. 11.
[2] Editorial, *Catholic Bulletin*. Vol XIII, No. 3, 1923, p. 131.

comment from the religious press there does not appear to have been much opposition to the idea, due probably to a combination of the aftermath of political upheaval, the failure to realize the communicative potential of film and lack of an awareness of its commercial exploitability. However, its passage was a harbinger of the increased impetus to bring about reform in the printed media. The way was now clear, as will be seen, to concentrate on the English Sunday press which 'In very many cases ... is a repertory of sordid crime, and of every form of moral filth and unclean suggestion.'[1]

The main target was, and remained, anything immediately accessible to the Irish public that tended to undermine the ideal of strict family morality. A secondary objective for attack was the Ascendancy, legal, medical or literary, whose interests and values were remote from those who were considered to be the true inheritors of independence and whose leaders were, at least in the domain of books (this was the time of Joyce, Moore and Shaw), nothing more than 'exhibits of literary putrescence.' Even the signal recognition accorded Yeats by the Nobel Prize for Literature was not enough to make the *Catholic Bulletin* pause at the thought of an award that bruited the reputation of Ireland far and wide and paid tribute thereby to a literary movement that has taken its epoch-making place in the history of the literature of those who spoke the English language. Either because the logic of the liberals was irrefutable or because there were no plausible polemicists on the side of the angels, at all events these custodians of Irish morality had recourse to a campaign of vilification that pre-empted the need for reasoned argument.

Paganism in prose or in poetry has, it seems, its solid cash value: and if a poet does not write tawdry verse to make his purse heavier, he can be brought by his admirers to where money is, whether in the form of the English pension, or in extracts from the Irish taxpayer's pocket, or in the Stockholm dole.[2]

However, for the moment, this was a problem that was not so pressing. Slowly but surely, outside the metropolitan area in particular, there was a growing conviction that the foreign press which had so maligned the efforts of Irishmen to achieve independence was now seeking to regain a place in the minds and moral outlook of those who, it was claimed, had preferred death to dishonor and a life of modest means to one of hedonistic naturalism. The first really to put a shape on these arguments was a Rev. R. S. Devane, S.J., who contributed an article that exemplified the intensity of conviction among some representives of the clergy, by quoting with approval the Bishop of Clogher:

It would be somewhat reassuring to our sense of moral rectitude if we read of an

---

[1] *Ibid.* p. 131.
[2] *Ibid.* Vol. xiv, No. 1, 1924, p. 6.

Irish Catholic newsagent being sentenced to imprisonment or the lash by an Irish
Catholic Judge for purveying such filth.

and Lord Aberdeen in praise of the activities of the Vigilance Committee
of Limerick:

Twenty-two newsagents in the city have pledged themselves to sell no copies of
the undesirable publications; the newsboys too, have been organized, and they
have promised they will sell none of the objectionable prints.[1]

He next commended the attitude of the Irish Government for its subscrip-
tion to the 'International Convention for the suppression of the circulation and traffic in obscene publications,' and finally detailed the remedies
that appeared appropriate. First, a new definition of 'obscene' was required that would be broad and comprehensive enough to include many
things permissible in English law. Second, all birth control literature was
to be declared obscene ('Is any good purpose served by adopting the os-
trich policy toward this deplorable evil, and maintaining a prudent (?) silence while moral cancer eats in?').[2] Third, a Black List of books and papers similar to the lists drawn up in Australia and Canada should be com-
piled ('and, as a deterrent to the Dublin Cloacal School, open it with a
volume of a well-known degenerate Irishman').[3] Fourth, new legislation
should provide for certain advertisements to be declared indecent which
the British Indecent Advertisement Act of 1889 was unable to control,
namely the promotion of the sale of contraceptive pills and appliances
and the blacklisting of an unidentified number of papers.

It was in vain for *The Irish Times* to protest at the exaggerations that
must inevitably ensue unless some balanced perspective were retained in
the face of such proposals:

The things that defile Ireland come not from within, but without. If the vulgar and
indecent contents of a few English newspapers have power to warp Irish brains
and damn Irish souls, we are brought back to the point from which we started.[4]

An attack was now mounted by the religious press which was all the more
persistent and remorseless in that some English newspapers and American periodicals did give grounds for serious objection. Some of the civic–
minded publications expressed themselves with sincere but moderate
alarm at this unwanted presence of prurient reading material in Irish society. Others were nothing more at times than libel sheets, or as one irate
observer put it:

They deceive the ordinary, average, ignorant reader into believing ... that they
are orthodox publications approved by the authority of the Church, and that consequently what they say should have considerable moral weight. Sectarian bitter-

[1] R.S. Devane, 'Indecent Literature,' *Irish Ecclesiastical Record* 25 (1925), pp. 182–204.
[2] Ibid., p. 195.
[3] ibid., p. 197.
[4] Editorial, *Irish Times*. 1/2/1927, p. 9.

ness and animosity are favored and encouraged by these papers. They preach and practice a code that is as far removed from the Christian religion as barbarianism is divorced from civilization.[1]

This assessment, unusual for the period, was an indication of the lengths to which passionate conviction was prepared to go in its endeavor to ensure that its point of view would triumph.

For now, however, Fr. Devane's article, which truly reflected the mood of the activists of the period, must be read and understood against the background of its times. In the United States federal legislation had been drawn up to limit the sale of all contraceptive articles. A Joint Select Committee of the British House of Parliament had recommended that it should be made illegal to advertise drugs or articles for the prevention of conception. The Church of England at its 1925 Conference at Lambeth comdemned practices connected with birth control. Other member states of the English-speaking would such as Canada and Australia had adopted similar attitudes to the same issue. What was unique about Ireland was that all expressions of disagreement or diffidence as to the appropriateness of certain proposals were often treated as insidious attacks on the Church as a whole, and therefore indicative of a less than total commitment to the Irish identity in its spiritual nationalism. What was disturbing about Fr. Devane's article was not the special pleading inherent in his organization of authoritative and prestigious opinion in order to argue his case but his approval of paragraph 40 of the Report of the Select Committee of the British Houses of Parliament which dealt with legal procedures to be adopted for those charged with publishing obscene materials,

The Committee believe that not only would the cost of prosecutions be greatly reduced but also an effectual remedy would be found for that which they believe to be a serious and growing evil if cases of this kind were left to the decision of the magistrates.[2]

This proposal to remove the right of the accused to have his guilt in a libel action determined by jury, won over a hundred years previously, was a disquieting indication of a willingness to subordinate civil rights to theological conviction.

The combined pressures alluded to above resulted in the then Minister for Justice setting up a Committee of Enquiry on Evil Literature in 1926 'to consider and report whether it is necessary or advisable in the interests of public morality to extend the existing powers of the State to prohibit or restrict the sale and circulation of printed matter.' While the Committee showed commendable expeditiousness in completing and reporting on its findings, Fr. Devane published three accounts of the evidence submitted

---

[1] Senator O'Farrell, *Senate Debates*. Vol. 12, April, Col. 106, 1929.
[2] *Report of Joint Select Committee on lotteries and indecent advertisements*, pp. XVIII, 106, 1908.

to them, and the authorities consulted, in that same year of 1926. He felt there was a danger that people might lose contact with, and interest in, the important matters with which the Committee was dealing.

Moreover, the Government needs an informed public opinion to facilitate its efforts in introducing legislation, and to help countering in advance a certain opposition which cannot be burked and must be faced.[1]

To marshal Irish opinion, a motley crew of arguments was assembled. Condemnations by the Lord Chief Justice of England. by the House of Lords, by Select Committees and by Royal Commissions were quoted as evidence of the unsuitability of the gutter English press. Sir William Joynson-Hicks, the British Home Secretary, is reported in the *Daily Mail* (17.4.1926) as saying:

In one year two London daily newspapers with 310 issues gave, respectively, 85 columns and 35 columns of reports of divorce cases, whereas of two weekly newspapers, the *News of the World* gave 174 columns and the *Umpire*, 311 columns in 52 issues.[2]

When the very Minister who had set up the Committee said that there were ample powers under the existing law to deal with the sale and distribution of obscene literature, the Lord Chancellor of the United Kingdom, a former Public Prosecutor, a President of the Divorce Court, as well as Special Reports of Select Committees, all authorities in a foreign country, were adduced as proof that existing legislation was inadequate. As regards the liberty of the press, Law Lords and journalists alike were reported as having condemned the failure of those of their colleagues who refused to distinguish between liberty and license. Finally, as a means of ensuring that cultural protectionism was well worth any draconian censorship, an appeal was made to correct the folly of allowing English newspapers to take the bread out of the mouth of Irish printers, and at the same time to abort the Gaelicizing influence so essential to national identity.

Fr. Devane in his second article made some quite sensible proposals as to the composition and character of a possible censorship board which might be entrusted with maintaining a permanently vigilant eye on what was being offered to the reading public. His reference, however, to the great difficulties experienced in getting people actively interested, his account of the inefficacy of moral suasion in the case of mercenary newsvendors, and his relief that so eminent a legal authority as Sir Edward Carson had promulgated the apposite dictum that 'there are illegalities which are not crimes' to justify appropriate action being taken with the recalcitrant, bear witness to his alarm in the presence of what would appear to have

[1] R. S. Devane, 'The Committee on Printed Matter – Some Notes of Evidence' *Irish Ecclesiastical Record* 28 (1926), pp. 357ff.
[2] Ibid., p. 360.

been signs of moral inertia. He expressed a rueful indignation at the dup-
licity of English representatives of objectionable newspapers travelling to
Ireland to give them gratis to newsboys in order to promote their sale, alleging from his experience of working with the moral unregenerates of
Limerick that 'While demand creates a supply, supply creates a demand
out of all proportion.'[1] Throughout the article the emphasis is on newspapers, and their handling of sexual matters, whether treating of cases
dealt with in the Courts or treating of advertisements for contraceptive
devices. When it comes to literature there is either an emotional appeal to
protect the young against 'traffickers in moral poison,' or a quotation
from an eminent British lawyer attributing the decline in morality to exposure to unsuitable literature, or an array of possible definitions of 'indecent,' 'obscene.' And yet Devane was writing in a climate of opinion that
was more the norm than the exception for a country which had gained its
independence.

The history of all emergent nations had shown that control of communications could not be left to the play of market forces when the market itself attracted interests that were assuredly not limited to the national
territory, but were eager to establish themselves in a society that had yet
to define its own political and social norms. The Committee of whose deliberations Fr. Devane so assiduously kept his readers posted had indeed
found evidence of restrictions in the sale of obscene literature in eleven
other countries. In the 1920s, many anglophone governments had
thought fit to introduce some legislation by way of protection for its citizens. What was transparently clear was that the main intent, initially, in
any event, was to limit the influence of certain newspapers and
magazines, not to attack books of social or literary interest. What was disturbing were the outriders in the garb of Vigilance Committees, and articles by well-intentioned people, who in their zeal to carry their point of
view opened up possibilities of a constitutional derogation that would affect even more basic rights than the freedom of expression.

The Irish Times might well adopt a conciliatory note and agree that a
censorship, if conducted discreetly, could well do good work, but even in
the hand of balanced, mature and reasonable men, it could 'be only a desperate and insufficient remedy.'[2] The very fact of finding certain exam-
ples of literature to be unseemly, it argued, must inevitably have the undesirable effect of advertising their existence. This, across some six decades, may well appear a judicious observation but to the Editor of the
Catholic Bulletin, it was the typical sneer from the Ascendancy who chose
to see anyone who did not share its views on the idea of censorship as

---

[1] *Ibid.*, 1926, November, p. 464.
[2] Editorial, *Irish Times*. 1/2/1927, p. 9.

'those low creatures, vulgarians, wastrels, materialists, mere Irish scum.'[1]

The Committee of Enquiry into Evil Literature published its *Report* in the Spring of 1927. Its recommendations were in keeping with the prevailing mood as expressed by the majority pro-control lobby, but without some of the more unbalanced opinions that had inevitably crept into the campaign. Some necessary administrative improvements were recommended, considerable thought was given to the extension of the meanings of 'indecent' and 'obscene' that might be legally sustainable, and the whole question of the dissemination of information on birth control was reviewed with the not unexpected recommendation that it should be more rigorously prohibited. The Committee proposed that the police, without having proof that a sale had taken place, would now be able, on foot of a warrant issued by a district justice, to enter any premises where they believed indecent articles were being kept.

Reaction to the Committee's *Report* was varied. The indefatigable Fr. Devane, who was the only private individual to offer evidence, might well have been disappointed that the Committee had disregarded his proposal that tariff ranging from 33% to 100% should be imposed on foreign magazines and dailies had been rejected. He returned to his theme of linking national revival with the exclusion of alien influences:

We are at present engaged in an heroic effort to revive our national language, national customs, national culture. These objects cannot be achieved without a cheap, healthy and independent native press. In the face of English competition such a press is an impossibility... .[2]

Another cleric, the editor of the *Irish Rosary*, a Fr. MacInerney, echoed Devane's summons of profit in support of a censorship policy that would correspond to the sexual code of morality with which the Irish Catholic Church identified. Having first eliminated 'a great mass of prurient and demoralizing publications,' he then argued,

For economic, national and cultural reasons of the highest moment, the Oireachtas ought to pass a resolution imposing a heavy tariff on the remainder of what Fr. Devane calls the 'popular' class of imported publications.[3]

As has been said, independence was bound inevitably to bring in its wake a review of institutions, practices and customs that had persisted without attracting critical appraisal for many, many years. It was one thing to reverse the conquest of the land mass by feat of arms or by negotiating skill, it was another to take counteractive measures against the conquest of Ireland by English newspapers, which continued long after the British flag had been lowered. It is of interest therefore to note

[1] Editorial, *Catholic Bulletin*. Vol. xvii, March, 1927, p. 233.

[2] R. S. Devane, 'Suggested Tariff on Imported Newspapers and Magazines,' *Studies* 16 (1927), p. 556.

[3] M. H. MacInerney, Comment, *Studies*. Vol. xvi, (1927), p. 556.

throughout the critical year of 1928, how the *Catholic Bulletin* maintained an attack against Ireland being made into a 'free country for the disposal of British merchandise.' What Irishman, it asked rhetorically, ever 'foresaw or imagined an Ireland so debased and despicable as to be undistinguishable from England in the matter of its newspapers and periodical literature?'[1] It was not enough to campaign against England's Evil Literature when its Good Literature, published without censorship, or without regard to moral authority, continued to inflict on the Irish people the disputes, controversies and sentiments of free-thinkers.

The mind of England has been trained to criticize and think for itself; that of Ireland to believe and accept what it is taught. The respective newspapers of both countries reflect this fundamental distinction.[2]

What the *Catholic Bulletin* feared was that the other-worldly, intellectually dependent Irish (as it saw them), with their allegiance to the Church, dedication to the Commandments of God and regard for the sacredness of family life would be put at jeopardy if exposed to the materialism, the agnosticism, the non-confessional morality and divorce which characterized contemporary British life.

The existing position [according to the same leader-writer] is that Ireland is being overrun, a veritable Eighth Plague, with newspapers whose morals are absolutely at variance with the principles that have been the cherished characteristics of the nation.[3]

The next month's issue took up the attack with a subheading, 'The English Press Invasion,' this time levelling its charges at the relatively good newspapers. It quoted an article to underline how subversive their contents could be of the foundation of religion, but refused to identify the name of the paper or the author of the article. That the *Catholic Bulletin* thought it was a blasphemous production may be imagined from an excerpt it quoted as an example of how uncomprehending and deprecatory English agnosticism could be about the True Faith.

In the west, saints amazed the world with their austerities and self-scourgings and confessions and vigils. But Luther delivered us from all that. His reformation was a triumph of imagination and a triumph of cheapness. It brought you complete salvation and asked you for nothing but faith... He may be said to have abolished the charge for admission to heaven. Paul had advocated this: but Luther and Calvin did it.[4]

The popularity of the paper was unquestioned but did Irish people, the *Catholic Bulletin* asked, realize they were reading a paper owned by non-Catholics, written by non-Catholics, and published for non-Catholics?

[1] 'Far and Near,' *Catholic Bulletin*. Vol. xviii, Feb. 1928, No. 2, p. 124.
[2] Ibid., p. 124.
[3] Ibid., p. 126.
[4] Quoted in 'Far and Near,' *Catholic Bulletin*. Vol xviii, No. 3, 1928, p. 231–2.

Did they realize that anybody who read, retained or published matter that propounds heresy or schism incurred ipso facto excommunication reserved to the Holy See as provided by Canon 2318? Or that anybody who wrote or gave interviews to such organs of communication is infringing Canon 1386.2? The only thing to be done according to the *Catholic Bulletin* was to adopt Fr. Devane's proposal and, by imposing a tariff, make people really pay for their sins.

No doubt from this point of view something had to be done. Circulation of English Sunday newspapers among a population of 3 million was now estimated at 350,000, yielding a potential audience of one million adults. The *Catholic Bulletin* wondered what was the explanation for this popularity. The free insurance scheme? The layout and presentation? The advertisements? Or could it be, the periodical wondered, that London was brought to the doors of the Irish Free State with its advertisements and alternative life styles, some of which were repeated by Irish newspapers 'in the interests of the economic welfare of the enemy of this country... To our mind, the greatest force operating against Irish industrial revival is this big circulation press... We refuse to believe that the representatives of the people, elected on patriotic grounds, are going to lie down under this very real aspect of English domination.'[1] It is interesting to note that progressively this theme of the potential damage to Irish enterprise is stressed more and more as if native prosperity were a necessary concomitant to spiritual salvation. As the *Catholic Bulletin* went on to say: 'Economics are no less important than morals.'

What brought the concentrated examination of the English Press to a close in that year's issue of the *Catholic Bulletin* was the denunciation by the Bishop of Galway of the English *Daily Express*. That paper had incurred the wrath of the *Catholic Bulletin* in the past either because its proprietor, Lord Beaverbrook, counted the ex-Governor-General Mr. T. Healy among his friends, whereas the *Catholic Bulletin* counted the same gentleman as an implacable enemy of all it stood for, or because it had published an attack on the Catholic Church and its sacraments. At all events, the *Daily Express* decided to serialize over a period of two weeks a Life of Christ written by Emil Ludwig. The work was not thought highly of in Galway. The Bishop said it was the most blasphemous production he had ever read; that the paper itself was a poisonous rag; a positive danger to youth, and even to the grown-ups and aged people of this country; and finally that the good people of his diocese should send it back to England.

The Bishop's words and admonitions were, according to the *Catholic Bulletin*, duly reported in the Catholic Press, which to everybody's con-

[1] Ibid., Vol. xviii, No. 4, April, 1928, pp. 342–3.

sequent discomfort also advertised that the much-vilified *Daily Express* was going to print a series of articles by the same ex-Governor-General Healy, who had already denounced Ludwig as a 'biographical liar,' and by a Fr. John J. Hannon S.J., who was a leading theologian respected in both England and Ireland. 'What,' says the *Catholic Bulletin*, 'were the people of Galway to do?' Were they to disobey the Bishop who had forbidden them to buy or read the offending *Daily Express*? Were they to deny themselves the contribution of two very distinguished Catholics who most certainly would not lend their names to any articles that did not reflect orthodox Catholic teaching? What, and the frustration of the *Catholic Bulletin* is almost palpable, does it all mean? The answer Irish readers were offered

It means that for the future no member of the Irish hierarchy can condemn, by name, any English newspaper circulating blasphemous articles in Ireland, without running the risk of having prominent personages of his own race and faith exploited against him.[1]

This account, in the year in which the Censorship of Publications Bill was being debated, of the English press and its place in Irish culture at the time reveals a point of view that is rigorously Catholic orthodox, conservative and dogmatic, protective to the point of being obscurantist, insular, nationalist and satisfied with its Little Ireland cosmology. Not at all ill-disposed to buttressing theological with economic arguments, it was throughout single-minded in its determination to run up the danger signal, alerting those Irish to whom it might appeal that English newspapers constituted the one threat that could not be ignored, and that Irish newspapers, with the renegade *Irish Times* as the most coherent adversary of all, were unable unaided to act as a bulwark against their apparently Godless neighbor. The mentality it demonstrated was a far cry from Cleary's appeal that truth should not be adulterated so as to affect its potency or Gwynn's aspirations for a press contribution to the common good.

Opinion was of course not unanimous. In an Editorial, the *Dublin Magazine* denied the compatibility of 'evil' and 'literature' on the grounds that

Literature cannot be evil, for it is the artistic expression of those imaginative faculties which are akin to the life of the soul, and evil is primarily the principle of negation, which if not overthrown destroys the life of the soul.[2]

After this piece of didactic positivism, it distinguished literature from other forms of writing, declared a man's mind to be the last bastion of liberty which needed to feed on the aliment of another's intellectual endeavors and warned:

[1] Ibid., Vol. xviii, No. 8, August, 1928, p. 794.
[2] Editorial, *The Dublin Magazine*. Vol. iii, No. 2, 1928, p. 3.

If some Committee or Board or individual could doom to extinction a book of genius because its morality was suspect, or not cut according to recognized pattern, the real sufferer would not be so much the author as humanity at large. No man liveth to himself … he must also retain the immemorial right to communicate his vision to his fellow men. The majority instinct of rigid morality must not be allowed to usurp the throne of imaginative intuition.[1]

It was left however largely to Æ in the *Irish Statesman* to provide an alternative view based on a reasoned mixture of appeals to common sense, to national heritage, and to the reality of the world in 1928.

We have never believed that a people could be made moral by an Act of Parliament. Real virtue exists only when the soul, having vision of both good and evil, exercising free will, chooses what is good.[2]

However, anticipating the morality of Vatican II was perhaps not enough to persuade a people whose religion relied for guidance on authoritative interpretation. Did the Irish fear Gresham's law in literature, that bad literature as represented by the English Press would drive out noble literature? But surely, Æ continued, the best safeguard against evil was goodness. America had shown with Prohibition the inadequacy of legislating against a gift that was susceptible of being perverted. Instead of banning books, the Irish should be building libraries in the numerous counties where neither they nor bookshops existed.

We are one of the most uncultivated of races, if the quality of our culture can be judged by the number of books read in the Irish Free State. But little could be expected in a country where, until a year ago, ninety per cent of the boys left the national schools at the age of twelve, few of them caring to read or think after.[3]

Whatever the accuracy of his statistics, Æ highlighted the consequences of a rigid exclusionary policy that would deny whole issues of a periodical because of a blemish found in one article, that would make an enemy of Ireland out of every author who found his works were barred entrance, and that would give to the Irish in the eyes of the world the same mental set about humans relations as the bishop who used to declaim against the degrading passion of love.

He printed articles from Yeats and from Shaw. The former confirmed the populist view of the arrogant Ascendancy intellectual,

If you think it necessary to exclude certain books and pictures, leave it to men learned in art and letters, if they will serve you, and if they will not to average educated men.[4]

and the latter who as usual forgot that home truths should never be heard above a whisper,

---

[1] Ibid., p. 4.
[2] Editorial, *Irish Statesman*. 10, 1928, p. 456.
[3] Ibid., p. 486.
[4] W. B. Yeats, 'The Censorship and St Thomas,' pp. 47–8.

But if having broken England's grip, if she [Ireland] steps back into the Atlantic as a little green patch in which a few million cowards are not allowed to call their souls their own by a handful of morbid Catholics, mad with heresyphobia, unnaturally combining with a handful of Calvinists, mad with sexphobia, (both being in a small and intensely disliked minority of their own co-religionists) then the world will let these Irish go their own way into insignificance without the smallest concern.[1]

Yeats came back to the attack in the columns of the *Spectator* alleging that the Irish Government had drafted a 'Bill which it hates, which must be expounded and defended by Ministers full of contempt for their own words,' and just to make sure that the red rag would goad the Irish bull, he added loftily, à propos of those Sunday papers (which even his readers in England would not admit into their houses), 'every country passing out of automatism passes through demoralization and ... has no choice but to go on to intelligence.' Eliot writing in *The Criterion* was sufficiently taken with the problem to muse that it would be strange if a movement towards censorship legislation were to result in Protestantism in England making common cause with Catholicism in Ireland. He did, however, feel that

the support of such a Bill by Roman Catholics in Ireland is more intelligible than would be the support of similar oppressive measures in England by liberal Protestants. The tyranny of religion is bad: if religion should prosper, it should not prosper by such means. But the tyranny of morality, with some wholly vague religious backing, or wholly divorced from any exact religion, is still worse.[2]

The anonymous Irish correspondent of *The Round Table*, an English quarterly that dealt with the politics of the British Commonwealth of which the Irish Free State was then a member, pointed out that the establishment of censorship

is in effect to take from the individual the right to choose between good and evil and to seek to make universal particular standards of taste and criticism which cannot have a general application and which may be both ignorant and offensive ... Evil things flourish in the dark, and curiosity nourishes what is forbidden.[3]

The Round Table followed the Bill through all its stages. Its comments were insightful. It recognizes the attempt to steer a middle course between 'the quasi-intellectuals who would condemn nothing, and the ignorant zealots who would prevent all independent thought and allow no foreign book of any kind to enter the country.' It identified the worst type of English Sunday newspaper as being the real object of moral concern, and was pleased to note in spite of its predictions that discussion in the Dáil and Senate had resulted in the worst features of the Bill having been eliminated. It predicted an anti-clerical reaction which would increase as

[1] G.B. Shaw, 'Censorship', *Irish Statesman* 17.11.1928, p. 208.
[2] T.S. Eliot, A commentary, *The Criterion*. Vol. XIII, No. XXXI, 1928, p. 187.
[3] Ireland: Events in the Free State, *The Round Table*. Dec. 1928, No. 72, p. 830.

more people received higher education, but expressed the hope that should the powers under the Bill be used intelligently only literature that was manifestly pornographic would be suppressed.

But for all that Æ, Yeats, Shaw, the liberal journals and whoever else said, who heard them? A limited few whose extra inconvenience in procuring the forbidden fruit was probably more than compensated for by the pleasurable guilt associated with a socially daring misdemeanor. For the rest, too many subscribed to the ethic of the *Catholic Bulletin* or the *Irish Rosary*, which saw in the Anglo-Irish school of literature the not-so-thin end of a wedge that was humanist, international and ambivalent as regards the characteristics of what the Christian existence in Ireland should represent. Their editorial comments were typical of a puritanical isolationism that often descended, as has been observed, into a personal abuse that belied the religious pretensions enshrined in their mastheads. In the polemics that ensued, Irish Ireland was a star to which many wagons might be attached, and if in their progress the chariots of Catholic power and the Catholic way of life should collide with standards deemed to be obstacles to their realization, the destruction of reputations might be explained, if not condoned, by the profession of a patriotic fervor and a purity of ideals. People who had denounced Synge's *Playboy* were not slow in promoting the notion that no great loss would be experienced if the writings of certain authors were unobtainable. According to this cultural exclusivism, any literature that might incur moral disapprobation by the Catholic Church could not be guaranteed to be nationally authentic. In addition to theoretical justifications of condemnation, there were the concrete instances of demands for censorship by the Catholic Vigilance Association, later joined by the Catholic Truth Society (a publications agency founded by the bishops); there was the harassment of newsagents and the burning of newspapers, referred to above; and finally there was the *Madonna of Slieve Dun*, a harmless short story which resulted in the withdrawal from the library service of monies from the Carnegie Trust.[1] Generally, throughout many sections of the population there was a tenaciously held belief that the basis of Irish society would never be firmly secured until the State decided to statutorily establish the Catholic moral code as the law of the land.

From the vantage of hindsight, and bearing in mind that totalitarian regimes like Italy and democratic republics like France were equally opposed to contraception, it would be difficult to say that the Act – if one is to judge its intentions by its language – went far enough to satisfy the bigots. The definition of the word 'indecent'

---

[1] Brown, *ibid.*, p. 74.

as including suggestive of, or inciting to sexual immorality or unnatural vice or likely in any other similar way to corrupt or deprave,[1]
while it did not shed much light that would discover plainly, or reveal beyond doubt, the existence or non-existence of that which would 'corrupt of deprave', was the best Irish legislators could do, and sooner than seek to improve on it, subsequent Acts have left it unchanged. Of more significance were the grounds on which the Board was to consider complaints brought against a book which was alleged to be indecent. The Act laid down that regard should be paid to all or any of the following:

(a) the literary, artistic, scientific or historic merit or importance and the general tenor of the book or the particular edition of a book which is the subject of such complaint,

(b) the language in which such edition or editions is printed or produced,

(c) the nature and extent of the circulation which in the opinion of the Board, such book or edition is intended to haver,

(d) the class of reader in Saorstát Éireann which, in the opinion of the Board, may reasonably be expected to read such book or edition, and

(e) any other matter relevant to such book or edition which appears to the Board to be relevant.[2]

In addition, medical and legal books were excluded from consideration, periodicals were required to 'have usually or frequently been indecent' before it became incumbent on the Board to examine them, and the Customs were to continue to act as public watchdogs by referring books upon suspicion to the Censorship Board, which consisted of one Protestant, three Catholic laymen, and one Catholic priest who was nominated its Chairman.

It has generally been agreed that the Dáil treated the passage of the Act with considerable thoughtfulness, if the number of amendments is any gauge and the signal by the Opposition of its intention to collaborate is to be interpreted positively. However there were warnings that did not perhaps receive the attention they should. Mr. Fitzgerald-Kenney, the Minister who had replaced the murdered O'Higgins, was somewhat ambiguous as to whether a book would be condemned on a *virginibus pueris-que* basis, or only when it was clearly, *ex professo*, immoral, and indeed not merely immoral *obiter*. This prompted Senator Sir John Keane to utter prophetically about how inaccurately the Minister was foretelling future events:

He drew a totally imaginary picture of what the censors would do. As far as I can understand it, when the censors are set up they will be in the position of a quasi-juridical body. They will form their opinions on their own judgement and they will

---

[1] *Censorship of Publications Act*, 1929. Section 2, Dublin, The Stationery Office, p. 5.
[2] Ibid., p. 9.

in no way be bound by what the Minister said here ... or in the Dáil as to what he thinks they should do.[1]

Other contributions indicated the attitude, temperament and thinking of the nation's elected representatives. The sectarian aspect of the control of what might be read, everyone was glad to note, was no longer said to be an issue, a conclusion that made members of minority faiths shake their heads in disbelief. One member expressed his satisfaction that it would ensure a repatriation of the intellect. No discussion was allowed on the prohibition of birth control publications, a democratic lapse that had to await fifty years to be corrected. A distinction was drawn between the obligation imposed upon members of the Board to 'read and examine' and the obligation to 'examine,' deputies deciding eventually in the interests of the unpaid Censors, if not of literature, to limit their duty to the latter. These analyses in the Dáil were supplemented by another rigorous review when the matter came before the Senate (which at that time was largely appointive). Of the seventeen amendments proposed to the Bill, nothing emerged to highlight a divergence of opinion like the speech of this same Sir John Keane who again, more than most, seems to have grasped what might be its eventual role. He argued that to oppose the Bill would be to court public opprobrium, but that for all its popular appeal, the intelligentsia were as divided about its merits as they were reluctant to reveal their opinions. He then went on to speak of access to reading matter:

There is the method of repression and control and the method of selection and liberty. We know the method of prohibition and control. I do not wish to say anything ungracious, but I may say that is generally the method of the majority church in this country. It is a method which tries closely to control reading, which fosters good and discourages bad, which sublimates some things and conceals others, and which calls upon the will to surrender its ordained power.[2]

The other way was of course the Protestant method of liberty of thought and freedom of choice. Keane's fellow Protestant senators refused to associate themselves with his remarks so that the dust raised by his accusations of theological dominance, and by his imputations of unconstitutionality, was allowed to settle in silence.

Outside the Dáil, the Catholic press made sure in their columns that in the months preceding the signing the Bill into law, legislators would remain firm in their resolve. In January the *Catholic Bulletin* takes Pádraig Colum to task for saying that Ireland should be importing ideas not restricting them. In February, it attacked Professor Tierney and warned that a careful eye would be kept on how the representatives of the University voted. Behind the Professor's conclusions that censorship was im-

---

[1] *Seanad Debates*. vol. 12, col. 58, 11/4/1929.
[2] Senator Sir John Keane, *Senate Debates*. vol. 12, col. 68–69, 11/4/1929.

practical and reflected badly on the maturity of the Irish people there stood the 'Sewage School' which everybody knew 'prefers books as a medium of infection.'[1] The *Catholic Bulletin* did not wonder he had experienced 'curative deflation' in failing to get himself elected to the Governing Body of University College, Dublin. It suggested, in the meantime, that the 'common and decent people' of Ireland would be relieved to have the opinion of 'A mere Protestant Professor' who had described James Joyce whom Professor Tierney chose to champion as 'having raked hell and the sewers for dirt'[2] in the writing of *Ulysses*. In March, it quoted extracts from speeches given by different bishops attacking those who objected to 'any legal interference with the circulation of printed matter.'[3] In May, *The Irish Times* was itself attacked for its arrogance in claiming to speak for the 'educated classes' and for the 'liberal culture' that even at this eleventh hour was seeking to wreck the working machinery of the Bill. What the *Catholic Bulletin* was purveying was being replicated in the other periodical literature of the time, the *Irish Rosary*, *The Standard*, the *Catholic Mind*, *The Leader*, *Studies* and others with varying degrees of acerbity, and at a time when it was considered the duty of every priest to work for their widest diffusion.

The Catholic press had certain advantages. Its readers were a uniform, solid mass whose range of opinion on any matter that would come within the scope of confessional reporting was predictable. It was a press which measured itself against a similar press in the United States, England and Belgium with an objectivity that ensured it did not suffer – to its own disadvantage at least – from an insular approach. It was charged with a mission that guaranteed a readership who came to regard the weekly purchase as part of its religious ritual. And finally in areas of morality, it represented a pressure group that elected representatives, regardless of their affiliation, ignored at their peril. Its message was heard by all activist Catholics, irrespective of socio-economic class and political conviction, and was generally attended to.

When the Bill was eventually passed in the summer of 1929, there was a general expression of relief. Even periodicals hostile to the idea such as the *Irish Statesman*, *The Irishman*, *An Phoblacht*, and *The Nation* were of an opinion that the Act as it finally emerged was an immense improvement on the original Bill. Definitions had been modified; the proposal to have officially appointed watchdog committees up and down the country had been abandoned; the concept of the 'general tendency' of the contents of the book in assessing it had been adopted. It seemed to satisfy the need for the young State to affirm another aspect of its nationalism. 'The

---

[1] Editorial, *Catholic Bulletin*. Vol. XIX, 1929, No. 1, p. 9.

[2] Ibid., Vol. XIX, 1929, No. 2, p. 102.

[3] Ibid., Vol. XIX, 1929, No. 3, p. 205.

Bill seems to me to need no defense. It is but a step in the realization of that intellectual autonomy which has already had its counterpart in other domains...,'[1] was not an uncommon reaction.

One matter escaped all but the *Irish Statesman*. As far back as 1923 Æ had written:

We say we cannot merely out of Irish tradition find solutions to all our modern problems... We shall find much inspiration and beauty in our own past but we have to ransack world literature, world history, world science and study our national contemporaries and graft what we learn into our national tradition, if we are not to fade out of the list of civilized nations.[2]

This approach accurately predicts most of the liberal protest that was to be heard for the next six years. Its logic seemed incontrovertible, and was urged with as much conviction as *The Leader* and the *Catholic Bulletin* argued the contrary. What Æ however did not allow for in his protest against barriers was the fact that all post-revolutionary situations are haunted by the ideals of those who are no longer around to profit from the victory they had contributed to winning. Perhaps he did not recognize that even as they heaved a sigh of relief at the ending of the bloodshed, the Irish people were looking for outlets to accommodate the continuance of the revolutionary energy. There were tensions with the outside powers as the country sought to establish itself in the world and eventually in the British Commonwealth. At home there was a vacuum in which Griffiths' industrial policies remained as inert as Connolly's idea of social justice. There were frictions like the National Anthem, the Irish revival, land annuities, Trinity College and other matters which one way or another always were liable to blow up into major confrontation. Too much had been achieved by the gun to discount its presence as a logical response to what might be conceived of as an intolerable betrayal of the aims of the 1916 rebellion. It was one thing for Æ to ask rhetorically 'To what must we attribute the Bill? It is, I think, a consequence of arrested growth; or in other words moral infantilism.'[3] It was another to challenge a belief, perhaps the outcome of centuries of ignorance but nonetheless tenaciously held, that literature of any sort had no rights that could stand out against what was owed to God.

This was a country that in one decade had known arson, robbery, murder, political assassination, and most traumatic of all, as has been noted, had had through force majeure to accept an unnatural division of its territory. To counteract these pointers to anarchy, all political parties had come to realize that the machinery of government had to be set in motion, law and order restored, the economy regenerated and the status of the

[1] Deputy Doyle, *Dáil Debates*. Vol. 26, Col. 658, 18/10/1928.
[2] *Irish Statesman*. 3/11/1923, p. 230.
[3] Æ 'The Censorship of Ireland,' *Nation and Athenaeum* 22/12/1928, p. 435.

Oireachtas affirmed as the legislative body to which the executive was immediately responsible for the running of the country. To ensure that public peace, health and safety were preserved the Government of the day frustrated by Article 48 the personal contact the voters might have had in the making of the laws by which they were to be governed. The Censorship Act was of the same stuff. Both were measures to be justified on the grounds that freedom in the bosom of the evolving, ever-perfectible citizen of the revolution might even break out into license. Underlying the political dialogue was a perilous contradiction: all lawful authority coming from God to reside in the people had still to be interpreted in the interests of a third party, the British Crown, which neither honored the Irish faith nor recognized Irish sovereignty in a manner that was acceptable to all of the people. To contain that sentiment within the bounds of parliamentary exchanges, to offset the absence of even the pretense of providing work or redistributing income by creating an issue identifiable with the ancient enemy, and at the same time inhibitive of new and disturbing ideas, must have appeared an excellent substitute for welfare legislation.·

The Catholic periodical press if they did not appreciate the reasons behind the reasons for the Censorship Act were more astute and more perceptive than Æ in realizing that they represented for many,

an attempt to translate into reality the puritanism that often goes with revolution – to establish so far as laws could establish it, that the new Ireland should shine like a good deed in a naughty world.[1]

What Æ did realize was that the Executive had decided that it was not going to be satisfied just with acting against newspapers and periodicals about which all the clamor had been raised. To do so, all that was required was either a prohibitive tariff (as suggested by Fr. Devane) or an extension of existing judiciary powers. The government of the day, however, disliked the idea of moving against the Press (still today the freest of the media in Ireland). Instead it sought, by offering the clergy more than it had asked, to identify itself more firmly with the one stable institution the country had ever known (and thus wrong-foot, if possible, its opponents). In effect, what happened was that the opportunity was grasped not alone to suppress pornography but to give the fanatics of the Catholic press powers the future use of which not even they were able to visualize. In the long run, did it matter since the mass of the Irish people hardly seemed to care one way or the other? But they, too, were to learn. The Church had begun a justifiable campaign against the distribution of certain English Sunday newspapers, the contents of which it found offensive. It ended

[1] F.S.L. Lyons, *Ireland since the Famine* (London: Weidenfeld and Nicholson, 1970), p. 675.

with its moral teaching being reinforced by statutory law to cover areas where, by the very nature of the phenomenon, consensus was most unlikely. For the sake of its immortal soul, the Irish people were to be denied some of the means to find it. Instead, its tutelage had begun.

CHAPTER 4

CENSORSHIP IN ACTION

The nation had survived its first decade of independence. Power had passed peacefully from one civil war foe to the other. A new economic strategy was implemented, and a new definition of the national ethos was to be enshrined in a Constitution which the people would freely vote themselves. Self-sufficiency, a return to traditional values, and, above all, a consolidation of those familial and simple virtues upon which Irish civilization was allegedly based were to be the accepted guidelines for those who aspired to be conscientious, God-fearing and patriotic. Censorship was one of the mainstays of such an approach. A list of prohibited books was begun that would remove from public access old and modern classics without which the human spirit would be the poorer. There were protests at this tendency to opt out of the mainstream of world thinking just as the gathering clouds of World War II presaged greater misfortunes for mankind than immoral books. Radio and film continued to provide messages intended to distract rather than to inform. The neutrality that ensued raised control of the media to be a matter of public security. The Irish withdrew behind their Celtic mists and now had time to examine the consequences of writing for themselves according to imposed criteria which only a few cared to challenge. Cut off from a wider dimension of reality, censorship soon lost whatever sense of proportion it possessed. Discussions in the legislature and attempts to achieve an accommodation in the journals were to prove of no avail. A passionate intensity was dominant that would discover evil even in literature approved by the Catholic hierarchy. Such excess of zeal was to lead to the first indications of disaffection and doubt among those who had been prepared originally to welcome censorship as a social earnest for a spiritual ideal.

It is not in the nature of pressure groups to celebrate a victory, then fold their tents and steal away into oblivion. The passage of an Act by the Oireachtas does not change the mind and hearts of the citizens whose actions it proposes to control. In the conservative nationalism that best describes the climate of opinion in the late twenties and early thirties, there was no outward-looking cosmopolitanism, no revolutionary humanism, no political egalitarianism, ready to rise and protest censorship by way of reflex action as an insult to the movement which had brought independence and generated the finest literary movement the twentieth century had known. Illegal drillings, summary executions by the IRA, the emergence of Saor Éire as an organization dedicated to overthrow Irish capitalism (or what was left of it after the repercussions of Wall St.), the passing of the Constitution (Amendment No. 17) Bill, which was rightly regarded as a rigorous and harsh Public Safety Bill, the change to Dominion co-equality with the United Kingdom as a result of the Statute of Westminster, the ruinous decline in agricultural exports, the reduction in state employees' salaries and in the old age pension, all these and many other issues were to be topics of conversation, but not the Censorship of Publications Act. The party of austerity in fiscal, as well as in moral, attitudes had run its ten year course and now the 'slightly constitutional Party' under de Valera was waiting in the wings to begin a sixteen-year period of government. In the meantime, the machinery of the Act got under way in 1930. The members of the Board were appointed, regulations governing the submission of suspect publications were drawn up, and the Minister for Justice's worst prognostications were proved to be quite accurate – few bothered to avail themselves of the opportunity to eradicate the alleged evil in their midst.

The Catholic Truth Society did what it could to correct this default. It invited cooperation in the work of detection and endeavored to found voluntary recognized associations in various parts of the country with whom it would collaborate. It baulked, however, at the idea of spending its own meagre resources on the acquisition of such literature, holding that its purpose was to propagate what was good in writing, not to unmask that which was evil. The *Catholic Bulletin*, the *Catholic Mind* and other organs of the Catholic press continued to be unremitting in their efforts to ferret out peccant publications, particularly those which promoted birth control. The *Irish Book Lover*, rather inappropriately, congratulated everybody that the Act was 'in full swing' and that while so far only non-Irish publications have been banned, 'it may be that an Irish author will one day attain the doubtful distinction of being included in a subsequent list.'[1] But then there was such a backlog! No, a more accurate estimation of the impact may be found elsewhere. Adams writes that 'comment and controversy on the subject of censorship were somewhat meagre'[2] in the thirties both in parliament and in the newspapers as distinct from criticism

[1] Séamas Ó Donnabháin, *The Irish Book Lover* 18 (1930), p. 74.
[2] Michael Adams, *Censorship: The Irish Experience* (Dublin: Scepter 1968), p. 64.

brought to bear on particular issues like the banning of specific books. What was apparently happening was that private individuals not unexpectedly were unwilling to lodge complaints in the volume needed to justify the existence of the Censorship Board. One reason was that they would have to forward a copy of the publication and go to the trouble of marking passages and composing comments to justify their objections. Another more probable reason, and one that explains the calm that succeeded in the legislature for the next ten years, was, as Horgan pointed out,

that very few people in Ireland read any modern books at all, and that those who do are not likely to take the trouble of acting as literary informers to the Censorship Board. In any event, to attempt a censorship of modern literature, even in one language, is not unlike trying to drink a river.[1]

When it is recalled that the Customs Consolidation Act of 1876, Section 42, had not been repealed by the 1929 Act so that the Customs Officials, by operating along guidelines, then and now, of their own invention, were all the time keeping a watchful eye over imported literature; that the members of the Board were and are unpaid; that the notion of informing to authority was and is particularly distasteful to a people who have known civil strife; and that while there may well have been pleasure expressed in parochial houses and episcopal palaces with a report in *The Tablet* of February 22, 1930, that Pope Pius XI 'was very glad that the legislation had been passed for the censorship of publications,' none but the most militant Catholic was likely to find the trouble in any way rewarding. These confessional Comstocks were to appear, but not in the first few years of the thirties.

The reason was simple: there were too many other issues of much greater importance. Considering the reputation of the new Head of Government it is not too difficult to understand why the book-buying, middle-class public would have been more preoccupied with fears of a communistic assault upon property, of a settling of old Civil War scores, of a bellicose confrontation with Britain, and of unthinkable reprisals in education and health against those who had excommunicated his brothers-in-arms, than with the loss of Sherwood Anderson's *Horses and Men*, of Frank Harris' *Bernard Shaw* and of Sinclair Lewis' *Elmer Gantry* which were among the first to incur the Board's displeasure. No, in the seven years that intervened between de Valera's accession to power and the outbreak of hostilities in Europe, more significant events were to occupy the foreground. The process of dismantling the Treaty began by neutralizing or removing those symbols with which popular thinking identifies the alien influence so easily; the degradation of the office of Governor-General;

---

[1] J. J. Horgan, 'Ireland: Events in the Free State' *The Round Table* Vol. xx, No. 80 (1930) p. 835.

the abolition of the oath; the denial of the right of appeal from the Irish courts to the Privy Council in London; the careful eschewing of a formalism that might be associated with the ascendancy; the removal of all references to the King in the 1922 Constitution; and finally the modification of the relationship between the two countries to one of external association, all these measures contributed to satisfying the separatist sentiments so necessary for national self-confidence. Free trade was replaced by economic nationalism; the retention of annuities payable to Britain was determined; the drive to establish national self-sufficiency through the erection of high tariff walls was launched so that there ensued

a serious and prolonged attempt to redress the balance between the different sectors of the economy – to free the countryside from the dominance of the cattleman, to extend the area of tillage, to develop home industries and thus provide employment for those who might otherwise be obliged to emigrate.[1]

In addition widows' and orphans' pensions were introduced, unemployment assistance made available, the construction industry was encouraged, new factories were located in rural areas and capital was injected by state-sponsored bodies into the economy to improve the infrastructure necessary for the advance of manufacturing enterprises. By contrast with its predecessor a caring, socially-sensitive government was emerging. In the previous administration the Irish identity had been articulated by asserting dominion co-equality and a cultural differentialism through the negativity of the Censorship Acts. This administration showed itself to be more aggressive by loudly and roundly proclaiming an ideal that stood in sharp contrast to everything that was associated with a British way of life. Ireland was to be a land where money was to be valued only as a means for purchasing basic commodities. The dream was,

of a people who were satisfied with frugal comfort and devoted their leisure to the things of the spirit; a land whose countryside would be bright with cosy homesteads, whose fields and villages would be joyous with the sound of industry, the romping of sturdy children, the contests of athletic youth, the laughter of comely maidens: whose firesides would be the forums of the wisdom of serene old age.[2]

Of course such dreams carry a price tag when they are to be translated into reality. The Economic War that ensued and the protectionist policies the followed the retention of annuities led to a serious slump in trade, with a huge increase in unemployment and a severe decline in wages. Again there were serious threats to law and order as a result of the unrelenting hostility that initially began as a feud between those who had supported and those who had opposed the signing of the Treaty, but later developed into an ideological war (not unaccompanied by physical vio-

---

[1] F.S.L. Lyons, *Ireland Since the Famine*, p. 614.
[2] Eamon de Valera, as reported in *The Irish Press.* 18/3/1943, p. 1.

lence) between those who wished to consolidate what had been won and those who wished to continue the struggle for what remained to be achieved; between corporativists and socialists; between 'big' farmers and landowners affected by the Economic War in terms of their shrinking profits on the one side, and 'small' farmers and farm laborers who were equally affected but in terms of an income barely enough for their simplest needs on the other. Violence in the form of beatings-up, floggings, civil commotion and shootings was commonplace. Parliamentary debate provided no model of how opposing views might agree to differ. And to pile Pelion upon Ossa there was an autochthonous constitution that managed to be republican without breaking the external link with England, that combined a secular liberalism and an acceptance of Catholic social teaching on the nature of the State, and that asserted inalienable rights to property at the same time as it promoted Irish idealistically to the status of first national language. But these were not inconsistencies to de Valera who presented his Constitution to the people as

a renewed declaration of national independence and its enactment will mark the attainment of one definite objective in the national struggle. It consolidates the ground that has been gained and forms a secure basis from which we can move forward.[1]

When the plebiscite was held on the ratification of the Constitution, the electorate gave a none too generous endorsement. But this grudging approval should be seen as reflecting a period when political convictions were held with an aggressive determination yet at the same time were sufficiently imbued with the democratic spirit to accept unquestioningly the decision of the majority. Certainly the physical force elements in the IRA and the uncompromising liberals protested and, as will be seen, continued to make their feelings and voices heard. For all their reservations, however, there was a growing feeling among most Irish that these pre-war years were witnessing movement, a domestication of the national impulse, a sense of presence at the birth of political structures that were indigenous. There were legislative measures dealing with social welfare; there was an economic policy that had clearcut nationally-minded objectives; there was industrial and agrarian activity of which the country had little previous comparable experience; if there was poverty, there was a directive to the legislators written into the new Constitution, Article 45.4:

1. The State pledges itself to safeguard with especial care the economic interests of the weaker section of the community, and, where necessary, to contribute to the support of the infirm, the widow, the orphan, and the aged.

Planning regarding currency, banking, state investment and financing of

---

[1] Eamon de Valera's address, quoted in The Earl of Longford and Thomas P. O'Neill, *Eamon de Valera* (Dublin: Gill and Macmillan, 1970), p. 298.

government spending was elaborated. In foreign policy de Valera, by worldwide agreement, was recognized as an impressive champion of the League of Nations against states such as Japan and Italy which disregarded the rights of other countries to independence. And, finally, on the eve of World War II, he not only regained possession from Britain of Irish ports without which future neutrality would have been a nonsense but also negotiated a settlement to the Economic War which was highly advantageous. The Church was more than satisfied with the Constitution (as well it might, with its 'special position' enshrined in Article 44), but the minority had also some grounds for satisfaction at that time not only because of the affirmation that 'Freedom of conscience and the free profession and practice of religion are, subject to public order and morality, guaranteed to every citizen'[1] but also because of the courteous and meaningfully effective manner with which they had been consulted.[2] All these measures were important in that they involved the people. That they continued to suffer from emigration, from pockets of economic stagnation, from frustration at the quality of social life engineered by the alliance of the Church and the petty bourgeoisie is true. Despite these drawbacks, they were still aware that there was a new political force abroad that was not satisfied that Ireland should merely evolve through time but was determined to move the country perceptibly in the direction of the ideal that had inspired the struggle for independence over countless generations.

In this period of national definition what role did the media play? As has been pointed out, the Censorship of Publications Board did not attract much comment. The *Catholic Mind*, the *Catholic Bulletin*, the *Irish Rosary* and their like were inevitably loath to let drop the issue of safeguarding Irish morals against evil literature, but it requires an exhaustive study of the files of this confessional press before there can be found material of an activist nature that compares with the pre-1929 diatribes. There is an ongoing criticism of Yeats, of Shaw and of the effrontery of the newly-formed Irish Academy of Letters in protesting to the Minister against banning *The Adventures of a Black Girl in Her Search for God* before the Board had had an opportunity to pass judgement on it.[3] There are quotations from Lenten Pastorals, for example, the Archbishop of Tuam in 1934, warning about blasphemous and immoral books:

The evil recently became so menacing that a kind of censorship was set up, but unfortunately it was altogether inadequate. It was only when some conscientious casual reader reported a bad book that the Censorship could act.[4]

[1] Constitution Article 44.2.1.
[2] Longford and O'Neill, p. 297.
[3] Editorial, *The Catholic Bulletin*, Vol. xxiii, No. 9, (1933), p. 693ff.
[4] Editorial, *The Catholic Bulletin*, Vol. xxiv, No. 3, (1934), pp. 181–2.

What is interesting about this admonition and those of his fellow bishops is their mildness and infrequency. Late night dances which were castigated without fail throughout the thirties were correctly adjudged to be more of a source of evil for the Irish than were books. Whatever the deficiencies of members of the Censorship Board, the episcopal bench could rely on the Customs to control the flow of literature. Indeed that very year there had been a debate in the Senate on the vagaries of that branch of government, drawing attention to the fact that books like *Straphangers* and *The Postman Always Knocks Twice* were being banned at one port and admitted at another. The Minister in reply had made it quite clear that the aforementioned Act 'gives power to the Customs people to examine and to remove anything in the nature of obscene literature or other material' which in the case of books they passed on to the Censorship Board, as laid down by the Act of 1929.[1]

As regard public libraries, the more likely source of reading, since membership was free, a little insight into how scrupulously these local government officials discharged their tasks eliminates any impression that they at least were undermining the fabric of Irish society. One County Librarian, writing in a professional journal, listed his criteria for determining the suitability of an item before placing it on his bookshelves. Was it in the **Index Librorum Prohibitorum? Was it against the Revised Code of Canon Law? If it was a novel, did it contain propaganda 'subtly veneered?' Was it one of** 'the psychological-cum-biological efforts of the declared elite?' Was it a romantic novel, a detective or adventure story 'into which there is introduced extraneously pornography in various forms, blasphemy...?' If fiction must constitute the main bulk of the stock in Irish Libraries, the librarian protested,

Why can it not be kept within the wide bounds of what is legitimate? A novel can provide healthy pleasure as well as exerting a bracing influence on character, and the latest tendency to utilize the novel as a process of influencing public opinion must be regarded with a good deal of suspicion.[2]

County Librarians, then or now, in Ireland or elsewhere, were unlikely to seek public confrontation over the choice of reading material. However, they appeared, as will be seen, to require watching.

It should not be understood that thinking Catholics at this time were indifferent to, or unaware of, certain aspects of Irish life which sorted ill with the notion earlier elaborated of a nation endeavoring from small resources to plan what it wanted independence to mean. One bishop demanded, 'Why should the rural population alone be in the war trenches?' in the battle for nation economic survival, when 'The rich, the men of

---

[1] *Seanad Debates*, Vol. xviii, col. 1667, 20/6/1934.
[2] Samuel J. Maguire, 'Censorship in Irish County Libraries', *Leabharlann*, Vol. 3, No. 4, (December 1933), p. 126.

high Government salaries, of high commercial salaries, of sheltered high wages, go free.' There were others in the Church who looked past the all-night dances to other social considerations, among which were the dangers of intellectual protectionism, every whit as real as the dangers of economic protectionism. On the one hand, there was the view that 'our literature cannot be truly national unless it is Catholic,'[1] which explained the comparative neglect of authors and poets held in high esteem elsewhere. On the other hand, and within the same orthodox Catholic fold, there was a growing opinion that while native literature, play and work had value in the construction of an Irish culture, yet 'in intellectual thought, like all philosophy and some poetry, this kind of particularist confinement, identifying reason with prejudices, ends in Babel.'[2] To those who belonged to no Church but who took religion seriously, the Censorship law remained

repugnant to every instinct of a free man, ignorant in its conception, ridiculous in its method, odious in its fruits, bringing the name of self-governing Ireland into contempt where the freedom of literature is understood,[3]

second in its offensiveness only to the Military Tribunal law which had suspended the right to trial by jury.

The Catholic press, however, was unlikely to be troubled by what the world thought, or indeed to be unduly influenced by what other non-Irish Catholics thought. The Irish have a sensitiveness, one learned judge wrote, that was peculiar to themselves alone in matters of sexual morality. 'Experience of life,' he said, 'would teach any man who thinks that wicked or suggestive books and plays are responsible for more wrecked lives than any other human agency.'[4] Another writer argued

For as the spiritual health of a society is immeasurably more important than its physical health, so the suppression of heretical theology is immeasurably more incumbent than the suppression of heretical therapeutics.[5]

What salvific perversion these represented the writer does not specify, but the Irish reader was no doubt to understand that it was as nothing compared with the exercise of an independent conscience in its choice of what it read. However a first serious reappraisal from the pro-censorship lobby did appear in 1936. A Jesuit priest writing in the *Irish Monthly* asserted that the Government was acting within its rights in establishing a

[1] Riobard Ó Faracháin, 'Irish Literature and the Catholic Inspiration', *The Irish Monthly*, Vol. LXII, No. 734 (August 1934).
[2] T.J. Kiernan, 'Intellectual Protectionism', *The Capuchin Annual*. 1934, p. 141.
[3] Francis Hacket, 'A Muzzle Made in Ireland', *The Dublin Magazine*, Vol. XI, No. 4, 1936, p. 179.
[4] Louis J. Walsh, 'Catholic Standards in Criticism', *Irish Rosary*, March 1935, p. 174.
[5] Riobard Ó Faracháin, 'Are we entitled to our opinions?' *The Irish Monthly*, Vol. LXIII, No. 743, (May, 1935), pp. 311–12.

censorship just as it was obliged to take measures against any anti-social act. As to whether such restriction on human liberty was justified, he quoted Maritain, 'The sole end of art is the work itself and its beauty,' and, in the case of objectionable matter, 'prohibitive measures, however necessary they may be, remain by nature less effective and less important than a robust, intellectual and religious training, enabling mind and heart to resist vitally any morbid principle.'[1] What the Government's Censorship Act therefore was doing should be regarded as a matter of 'simple scavenging, more difficult no doubt, than the cleansing of the streets, but none the less necessary.'[2] The arguments about the corruptive effects of evil literature were rehearsed; the deleterious consequences for youth exposed to immodest books and periodicals were enumerated with assertion replacing evidence; but there was, throughout the article, a recognition that a right principle may be applied unreasonably, and even D. H. Lawrence's definition of pornography as 'the attempt to insult sex' was quoted with approval, an approval, of course, not extended to his novels. After all, the good fight had been fought, the battle won, and a different language based on an appeal to reason was likely to be more cogent in the long run. Even the *Catholic Bulletin* in commenting upon the short-lived appointment to the Board of a minor author, Lynn Doyle, who had written that under Censorship, 'A sincere and courageous writer in Ireland may be compelled to emasculate a work of genius, or starve ... The warmth of the unfortunate writer's imagination will be chastened by hunger... The empty ass keeps his kicking end down,' limited itself to the comment that the empty asses with warm imaginations now had a friend among the censors.[3]

The *Irish Monthly* returned to the theme of censorship the same year (1937) in an article written by another Jesuit, Father Gannon. He began by confessing his reluctance to admit that censorship was necessary and as such was at best a partial remedy that could provide no fundamental cure. He ended his article by recognizing that censors were fallible and that he would gladly lend his support to any movement that ensured redress for those unfairly penalized. In between, he argued that there was a morality to literature that could not be replaced in importance by its artistic qualities. Art which failed to elevate the spirit was a 'bastard product,' and to say that the end of literature was self-expression was a gratuitous absurdity, incapable of demonstration. The thesis that art holds the mirror up to nature was acceptable only as a half-truth, for depending on the setting of the mirror what it reflects may serve the vilest Soviet propaganda or the

[1] Jacques Maritain, *Art and Scholasticism*, quoted in Stephen J. Brown, S.J., 'Concerning Censorship', *The Irish Monthly*, Vol. LXIV, No. 751, 1936, pp. 30–31.
[2] *The Irish Monthly*, Ibid., p. 35.
[3] Lynn Doyle, quoted in the Editorial, *Catholic Bulletin*. Vol. XXVII, No. 1937, p. 20.

gratification of man's carnal desires. Literature that was intended to satisfy curiousity, or shirk sensibilities, or expose weaknesses was not art. A writer was free to subordinate his art to legitimate incentives of greater importance than an aesthetic production, but he did not thereby produce a work of art. Indeed, he asked, if a man or woman in pursuit of a vision produces art that 'may commingle beauty with moral deformity,' could not society suppress it? Not on aesthetic grounds, but there are transcending moral considerations which are as valid in their approach to literature as they are to the drug trade. 'No activity of men is free of ethical assessment and those who proclaim that they are a law unto themselves are to be banned lest they succeed in taking over from theologians and philosophers the formation and instruction of the Irish mind.'[1] The burthen of Fr. Gannon's thesis revealed a readiness to discuss rather than ordain, to posit (for its time) an intelligible rationale for the Irish people in the current state of their culture rather than deliver a pronouncement about the moral code, any infraction of which previously would have been treated as a serious moral offense. There was a latent recognition that people were beginning to think for themselves, and were therefore more likely to respond favorably to persuasive arguments than they would to discussions on morality which had not won their intellectual assent. An exhaustive search of the Catholic periodical literature reveals only two other articles dealing with censorship, both of which eschewed the personal polemic and imputations of un-Irishness in favor of a reasoned appeal for an ordered society. This restraint may have been dictated by the results which the operation of the Act was yielding.

During the five years 1933–37, figures are available which show that 3,975,877 bound volumes had been imported into the country. During that period the Censorship Board banned 667 titles, or an average of 133 a year. While the number of titles in the near 4 million is not known, it is fair to say that this incidence of banning could not be interpreted as being indicative of grave moral decadence in the nation's taste in literature. Regarding those works that were banned, certain factors should be borne in mind. In all the pre-legislation discussion, numerous works had been mentioned and these as a legacy of the past would obviously tend to inflate numbers for the first decade. The second consideration is the nature of the books banned. Adams examined the lists of books censored during the 17 years between the years between the first and second Censorship Act. Of these 1,700 odd he identified 153 which would be recognized as serious literature. They included books like Stella Gibbons' *Cold Comfort Farm* (1932), Erskine Caldwell's *God's Little Acre* (1933), Giovanni Boccaccio's *Pasquerella and Madonna Babetta* (1934), William Faulkner,

---

[1] Patrick J. Gannon, 'Literature and Censorship', *Irish Monthly* 65 (1937) p. 445.

7 titles (1935), Aldous Huxley's *Eyeless in Gaza* (1936), Ernest Hemingway's *To Have and Have Not* (1938), Seán O'Casey's *I Knock at the Door*
(1939), Frank O'Connor's *Dutch Interior* (1940), Hemingway's *For
Whom the Bell Tolls* (1941), Thomas Mann's *The Transported Heads*
(1942), Marcel Proust, 4 titles (1943), Margaret Mead's *Coming of Age in
Samoa* (1944), and nobody significant in 1945 when only 60 titles were
banned. The others Adams found included titles like *Nun in Jeopardy,
The Virgin's Progress, A Lover would be Nice*, etc. (about 80%) and
books which advocated the unnatural prevention of conception or the
procurement of abortion (about 12%).[1]

While some of these exclusions may well appear incomprehensible
today, it is arguable that their number and quality do not indicate for the
time that the attitude that brought about the passing of the Act in the first
instance had surrendered to an excess of zeal and had extirpated every
work of literature that might be thought to be indecent or obscene. There
were of course vociferous and well-articulated protests, and it was in reply
to these attacks on censorship that the moderate and reasoned defenses
were mounted. The Catholic press indeed had no option but to pitch their
arguments on the level of an appeal to the intellect. Some such effort was
necessary if the suffrages of the book-reading public were to be won for
control of reading and away from those who would take from 'theologians
and philosophers the formation and instruction of the Irish mind.'[2]

What was feared in the pre-war circles of orthodoxy was the type of
socio-cultural thinking of the *Irish Statesman* that had proved so trouble-
some in the Twenties. The moderates were proved correct in their sur-
mise that the dialectical process would ensure that the negative attack of
censoring would be followed by a positive defense of the intellect. The
vehicle for this affirmation was a short-lived periodical, named *Ireland
To-day*, 1937–1938, that offered an opportunity to writers and intellectuals to express themselves on matters not limited to a now intensely in-
ward-looking, self-preoccupied nation. It supported the Republican
cause in Spain, attacked Fascism, reported on the arts and literature in
government and administration, and tried to convey some awareness of
what was modern European Catholic thinking on social and political
problems.

There was an astringent impatience in its pages, a contempt for all mediocre aspects of Irish life, an inconoclasm that could be directed at the Abbey Theatre and
the Gaelic revival alike, and an uncomproming republicanism in some of its social
comments that made it an obvious target for suppression in the interests of a national complacency that thought Ireland had little to gain from modern European

---

[1] Michael Adams, *Censorship: The Irish Experience*, pp. 247ff.
[2] Gannon, 'Literature and Censorship', p. 445.

culture, and nothing certainly from the pretensions of a self-appointed intelligent-sia.[1]

Die it did not from censorship directly, but from a concerted attack led by some members of the Church who had been angered by articles written sympathetic to the Spanish Republicans, an attack duly reported in the periodical:

It is now common knowledge in Ireland that even this cautious and thoughtful periodical has been submitted to a violent series of ... attacks delivered in the name of religion.[1]

Such high-minded intolerance is not a phenomenon unique to Ireland, and while the country in the past had always found successors to carry forward the torch of radicalism, the experience of each such termination has left a vague sense of civic shame over failure to protect the alternative voice necessary to democracy. What had *Ireland To-Day* to say in its two years' existence on the topic of censorship?

Seán O'Faoláin's *Bird Alone* was banned in 1936. His article on 'The Dangers of Censorship' therefore must be read as the expostulation of someone who has suffered the public indignity of being declared a pornographer. His message was not, however, a condemnation of censorship which in fact he recognized and accepted as an instrument of last resort to be used with the utmost circumspection. What distressed him was a restrictive censorship under the control of the Gaelic Revivalist who feared the influence of any foreign literature, and of the Catholic Actionist who feared the promulgation of ideas direct to the Irish people without prior screening by the Church. The consequences of censorship are that it

preempts the activity of a healthy public opinion and prevents that public opinion from (so to speak) growing by exercise. It kills the national conscience by giving it no scope to take or leave, to praise or condemn, to exercise its will or exercise its freedom. By depriving morality of its freedom it reduces it to a machine without virtue.[3]

The words are prophetic. They foreshadow, first, the future decision of different Irish governments not to allow public opinion of the IRA to grow by exercise and secondly, by contrast, post-Vatican II recognition that obedience without choice is moral slavery which must lead to revolt on behalf of the very conscience that has been disenfranchised. He quotes Milton, 'that which purifies us is trial, and trial is by what is contrary.' Censorship on the other hand tries to keep the national mind in the protected state of perpetual adolescence. Hence, the State has legislated for the blank virtue of mechanical acquiescence in traditional values when,

---

[1] Terence Brown, *Ireland – A Social and Cultural History*, p. 170.
[2] Seán O'Faoláin, 'The Priests and the People', *Ireland To-Day* 2:7 (1937), p. 37.
[3] Seán O'Faoláin, 'The Dangers of Censorship', *Ireland To-Day* 1:6 (1936), p. 57.

on the contrary, as a young nation Ireland should be 'full of eagerness and the lust for discovery.'

There is a return to this theme of the dysfunctionality of literature under censorship in subsequent issues. In every community, Sheehy argued, there are those who believe that righteousness is static and those who believe it to be dynamic. The first, acting on the assumption that final certainty has been achieved, will seek to maintain the status quo: the second who know that they are the cartographers of tomorrow's possibilities act on only one assumption, that they dare not stand still.[1] This same idea was later developed by Geertz in his description of the tension between two political tendencies in countries that have newly won their independence. On the one hand there is what he describes as 'essentialism' – the impulse to elevate traditional norms and beliefs to such a position of dominance that existence only becomes significant and valued insofar as it conforms to the consensual image of religion, morality, language, family life, etc. On the other hand there is what he calls 'epochalism' – the urge to participate in the current flow of thought and events in one's time, to belong to a wider community and to play a role on a stage not limited by the traditions that are not of one's making. Essentialism and epochalism are not historiographic concepts to explain societal movements. Yet they are

as concrete as industrialization and as tangible as war. The issues are being fought out not simply at the doctrine and arguments level – th~ ~rh there is a great deal of both – but much more importantly in the material transformations that the social structures of all the new states are undergoing. Ideological change is not an independent stream of thought running alongside social process and reflecting (or determining) it, it is a dimension of that process itself.[2]

A moment's consideration bears out even today, sixty years on, the accuracy of the analysis for contemporary Ireland, with its rejection of abortion and yet growing demand for divorce, its rejection of obligatory Irish and yet its demand for traditional music, its rejection of book censorship and yet its tolerance of political censorship in its fear of the recrudescence of violence.

As regards the response of the Press in Ireland to censorship, the role played by *The Irish Times* was that of its indefatigable enemy. Still associated with the Ascendancy, it stood for much of what was fine in the old liberal and parliamentary traditions. Unfortunately for the better conduct of public discussion its opponents such as the *Catholic Bulletin*, the *Catholic Mind*, etc., persisted in associating its protests on behalf of tolerance with an alien culture whose gifts had been forgotten in the keen

---

[1] Edward Sheehy, 'Attitudes', *Ireland To-Day* 2:1 (1937) pp. 75–76.
[2] Clifford Geertz, *The Interpretation of Cultures* (London: Hutchinson, 1975), pp. 243–4.

remembrancing of the miseries for which it had also been responsible. And *The Irish Times*, seeing that it was not going to get a fair hearing for the contributions it wished to make to political thinking in the country, drew closer to the caricature by which its enemies represented it – the puppet of the West Briton, the lapdog of the Ascendancy, the enemy of Irish traditions and beliefs. As such, however, it did not fail through its editorial columns, features, and correspondence to remind the electorate of an Act that 'has made our country a laughing stock in the eyes of liberal peoples; and its administration ridiculous in the extreme.'[1] It opened its columns for three weeks to correspondence on the banning of O'Faoláin's *Bird Alone* as it had done five years earlier when Miss Laetitia Dunbar-Harrison, a Protestant graduate, was obliged to resign from her position as County Librarian on the grounds that her religion would make her an unsuitable person to be selecting books for the Catholics of Co. Mayo.[2]

What of other newspapers? Fr. Devane, despite the fact that his plea for a tariff on non-Irish publications had now been accepted, continued to keep an eye on the newspaper situation in Ireland. Quite properly he pointed out the dangers of a takeover by Camrose, Beaverbrook or Rothermere, and the consequences such a move would have for Irish culture. The vast bulk of newspapers, periodicals and books came from England and as long as this practice continued, 'it is not common sense to hope for a cultural and linguistic revival.'[3] Let the responsible Minister put up effective barriers to protect Irish communications. Why this should be necessary was due, in the opinion of *The Irish Monthly*, to the fact that 'The daily newspaper puts a pair of spectacles, with lenses of its own special manufacture, on Everyman's nose, and it is only by accident that he ever manages to see things as they really are.'[4] But were the Irish so gullible, so desperately in need of protection that they had to dig economic ditches and not expose themselves to news that had not been decontaminated by a Catholic filter? Obviously the majority felt no such need if Fr. Devane's figures about the circulation of British newspapers are to be believed. But how did the Church view the native secular press which after all was commercially Catholic,' as *The Irish Monthly* described it, and therefore unlikely to give serious offense?

It has been noted that the bitterness and abuse that characterized exchanges in the periodicals prior to the passing of the 1929 Act appear to have been replaced by a new thoughtfulness, either as a result of preoccupation with economic and political matters, or in consequence of the ob-

---

[1] *Irish Times*, 12th March, 1936.
[2] *Irish Times*, 6–22 January, 1931.
[3] R.S. Devane, 'The Menace of the British Combines', *Studies* 19 (1930), p. 69.
[4] James J. Campbell, 'Catholics and the Press', *Irish Monthly* 44 (1936), p. 716.

vious liberal discomfiture, or the Church's satisfaction with the unobtrusive working of the Board. The newspapers manifested a similar maturity of approach. Whether, therefore, as a result of the writings of 'epochalists' of *The Irish Times* and of *Ireland To-day* or those of the essentialists in the new party paper, *The Irish Press*, or more likely, as a direct reaction and response of their own, the Church in the last years of the decade began not only to avoid stressing the negative aspects of censorship but also to affirm the positive notion associated with a freedom of speech that would be compatible with Christian morality. A Professor Lucey of Maynooth was probably among the first of the secular clergy to discuss what freedom of expression should mean in a democracy. To him, truth was valuable, and the freedom of the press was necessary in order that it should be heard. It was of course subject to moral law since no one might say that which was false or was likely to lead to falseness or wrongdoing. A free press was impartial. It not only gave the true and complete news but also declared where its interests lay. When Lucey came to who was to decide what views were fit for publication he claimed that on faith and morals the Church had the right to decide, and the duty to make its judgement heard. Until any such statement, however, 'everyman is endowed by˙nature with the power of acquiring truths and conveying them to others. Hence, every man has a natural right to share what truths he may have with his fellow man. Nor should the State venture to suppress this right, since it is his by nature ... *Magna est veritas, et prevalebit.*'[1]

What Lucey was groping towards in the Ireland of his time was the growing conviction that a free press was one of the major safeguards any democratic country possessed, if it were to withstand the fascist dictatorships with their control of information, their distortion of fact, their concealment of events, and their dehumanizing propaganda which was a blasphemy against God and all His creation. There could be no State monopoly of the press, therefore, otherwise the liberty of the individual would perish. Freedom which was essential to sustain democracy meant its being independent of combines, of advertisers and of news agencies. It was an exacting demand to make of the press of a small, poor country like Ireland, but two years before the holocaust it seemed to be based on a premonition of the need to know, and the importance of knowing the truth. The *Irish Rosary* reversed the sequence but in effect came to the same conclusion about the loss of personal freedom which any curtailment of expression might entail:

For in a world in which the conception of man's moral nature and right has been undermined by indiscriminate propaganda, as in Germany and Russia, the con-

---

[1] Cornelius Lucey, 'The Freedom of the Press', *Irish Ecclesiastical Record*, 5th ser., 50 (1937), p. 588.

ception of liberty of opinion is driven out and force used not only to make physical seizures but to seize and hold conscience and freedom in bondage.[1]

Two months later it was pessimistically concluding that 'truth is not a primary consideration in a large section of the free press, in the big Press particularly,' intimating in fact that truth was being censored in the interests of 'Plutocracy, Publicity and Pornography.'[2] Obviously it did not like the accounts that were coming out of Spain, but there was this difference, that the range of its interests and the basis of its judgement had been extended. The British Press remained untrustworthy in the main, but when Irish papers began to report the same stories, then it became time to look at the nature of news, its purpose and relevance, and how to accommodate ugly facts, the immorality of which no one now could with justice claim he should disregard.

The critical approach to films in the thirties in a way reflected the conviction that as an art form it had a place, carried a message, made an impact, but fell very far short of being a benevolent and moral force in society. Normal enough for its time and inevitable, given the kind of periodical in which they were found, all appraisals of the cinema were seen under this moralizing light, save of course the comments that appeared in *Ireland To-day*. There, one does not find the jeremiads about corrupted youth, vacuous adults and perverted innocence but rather the sad commentary on what need not have been.

The Cinema is not the champion of corruption; it is the unwilling victim. It can be as potent an agent of Good as of Evil; and these potentialities are directly proportional. As evil is the irrational, anarchical and unnecessary element in Life, so is the plight of the Cinema reflected in the cult of the unnecessary, irrelevant and superficial in the structure of the film today.[3]

But other comment was less original and more condemnatory, too disposed to quote the Encyclical *Vigilanti Cura* on the moral degradation which films were always likely to cause, very unwilling to admit that *homo faber* was also in need of relaxation. The Film Censor obviously did not regard his work as a sinecure. 'Of the 1,587 films submitted in 1935, 1,271 were passed without cuts, 258 were passed with cuts, and 58 were totally rejected.'[4] The 18 million who paid admission to the cinema in the same year must have felt reassured that Ireland had its own fall-back position from the League of Decency, given that 80% of the films shown were American. Not everyone of course, was prepared to leave the task to local or foreign censors. The *Catholic Bulletin* reported that so dissatisfied

[1] Editorial, 'The Bedrock of Democracy', January 1939, p. 5.
[2] Editorial, 'The False Press', *Irish Rosary*, March, 1939, p. 169.
[3] Liam Ó Laoghaire, 'The position of the Cinema in Ireland', *Ireland To-Day* 2:10 (Oct 1937), p. 72.
[4] Gabriel Fallon, 'Celluloid Menace', *The Capuchin Annual* 1938, 249.

were some Irish with the papally-approved American Catholic Examining Board that they had decided to go ahead and build their own 'Hollywood,' a proposal that prompted the Editor to suggest rather hurriedly that 'an intensification rather than modification of the censorship'[1] might achieve the required effect. How the censor might be more censorious was not indicated.

Whatever about expansion in the film industry, contraction, to judge from the comment inside and outside the Dáil, appeared to be responsible for such a poor standard of broadcasting that listeners too often were driven to twiddle the knobs in a desperate attempt to pick up something from the BBC that was worth listening to. This comparison with its powerful neighbor's system worked always to the home country's disadvantage, indeed the outcome could not have been otherwise. Kept by deliberate government policy dependent for finance to run its programs, it enjoyed an income equal to 1% of that of the BBC and was supported by license holders who represented 2.5% of the population, whereas the corresponding figure in the U.K. was fifteen per cent.[2]

As regards performance, the reputation the station made for itself in 1932 with its worldwide broadcast of the Eucharistic Congress eventually convinced the Government that radio was here to stay. A new director was appointed in 1935, who was sufficiently independent to introduce some innovations in program content and insist on certain standards of entertainment being maintained. However, in the transmission of news and views the opposition was to remain persuaded that it had grounds for criticizing the running of the service. Their suspicions were probably inevitable given that the Assistant to the Director was a man very much identified with the party in power.[3] The annual presentation of the estimates for current and capital expenditure for approval affords in Irish parliamentary practice an opportunity for the elected representatives to air their opinions, grievances, and disappointments (and occasional commendations). One member of the opposition took the opportunity to complain that under the present Government, 'The Station and its political uses have gone to a point that has probably not been excelled anywhere except in Fascist Italy or Nazi Germany.' He accused the Minister of being responsible for suppression of unfavorable information, of selecting friends of the Government to give their opinions, for emending and censoring of texts, or if such a course were not politically convenient, for arranging that the person about to go on the air has 'put into his hands a document which is part of his own manuscript with parts blotted out and

[1] Gleanings, *Catholic Bulletin*. Vol. XXII, November 1932, p. 891.
[2] T.J. Kiernan, 'The Developing Power of Broadcasting', *Journal of Statistical and Social Inquiry Society of Ireland, 1935–36*, pp. 37–47.
[3] Maurice Gorham, *Forty Years of Irish Broadcasting*, p. 93.

he has got to extemporize to fill the gap.'[1] For all the Minister's demurrals, there was some substance in the accusations as Frank O'Connor was to find (though presumably not for political reasons) when a talk he intended to give on James Joyce was summarily rejected.[2] The basis for interference had been laid by the Broadcasting Act. Forty years later, as will be seen, the Government of the day had still not discovered any reason to revise its conviction that a State-subventioned organization should conform to its current thinking, and that any opinion or any view deemed to constitute a fundamental challenge to its basic policy should be censored out of hand. Their skill in unofficially controlling news and information was going to be put to the test when the circumstances of World War II made such intervention the overt and considered expression of the will of the people.

Ireland's neutrality in the conflict that was to engulf Europe is important to understanding the evolving attitude toward censorship. What had begun as an endeavor to limit (and, if possible, exclude) English newspapers whose contents and tone constituted an affront to a society with a strong familial basis and a need to explore its own national psyche before adapting external life styles, had taken the form of a ban on books and films according to standards that, for their day, could the difficulty be described as draconian. Interpretation and implementation of the Act had their moments of inanity, but the country was too involved with coming to terms with the definition of its future in regard to its own needs and resources to be unduly preoccupied. The flag of liberalism was not hauled down, and the Church far from trumpeting its victory appeared to be making an appeal to the intellectuals, and in the process modifying some of its more contentious arguments. The War was to raise obstacles to this *rapprochement*.

The decision to remain neutral was carried without a division in the Dáil. Its affirmation was recognized as the voluntary act of a sovereign state declaring its intention after centuries of bondage to go its own way, even if such a course were to jeopardize what freedoms had been achieved. Self-sufficiency was no longer an economic ideology, it was an ineluctable fact of life. In its external relations, since it did not possess the firepower or historical traditions of a Switzerland or a Sweden, respect for its neutrality was to be at times precarious. Politics was, like all other activities, a victim of shortages, with the opposition parties obviously the greater losers. National security information was jealously guarded, paper was scarce, petrol unavailable and communications unreliable. A wartime censorship was introduced that appalled visiting English politi-

---

[1] Deputy McGilligan, *Dáil Debates*. 25/3/1936, col. 321ff.
[2] *The Irish Times*· July 21, 1937, p. 13.

cians by its rigor.[1] Whyte recounts that a bishop's Lenten pastoral was censored as was a statement from the *Osservatore Romano* which itself was merely refuting idle speculation.[2]

Newspapers were of course the hardest hit. Weather reports, reports on the progress of the war that were not balanced, commodity shortages and production, troop movements, political analyses, features and commentaries, all and much more were censored. However, even here a modicum of sanity prevailed. *The Irish Times*, when reduced to four pages a day, still offered Ireland's greatest satirist since Swift his weekly column – that same satirist who, commenting on the world's reaction to his country's neutrality, is reported by Share to have written: 'Ireland should take her place not among the nations of the earth (who surely are in no position to receive guests) but among the dim enigmas of history.'[3] If *The Irish Times* felt it had a grievance when a most innocuous picture of a Minister skating with his daughter in St. Stephen's Green was blacked out, one can imagine the less robust sensitiveness of radio which daily had to await decisions to determine what might or might not be reported in the news it still continued to pirate from whatever station it could receive. Letters were censored, of course, as were telegrams. The Film Censor, in addition to his statutory duty to protect Ireland from celluloid indecency or obscenity, had now the additional task of excising from film any war that was partisan. Information, if it was to exist at all, was exist in its most sterile form.

Isolation did not, however, mean stultification, apathy and stagnancy. The Irish did not lose whatever creativity they had, they simply had nowhere to present it, save within the rather narrow confines of their own small island. English and American publishers were obviously going to direct their energies and resources to supporting their respective war efforts. Ireland had chosen the lonely road of neutrality. Along the way it would find few with whom it might share ideas, literature and planning, just at the time when having proven to everybody its ability to conduct its affairs, it was ready for the next stage in its development. Instead,

It was as if an entire people had been condemned to live in Plato's cave, backs to the fire of life and deriving their only knowledge of what went on outside from the flickering shadows thrown on the wall before their eyes by the men and women who passed to and fro behind them.[4]

Thus left to ponder on the endless perfectibility of their own Catholic Ireland, what thoughts engaged the mind of its inhabitants as they concentrated on the joyless task of mere survival? If the making of the future

[1] Bernard Share, *The Emergency* (Dublin: Gill and Macmillan, 1978), p. 7.
[2] J.H. Whyte, *Church and State in Modern Ireland 1923–70*, p. 94.
[3] Share, ibid. op. cit., p. 27.
[4] F. S. L. Lyons, *Ireland since the Famine*, p. 551.

remained in the hands of the belligerents, what response did the country make to the challenge of its present position? The majority of the people who had accepted the ideology of a self-contained Ireland in return for doing without the more scurrilous English Sunday newspapers probably, but not certainly, did not grieve too much over the cultural isolation. But there were others.

Public opinion in the main in the thirties had at the very least refrained from adverse comment on the operations of the Board of Censorship. As has been said there were other matters which occupied their attention. In the last year of peace (1939) the number of students sitting the second level terminal school certificate was less than 3,000, an increase of 200% on the 1925 figure but hardly indicative of an educated, as opposed to a literate, population. However, on each edge of this indifference, as has been said, there were protests to be heard. To the right, the Catholic Truth Society printed an article in the *Catholic Truth Quarterly* of 1940, entitled 'Ineffective Censorship: Why the Act is not doing its work: Official Remissness' which in effect complained that the Censorship Board did 'not ban the highest possible percentage of the worst books within the shortest possible time after their publication.' Adams gives a detailed account of the proposals the Society made to improve the machinery of the Act: funds should be made available for the purchase of suspect books and periodicals; the regulations concerning the submission of complaints should be improved; delays in banning should be reduced to correct the current derisory situation which permitted half of the number of books, eventually to be banned, to remain in bookstores and libraries for up to a year; and finally, steps should be taken to ensure that those responsible for making books available are notified.[1] These were all excellent suggestions if the Government had itself been dissatisfied with the working of the Act. It was not, and the Society, in the national interest obtaining in 1941, decided not to pursue the issue any further.

Almost on cue, liberal opinion in 1942 began to make itself heard, mainly through the agency of *The Bell*, the cultural successor to *The Irish Statesman* and *Ireland To-Day*. Like them it proposed to provide a reflective analysis of contemporary Irish life in which the different influences and traditions which explained the current heterogeneous character of the nation might be assessed as to the relative significance of their contributions. Like life, the character of the magazine was to be shaped by events, by the interaction of its writers freed from the shibboleths of yesterday, by engagement with the problems of today, and by the new associations and meanings that would grow symbiotically among their readers. *The Bell* was so named because it was sensitive enough to tinkle at even

[1] Quoted in Michael Adams, *Censorship: The Irish Experience*, pp. 77ff.

the faintest breeze, and yet posessed of a deep timbre and resonance for those who pulled on its rope with the strength that matched the convictions of their message. The time for stock-taking had arrived. Windows were to be opened. The Celtic mist was to disappear in the hot sunlight of the contemporary reality of Western civilization. With it would go the nostalgic dreams of past glory and the utopian abstractions concerning a future national being that had been seeded in the thin soil of Know-nothingness. The meaning to Irish life would not be found behind closed doors and drawn blinds: it would be found by acknowledging that it was also the product of forces outside the country, economic, social, political and aesthetic forces which required first of all to be understood.

The Bell was therefore a vital organ of empirical, humanistic self-consciousness at a moment when the new state was entering on a period of profound challenge. As such it probably helped to make more generally available ideals of rational reflection and social analysis without which the country would not have responded to the post-war crises as capably as it did.[1]

In any analytical description of the Ireland of the forties and early fifties, one obvious obstacle to the expansion of the creative urge was that tocsin of the bourgeoisie – censorship. Intellectual and artistic Ireland turned in on itself perforce must start to take stock of where it stood in relation to its existence on the Statute Book. John Hewitt, Patrick Kavanagh, Brendan Behan, Denis Johnston, Anthony Cronin, Louis MacNeice, Austin Clarke, Aubrey deVere White and others were to create in the pages of The Bell, a literary force that convincingly, and without the hyperbole of some of the liberals of the Twenties, would progressively make exaggerations of that phenomenon more and more indefensible. Whatever about cultivating the national garden, it first had to be cleared of the brambles that stood for Anglophobia, Tartuffeism, Celtomania, prudery and cultural analphabetism.

In an Editorial in 1941, O'Faoláin declared that the revolutionary period had come to an end and the creative period had begun. In this situation, the Irish needed some notion of standards so that they could judge how far they had come. The provenance of these standards is due to an instinctual condition that changes, that errs, that disintegrates and that hardens betimes in an orthodoxy so alien to a people that the momentum of the cycle is of necessity renewed.

Take the Literary Censorship, for example. That was an effort to codify certain alleged instincts about literature, and what has been the result? Time has proved that these alleged instincts are not native.[2]

Joyce, Yeats, Moore, O'Casey, were they not equally entitled to claim

---

[1] Terence Brown, *Ireland: A Social and Cultural History*, p. 205.
[2] Seán O'Faoláin, 'Standards and Taste', *The Bell* 2:3 (June 1941), p. 6.

that they represented native standards as much as the five gentlemen who made up the Censorship Board? Whoever was right must await Time's final decision, as opinion appraised efort and judgment groped its way to a conclusion. But,

Time will not tell if we do not make it tell. As I say standards do not grow like grass. The intensity of our minds is the measure of the growth of our lives. And it cannot but be that by searching life for the material of literature – much as Taine did with English literature – we shall extract the instinct of our race for certain affectible things that is natural for us to like and praise.[1]

This credo was the inverse of the recourse to orthodoxy. It was an assertion of the mutancy of truth and the variability of morality. It pitched its appeal to the native genius to take those provisional decisions that would help determine those putative standards by which life should be assessed. It came most opportunely. The Anglo-Irish movement had been financed by English publishing houses so that no Irishman need feel obliged to acknowledge, never mind purchase, the product until he had been sufficiently reassured of its convertibility into his native currency. Now the war had pulled up the drawbridge across the Irish Sea that had led to a reprieve from lack of understanding at home, from intolerance and from the philistinism to be found in all newly-emergent societies. The Irish writer like everybody else had to forego certain benefices once he passed beyond the clausura of neutrality. Censorship in this situation was no longer just an embarrassing commentary on Irish maturity, no longer a negative cachet to stimulate sales. It was now an impediment to communication with practically the only audience the Irish writer had left, and with that non-Irish world he might invoke in support of his thesis.

There then appeared in *The Bell* a number of articles which neither denied the need for censorship nor failed to identify its aberrations. Why, one writer asked, are books approved in Catholic periodicals in Britain and are still condemned in Ireland? Why in the pursuit of Irish Ireland have the Irish been unable to shake off Victorian prudery in dealing with sexual matters? Why is it not necessarily a sin to read a book that has been banned? Why does Canon Law condemn only *'libri qui res lascivas seu obscenas ex professo tractant, narrant aut docent,'* the Censorship Act only books 'in general tendency, indecent,' but the Censorship Board members condemn books because they find fault with one sentence, e.g. Kate O'Brien's *The Land of Spices*?[2]

Murphy was to return to the theme of censorship twice in the following year. His reasons were clear. Censorship was based not upon argument, but on preventing all discussion of sex. The technique was to overawe

[1] *Ibid.*, p. 10.
[2] C.B. Murphy, 'Sex, Censorship and the Church', pp. 64–75.

anyone who dared to brave the conventions by campaign of calumny and detraction to which everyone is vulnerable within the narrow confines of literary Ireland. If this failed, one always summoned up the *virginibus puerisque* proposition in defense of the Irish family, despite the fact that this standard had been rejected as far back as 1926, by the Committee on **Evil Literature, one of whose members was a parish priest. Should Irish censorship, the writer continued, be stricter than canon law?** Catholic bishops have the authority and the duty to ban in their diocese books which they feel endanger faith and morals. They have not considered such a course of action necessary. Why? Because the Irish Censorship Board performs that function for them? Then why did they not use their powers prior to the passing into law of the Bill? Why are they not using them now in N. Ireland where Irish law does not apply? Murphy concluded by reiterating that he is not opposed to censorship. He knows 'that mistakes will be made by the best and most reasonable censors, and for the sake of the principle I agree that such mistakes ought to be let pass, up to a point. But there is surely a limit, and our Censorship is well beyond it.'[1]

There was another matter, however, which the writers in *The Bell* did well to advert to. The Church's law when it deals with recognizable externals is not lightly set aside in Ireland. More than civil law (which was law imposed, at least originally) church law had been assimilated into the pattern of social existence. What, the average intelligent Irish Catholic would have asked himself, should be my attitude to a banned book? The answer *The Bell* provided was clear. The Censorship of Publications Act did not forbid the reading of a banned book: it forbade its distribution and sale. And if the scrupulous Irishman had persisted that, according to Catholic theology, the State had the power to impose upon its subjects a true obligation in conscience to behave in accordance with its laws, the reply was that 'the Censorship having from the law no power to prohibit the reading of the books it bans, has a fortiori no power to impose an obligation not to read them.'[2]

The other question *The Bell* dealt with was the possibility of a banned author taking an action against the Minister in order that he might be compelled to show cause why. In Irish law, at that time, the Minister could not be obliged to prove his case for censoring a book: that was incumbent on the author, who, if he lost his case, heard not by a jury but decided upon by a judge, must meet his costs and those of the Minister. The dice were further loaded against the author in that it was the Minister who was given the benefit of the doubt and the book he had banned remained guilty of indecency, until it was proved innocent. The only feasible appeal

---

[1] C.B. Murphy, 'Censorship: Principle and Practice', *The Bell* 3:4 (Jan 1942), p. 301.
[2] Henry Bellew, 'Censorship, Law and Conscience', *The Bell* 3:2 (Nov 1941), p. 141.

open to the author was therefore an appeal to the court of public opinion, an appeal *The Bell* was supporting.

These articles give some indication of an approach that matched the reasoned apologetics found in the Catholic periodicals. Collectively they represented an attempt to find some balanced perspective on sex, on the artistic treatment of human nature that was at times corrupt, and on what the Irish mind might be exposed to in word and image without suffering irreversible moral degradation. They posited, in a society that looked askance at principles that did not emanate from a confessional source, the necessity for the artist to be true to his vision. They demonstrated that it was possible to support censorship and yet criticize its excesses; that logical argument while it might not convert at least had to be answered by language that was a few notches above abuse and vilification; and, finally, that reasoned protest might be regarded as a holy endeavor since, as one writer put it in a Catholic weekly newspaper, 'A crusader in search of strange errands might find congenial work defending the Church against the Censorship Board,' and, he might have added, its unsolicited coadjutors. The level of discussion then was raised as the professional communicators took store of the audience they must seek at least to sway if they were not to end up talking to themselves. Were they winning?

Almost at a midpoint between the beginning of World War II hostilities and the passage of the 1946 Act, there took place in the Senate a debate that lasted four days on the motion:

That, in the opinion of Seanad Éireann, the Censorship of Publications Board ... has ceased to retain public confidence and that steps should be taken by the Minister to reconstitute the Board.[1]

The motion when it was eventually put was lost 32–2. The outcome was never in doubt. No one wished to attack the members of the Board. No one wished to be identified as attacking the principle of censorship. No one wished to forego the opportunity of recording his reservations provided these were understood against his overall commitment to uphold religion, Irish Ireland and the spirit of liberalism, in that order.

As a cross-section of Irish opinion, the Senate was and is to a certain extent representative. The constituencies its members represent are small and confined in their interests. Senators are either ex-politicians or part-time politicians, members of professional bodies or have been elected by the two universities. Debate is leisurely, and though acrimony did appear during the 18 hours this discussion lasted, there is generally a courtesy extended by members to one another, not found in the Dáil where politicians are full-time professionals. More than one member adverted to their average age and each doubted his ability to be positive about the ap-

Senate Debates, Wed. 18th November 1942, Col. 16.

propriate standards by which decency might be measured in the contemporary situation. Nevertheless they were public representatives who took their responsibilities seriously enough to attend to a matter that had, in the opinion of many, a bearing on the quality of life at that time. Some appeared limited, locked into their own prejudices, unwilling, or unable, to see an Ireland other than that which matched their private, comfortable vision. Others were realistic, measured in their statements, and modest as to the value of their own cogitations. Speaking on the regard the Senate must have for youth, one said:

We must not act as if our offspring were degenerates searching for every possible obscenity that they can find in a book or sentence, but rather as if they were sensible young men and women with a genuine belief in the faith in which they were brought up and which will sustain them when they do happen to come on a book calculated to deprave.[1]

The debate centered on the manner in which the Board was discharging its function as censors within the terms laid down by the Act. Three books, all of which had been banned, were put forward as indicators of their approach. One was an account of *The Tailor and Anstey* written in a language that even then was regarded as Rabelaisian but not suggestive. It has today a certain sociological/folklore value as a documentary of a peasant-class man and wife in a remote part of Ireland. The second was a book by Kate O'Brien, entitled *Land of Spices*, which was banned on the strength of a one-sentence reference to homosexuality. The third book, Halliday Sutherland's *Laws of Life*, dealt with the question of the safe period and had received a *cum permissu superiorum* from the Catholic Archdiocese of Westminster.

Reading the accounts of these occasionally tediously verbose debates reveals certain attitudes that, collectively, explain why Irish censorship had then its own distinctive character. First there was a patriotism that resented any portrayal of the Irish and their way of life that was unflattering. 'Apart from the moral censorship I think there should be a censorship of books that portray us Irish people in the way I have indicated (damaging).'[2] Second, indecent was defined as 'disgusting,' 'tiresome,' 'unwholesome.' Circumstances could and did make the decent indecent, the wholesome vulgar, the parody smut, depending on the audience. There is evidence throughout of an unconscious drive to define reality in such a way as to make the force of the religious ideology more applicable. Third, there was a fear of allowing access to literature to those who were deemed insufficiently emotionally or morally mature. 'It is because we know that the masses of our people can hardly be called educated that censorship

---

[1] Senator The McGillycuddy of the Reeks, *Senate Debates*, 3rd December 1942, col. 258.
[2] *Senate Debates*, 18th November 1942, col. 32.

must be exercised to protect them from this pernicious literature.'[1] Fourth, senators still felt obliged to point out that opposition to censorship did not equate with the wish to destroy the state. Fifth, the readership of books was confined to less than 10% of the population, and that the real enemies were still English Sunday newspapers and American magazines.

Most of these comments, with small variations, had previously appeared in arguments about the validity of censorship as an institution. What was particularly Irish was what had been alleged about radio, and was 25 years later to be stated as the government view about television, namely the duty-conscious paternalism of legislators who in the domain of communications seemed to abandon laws which they had sworn to uphold. Commenting on *The Laws of Life* the Minister of Justice said:

Whether the Board was technically and legally correct, whether the book in its general tendency was indecent or obscene, may be open to question, but on the ground that it was calculated to do untold harm, I was perfectly satisfied it should be banned.[2]

He thereby relegated the statutory law to inoperative status and established his own opinion as law in its stead. It is not surprising, therefore, that this debate should witness the first occasion for the omission in the Senate report of quotations the Senators gave from the relevant books in support of their arguments. Censorship of the offending works was intended to be thorough. Another aspect that made the debate unique for its time was a four-and-a-half hour speech by the Senator Chairman of the Board, a professor of metaphysics, at University College, Dublin. His defense of the banning is ponderous, humorless, quibbling, contumacious and obsequious, and, for all that, compulsive. The academic's case was built block on consecutive block, ambivalences lost sight of in heady flights of rhetoric, and the personalities of those hostile to censorship picked over with the deadly precision of a seamstress intent on her sampler. In the course of the debate truth inevitably paid the price it must always pay when the purifier is persuaded of the long-term benevolence of his prudential algebra. He was however not allowed to have everything his own way. The Senate's patient, courteous and attentive ear was not to be mistaken for agreement. The self-defeating anomalies were of course pointed out together with the small number of worthwhile books which had been actually censored. Given, however, the quality of some of the contributions and the basis on which members formed their judgement, it is difficult not to share the view of one Senator who feared 'that Irish authors would ... have preferred prosecution – where the case would be

---

[1] *Senate Debates*, 18th November 1942, col. 45.
[2] Deputy Boland, *Senate Debates*, 18th November 1942, col. 55.

made and they could defend themselves – to being treated by their books being banned entirely without appeal.'[1] At all events, Irish parliamentary life had witnessed the dedication of a considerable amount of time and energy to ensure that the custodians of the Irish ideal, if not of the reality, were confirmed in their tutelage.

The response of the anti-censorship *Bell* group was thoughtful. They took heart that of the twenty Senators who had spoken, nine made sense, and forty Senators had expressed the depth of their involvement with the topic by not speaking at all. They noted the Minister's breathtaking 'I am the law' attitude with the rather empty satisfaction that at least its derogation and abuse were now on record. What even the most disinterested public could not help taking into consideration was the fact that mistakes had been made that would not simply disappear. Maybe English Catholicism was not Irish Catholicism but to ban a book approved by the Archbishop of Westminster, that was an error which would linger on in people's minds and not to the credit of its perpetrators. As Ó'Faoláin said,

No Minister likes public criticism: you never know where it ends. The Censorship Board will watch its step more carefully in future.[2]

A Council of Action was formed from organizations having literary interests with a view to securing the administration of the Act in accordance with its provision. A Memorandum was drawn up which claimed that though 'in theory the existing Censorship is not designed to prevent liberty of thought or discussions, ... reasons will be given ... to show that unconsciously it is operated to achieve this result.'[3] The cogency of their arguments, the wealth of detail and the articulate class they represented were enough. The Minister took notice that he was being watched, and would continue to be watched every time he gave effect to any of the Board's recommendations.

If the left drew some consolation from the reservations more and more people were beginning to entertain about the zeal with which the Censors were discharging their office, not so the right. Father Gannon who had appeared to be inviting an intellectual accommodation with censorship published an article in *Studies* that perhaps might have been more appropriately located in a religious pamphlet. The arguments have not changed, indeed they appear to have reverted to the pre-Act polemics of the *Catholic Bulletin*. Ireland has still a valid religion. Religion is the tutor of art. Art does not set up its easel in front of a sewer. The moral law is like the law of gravity: to break it is to be broken by it. People must therefore be protected from their own follies lest they do themselves and others an

---

[1] *Senate Debates*, 9th December 1942, col. 315.

[2] The Editor, 'The Senate and Censorship', p. 248.

[3] Quoted in Michael Adams, *Censorship: The Irish Experience*.

injury. Literary merit can never redeem indecency, and even genius when it choses to be salacious does so with a view to stirring up the silt of man's nature. Father Gannon was no doubt disturbed at the buffeting the Act and the Censors were taking. For all their *faux pas*, they had succeeded in banning 1,552 publications. Being challenged on three was almost a compliment to their efficiency. At a time when Christian moral standards needed support, when 'the ethics of nationalism were substituted for Christian asceticism and the Great God Pan came shambling in with all that follows jn his train ... it was something to have a barrier, however imperfect, against the inroads of open indecency.'[1] The process of sanitation must therefore go on. The interests of the common people of Ireland demanded that someone exercise the unpleasant and patently unrequited duties of censor.

But somehow the rhetoric is not convincing. The crime does not really justify it, particularly when the judges are seen themselves to be at variance, in the spirit and in the letter, with the law by which they assess others. It was growing more difficult to rouse the public conscience. Irish puritanism, unable to arrest its own momentum, had lost its credibility, not so much as a result of the liberal arguments put forward by Irish writers (though they had at least forced the topic of censorship to surface) as by its own inevitable logic that must in the end be self-defeating.

After the banning of *The Land of Spices* no Irish priest who knows his theology, can insist that the Censorship binds Catholics in conscience, and we know that legal obligations divorced from conscience get a thin time of it in Ireland.[2]

Human relations between the sexes have always been liable to distorted representation in Irish literature. Pick up any bedside book about Irish saints, and what they have in common in the hagiology is the distance they maintain from the company of the other sex. To achieve the virtue of chastity they fast and do penance. This ideal has been transmitted down through time so that the Roman-imposed celibacy became not a barrier to human evolution but a liberation of the human spirit whereby men and women could serve God and man the better. The heroic life took precedence over other forms of existence. The law which sustained it was regarded as inviolable. The crime of the Censorship Board was that in assuming the duty of promoting the social discipline which enhanced the celibate life they had brought into disrepute the law by which the successors to these legendary saints lived. That Irish Catholic Church had disappeared some fifteen centuries ago despite recurrent but momentary lapses into religious jingoism. Catholics who owed allegiance to Rome now were Roman Catholics, and a book which had been approved by the

---

[1] P.J. Gannon, 'Art, Morality and Censorship', *Studies* 33 (1942), p. 418.
[2] C.B. Murphy, 'Sex, Censorship and the Church', *The Bell* 2:6 (September 1941), p. 74.

highest Roman Catholic authority in England should not be, could not be, censored in Ireland without a loss to their sense of universal member-ship which as Irish Catholics they were not prepared to sustain. The Board in banning Halliday Sutherland's *The Laws of Life*, denied that it had made a blunder but was only being logically consistent with estab-lished policy. Irish commitment to the heroic life was not however pre-pared to match with an ideal a personal performance not imposed upon their co-religionists across the Irish Sea. Obvious conclusions were drawn; the ensuing silence marked a weighty dissent. *The Bell*, however, published an anonymous doggerel, *In Defense of Censors*, which re-flected in its inverted way the feelings of the 90% who did not read and the 10% who did.

> If foreign swine may choose to dish up
> What seems to please an English bishop,
> His Grace, we know, is much misled;
> He's no authority on *our* bed.
>
> In English smut we've not been sharin'
> Since first we founded Obstat Éireann,
> We got the power in the Treaty
> To liquidate our Aphrodite.'[1]

The war was now into its fourth year. No one abroad had time or paper for Irish prose or poetry. The home market was precious not only because of the audience it provided faute de mieux, but as a society which rep-resented in its inspiration his bread and butter, no writer, poet or playright could afford to let his public slide too far down the abyss of isola-tion where the signals of ordinary human intercourse would no longer be comprehensible. Collectively, they had jolted the Establishment's elbow, conceded the basic premiss of censorship, alerted the Minister to the danger of allowing his reputation to depend on the seekers after the Holy Grail of Irish purity, but they had as yet won nothing tangible, and this war was going to last for them long after the last bullet had been fired in Europe.

---

[1] *The Bell*, Vol. v, No. 4, January 1943, p. 323.

CHAPTER 5

THE CHANGING FACE OF CENSORSHIP

The cessation of hostilities created problems even for the neutrals. While emergency regulations were repealed, there was to be no sign of improvement in the quality of postwar life in Ireland. Emigration accelerated as successive governments floundered vainly in their search for the economic key to the material progress so long expected. In the absence of any guiding philosophy, earlier values were insisted on with renewed vigor even though circumstances had changed. Church and state were now to be found in open confrontation which was to confirm the proponents of censorship in their belief as to its worth at the same time as its credibility gap continued to widen as a result among those who heretofore had suspended judgement. A new Act is passed and the Censorship of Publications Board will assume an aggressive posture to match and justify the increase in the number of books prohibited. Protests continue, however, and the government will give its first positive indications of sharing some of the disquiet evinced by writers and intellectuals.

The war ended in May 1945. The process of standing down a quarter-million men began. The task of postwar adjustment of the economy was set in train. Problems there were a-plenty in the difficulties created by a labor market flooded by unneeded soldiers and by the end of the wartime boom in the United Kingdom that had provided employment for countless thousands of Irish emigrants. Initially conditions appeared to deteriorate. A disastrous harvest necessitated the introduction of bread-rationing in 1946; a drastic curtailment of transport and a seize-up of industry ensued; and, finally, a worldwide shortage of shipping was to deny raw materials, capital equipment and above all those manufactured goods the public had done without for six long years. Wages had been pegged too long, and the deprivation which had been tolerated while the war had lasted was to be sensed more acutely as the inevitable post-hostilities inflation, coupled with increases in income tax to pay for food subsidies,

further eroded what little purchasing power remained to buy the commodities the country had been so long denied.

And yet Ireland had emerged from neutrality a nation where before it
might have been more accurately described as a state, growing now progressively more integrated but still showing the signs of that travail which
attended its creation. The united response of the people to the dangers of
invasion and the tolerant acceptance of the discomforts of neutrality not
only underlined their homogeneity but reinforced their sense of community. There was, too, a sense of pride that the country had gone it alone; a
sense of confidence that grew from reflection on what had been achieved;
and finally out of their newfound awareness that theirs was a sovereign
state that had ridden out rumors and threats and isolation, there emerged
the will and desire that it reassume its place among the nations of the
democratic world.

During 1939–45 Ireland had closed a blind eye to violations of its neutrality by Britain. Now with the return of peace, friendly feelings could
begin. At home, however, a subsistence level economy was tolerable only
when life-and-death issues overrode all other concerns. While elections
had been held throughout the war, shortages and the priority of national
security had resulted in a diminution of the intensity with which alternative policies were urged. The repressive legislation that had become part
of the nation's law had simultaneously weakened the IRA to the point of
its being no longer effective, and at the same time strengthened the confidence of businessmen and the Establishment that a government that had
been feared as irredentist, socialist and republican was in fact a government exclusively intent on governing, and being continued in government
by the suffrages of the people.

A period of 16 years at the controls was however to take its political
toll. On both sides of the Irish Sea, those who had organized their country's survival were to experience electoral ingratitude. The period that
now ensued revealed growing dissatisfaction at the lack of economic impetus and social reform. Preferences were to be switched four times in the
next decade as voters made up their minds which policy or combinations
of policies were more likely to achieve the Good Society on whose realization the past sufferings and sacrifices had been predicated. New political
parties were formed, national strikes were called, housewives' associations were formed, and an unending barrage of complaints was mounted
to protest at emigration, unemployment and inadequate social services.
Another factor was the depopulation rural Ireland sustained as more and
more people rejected with their feet the boredom and hopelessness of
provincial life that stood out in stark relief once the dangers and lack of alternatives no longer existed to justify their decision to remain where they
were. In this postwar period, the outflow from the agricultural sector in-

creased 300%, men representing 87% of the decline. Every Census of Population from 1841 to 1966 – with the sole exception of 1951 – had shown a decrease in population. The marriage rate continued to be among the lowest in the Western World, due principally to the housing shortage and the low quality of amenities offered (particularly outside urban areas). Those who were not prepared to tolerate these conditions left home, usually one at a time, and made their way to Dublin, or kept on going to England which, for all its austerity, was still preferable to the drab monotony they had left behind. This exodus from the least anglicized, most conservative part of Ireland – the West and South – constituted in effect the abnegation of the viability of that Gaelic civilization for which many had died in the belief they were preserving it.

The failure marked by this emigration was a profound one, for the very people who flocked from the country in such numbers were the sons and daughters of those who had fought a revolutionary war (although not to the finish) in the early part of the century, and on whose behalf the revolutionary war had been fought. Their going made nonsense of the official ideology of the twenty-six county State, of what was taught in the schools and preached from the pulpits and platforms.[1]

In a way, neutrality had exorcised the demon of inverted nationalism. The people had stood by their country successfully without learning to speak Irish, or foregoing the pleasures of reading the English Sunday press, or forswearing listening to the BBC. There had, in the past, been too much traffic across the water dividing the two countries to persuade anyone that instead 'of a distinctive Irish way of life, the twenty-six counties had remained in many aspects a social province of the United Kingdom.'[2] This situation had now to change in response to a different set of social forces.

Such was postwar Ireland. A flight from the land, a stagnating economy, unemployment, emigration, a new definition of Irishness, a government too long in power, protests against shortages, housing and welfare services, in all these were the makings of a social upheaval with unpredictable consequences which would probably have materialized had not the English bolt-hole not been available for the 50,000 who left each year. As it was, the demographic concentration was eventually to result in one-third of the total population residing in the greater Dublin area. Whilst the capital grew progressively industrialized, and more and more the site where national decisions were taken, big business located and foreign agencies established, its work force came to be drawn from those newly-arrived city dwellers who had left behind them rural norms of social behavior which might have acted as a brake on change. Next, there

[1] Liam de Paor, 'Ireland's Identities', *The Crane Bag* 31 (1979), p. 25.
[2] Terence Brown, *Ireland – A social and cultural history*, p. 216.

emerged the nuclear family which, here as elsewhere, demonstrated, as part of that individual aggressiveness which characterizes a competitive economy, a readiness to off-load the past, to break the mold of tradition, and to seek some other basis for its beliefs than a no-argument authority. In short, the Irish people on the surcease of war was to propose to itself an entirely different agenda for consideration. In terms of public morality, on the macro-scale, there would be head-on clashes between the Church and State in which the former was for the time being to successfully define the limits of welfarism, and the latter, for its part, would quite expeditiously bury the corporativism of the papal encyclicals. On the micro-scale there remained, as part of this adoption of new values, of new intellectual criteria, and of new assertions as to the rights of the individual conscience, the question of censorship.

Enough has been written of *The Bell* to indicate that, alone in its time, it sought to portray an Ireland that was, that might be, and debunk an Ireland that never had been, that never could have been. It offered to be a midwife to the new national selfconsciousness; it proposed to offer a social analysis of the environment in which such would survive. It was humanistic; unlike the Catholic periodicals it was free of a priori concepts (apart from a dedication to examine the liberal point of view); it was empirical in its approach, objective in its analysis and community-minded in its direction. This evenhanded rationale explains why it chose to celebrate the first issue to appear in 1945 with an article which offered an apologia for the principle, if not the practice, of censorship. The author wrote: 'The case for censorship is, broadly speaking, the case for youth,'[1] and went on to point out that in every society, officially or unofficially, there is censorship at work, whether it is intended to promote national cohesion or prevent national deterioration. Writers influence mentality, and mentality affects morality, and the State which fails to take action should not be surprised if social disintegration ensues. The article is notable in that it insists that even in ideals there should be a sense of proportion, and since it is a legitimate assumption that the artist has been subordinated unconsciously or otherwise to the propagandist within him in the fashioning of his work of art, it is surely within the rights of the audience to comment on the message. Given the fact that the *virginibus puerisque* argument had been abandoned twenty years earlier and the range of omissions from the censor's net which the writer would recommend, it is difficult to see in this single defense of censorship to appear in *The Bell* anything more than the discharging of an obligation to the public to provide a balanced treatment of a topic, and at the same time to lodge a plea for an educated taste.

Of course setting up a target is intended to provide an object to aim at,

---

[1] Monk Gibbon, 'In Defense of Censorship', *The Bell* 9:4 (Jan. 1945), p. 313.

and when those invited to expend their energies included George Bernard Shaw, Seán O'Casey, et al., it was likely that there would be a few direct hits. Shaw was disarmingly moderate. 'No civilized person can be a freebooter, though everybody, civilized or uncivilized, would like to be let do what he or she pleases. Occupational privileges are unavoidable,'[1] he wrote. Just as surgeons commit murder in the name of medicine, biologists commit the most unspeakable atrocities in the name of scientific research, and parents abuse their children unmercifully under the guise of nurturing them, so too may one expect from even the civilized censor a failure to resolve problems which thankfully the average human being does spontaneously, without recourse to an official conscience. O'Casey is of course much less reserved, and launches his missiles in a wide enough arc to take in the Pope, Poland, Franco, the National Organization for Decent Literature in Fort Wayne, Indiana, and of course 'this pompous, ignorant, impudent and silly practice that is making Ireland a laughing stock among the intelligent of all lands.'[2] The remaining contributors, as liberal academics, were more restrained, save for one who observed that, 'Censorship of literature should be at the very minimum by comparison with the Censorship which the community enforces against various forms of political opinion.' The ominousness of this frightening statement coming from someone who purported to attack the system was not immediately apparent. These quotations from *The Bell* provide some indication of the ferment of thought that accompanied the cessation of hostilities, and of which the campaign for censorship reform was a minor but symptomatic protest against the status quo that it was felt could no longer be argued as essential to a mature and independent society. It was therefore no great surprise, and indeed provoked only desultory comment from the protagonists of both sides, when a Bill was introduced in the Dáil in February, 1945, 'to make further and better provision for the censorship of books and periodical publications.' The newspapers certainly reported the debates in the Dáil and in the Senate, but they also reported in those days of paper rationing 'mention after mention of parish hall bazaars and ordinations of priests and marriages of clergymen.'[3] The Dáil itself appeared to think that all the arguments had been adequately rehearsed, for the time they devoted to its consideration was minimal. Presumably, too the fact that the principle of censorship was not at issue expedited deliberations. After all, as politicians they could read the portents from the 1942 Senate Debate, and it would have appeared to them appropriate that the Minister would divest himself of the possible odium attaching to banning a book, and yet at the same time take the necessary

---

[1] G. B. Shaw, 'Censorship', *The Bell* 9:5 (Feb. 1945) p. 401.
[2] Seán O'Casey, *The Bell* 9:5 (Feb 1945), p. 404.
[3] Michael Adams, *Censorship: The Irish Experience*, p. 99.

precaution of setting up an Appeal Board that might inhibit the worst excess a future lax or puritanical Censorship Board might commit. The low-key mood is indicated by the Minister's tentative and hopeful expression for the Bill's safe passage, when he said, 'I hope that the new scheme will work. Like everything else done by human beings, it is only by trial and experiment that we can arrive at anything like an approach to a perfect system.'[1] The members of the Oireachtas were in no mood to shipwreck this nonpartisan venture. They had been nominated as being entitled to bring banned books to the attention of the Appeal Board (in addition to the author and the publisher) and their main concern now was to protest (futilely, as it turned out) at having to become involved with outraged authors, and even worse, with their banned books, which, as politicians, they saw as a typical no-win situation.

It was in character for the Senate to take the matter more seriously. There were the traditional reviews of arguments for and against the Board's conduct of its duties under the 1929 Act: the deploring of inadequate funding for conscientious Censors eager to seek out suspect material; the indifference of, and lack of support from, the Garda Síochána and District Justices; and the difficulties successive Boards had had in dealing with the mountain of objectionable literature in sufficiently expeditious a manner as to making a banning an event that did not occur until twelve to thirty-six months after the book in question had appeared in the bookstores. One Senator retailed the usual catalogue of the Board's aberrations and offenses against the human spirit, while another asserted that 'the pseudo-intellectuals ... are making a mistake if they think that the plain people are going to stand for a reintroduction of the vicious type of literature which the original Act was largely successful in keeping out.'[2] Certainly, as a result of these deliberations, the Irish were going to find it more difficult to get hold of their scatological English periodical newspaper. From now on, if any three issues were adjudged to be obscene within a fixed period, it would be summarily banned. Ninety-five amendments were put during the two days the Senate devoted to the Bill. Of principal significance was the withdrawal of the phrase that a book to be censored must be 'indecent or obscene in its general tendency' which had been intended to be a guideline in the 1929 Act. Passions became inflamed, as the semantics of lay metaphysicians challenged their opponents' grip on reality and arguments grew so stormy that one Senator was moved to say, 'Is Ireland to be Irish, or is it to be subjugated again by a foreign printing press by means of a spiritual defeat.'[3] Eventually the Bill passed and the Principal Regulations issued concerning the mode of

---

[1] Deputy Boland, *Dáil Debates*. vol. 98, col. 332, 17 October 1945.

[2] Quoted in Michael Adams, *Censorship: The Irish Experience*, p. 107.

[3] Senator Professor Magennis, *Senate Debates*, vol. 30, col. 1085, 28 November 1945.

making complaints and of addressing appeals. The second phase of censorship had begun. The reassessment made inevitable by the experiences which arose from the operation of the 1929 Act had resulted in new legislation. The Bill had contributed to forming a climate of opinion that had recognized the need for some form of control but which was now to launch its protest against interference with works that were by any reckoning to be counted as literature. Before sanity was to be restored, however, paradoxically there had to ensue for a conservative people arrived at a political crossroads an episode of relapse, restriction and repression. In the social challenges that were now to follow, the old restraints were reintroduced as if by way of reassurance that at least in this one field of sexual morality there was still continuity in the traditional Irish value system. An amendment of its ways had been proposed to the Censorship Board. By way of response it proceeded to confirm the fears of even its fiercest critics by compounding all the errors of which it had ever stood accused. Instead of a policy of tolerance and expansion in keeping with changing societal definitions, it regressed. Eventually, there was bound to be an implosion as negativeness fed on itself in an environment that neither sought nor could be offered a protection that would be permanently insulated against change.

The 1948 election brought to an end sixteen years of one-party government. A rather unlikely Coalition lasted for three years, made up of conservatives, republicans and differing representatives of the labor movement. While its duration was brief, it took Ireland out of the British Commonwealth; launched an international propaganda offensive against partition; reclaimed four million acres of land; developed agriculture; and virtually eliminated tuberculosis. Most importantly, in a major confrontation, the echoes of which still resound in the political consciousness of the Irish people, it surrendered over a piece of maternity legislation to the Catholic hierarchy who claimed it portended an invasion of family rights, the destruction of confidential relations between doctor and patient, the exposure to undesirable consequences as a result of the proposed sex education, and above all, the invasion of personal freedom by the State whose functional intervention could only be to supplement, not supplant, the responsibilities of the family. The government was to fall shortly afterwards but its period of office was to be recalled over time by this apparent failure to reconcile parliamentary democracy and ecclesiastical authority. At the time there ensued an exhaustive discussion of the nature of Church-State relations, which in the long term was to result in a readjustment, but for the moment served principally to give notice to legislators that creating a modern society was a hazardous enterprise, even though the benefits were, by any modern standards, as obvious as they were necessary.

Regardless of which party was in government the balance of payments crisis continued; emigration remained a drain on the resources of national pride, as well as on native skills and expertise; unemployment figures showed no signs of reduction; economic policy was still tottering on the aged and ailing legs of protective nationalism; both parties managed to combine wings of pre-Keynesian financial orthodoxy and varying degrees of expansionism, so that investment money had every reason for postponing a commitment until the political compass would steady. Steady it did when the country dropped its pilot and architect in 1957. Eamon de Valera now moved from parliamentary politics to assume the largely ceremonial role of President, and the moment at last had arrived to review

the old Sinn Féin ideal of developing our national resources with our own capital, our own skill and our own labor. There had always been a danger of economic penetration in regard to Irish industrial development, and that it has up to the present been avoided is as great a triumph as the development itself.[1]

The fact that this unrealism was now being discarded and that in its place there came an orientation of the economy towards the world market, the attraction of foreign capital and the integrated planning necessary to make native industry competitive meant that the mold of an Ireland purified in its revolution was forever broken. The detailing of what needed to be accomplished before economic development could become a reality pointed to all the defects that had hung like a blight over the period 1946–1958: a backward agriculture, a stifled and inert industry, a private investment that still preferred British consols and a public investment that had too often opted for the socially desirable rather than the commercially productive. Such was the social climate in which the activity of the Censorship Board was to rise to an average annual banning of around six hundred books a year. How much its endeavors were the product of these years of national uncertainty, of recognizing that traditional models of thought were no longer appropriate, but of not knowing a suitable social policy with which to replace them; how much they were due to a timid and tentative groping towards the deinsularisation of the Irish mind which knew little philosophy, less political science and, in all, had little practice in, and experience of, independent abstractions, are now imponderables.

The fifties were a decade in which the Church found more occasions to impress what it stood for on the Catholic consciousness than either before or since. It was the period of Maria Duce, an anti-semitic, pro-fascist, rabidly sectarian organization whose avowed objective was to expunge from the Irish way of life the religious indifferentism which it chose to read into the recognition the constitution afforded to all who were not of

[1] *Sunday Press* Editorial, 19 February, 1956, p. 11.

the majority faith. It was a time when Papal Nuncios could take umbrage at criticism levelled at any Catholic institution, when Trinity College, the nation's oldest university, was solemnly forbidden to Catholics by the National Council of the Church, when a racetrack could be brought to its financial knees because it refused to allow a Rosary Crusade, where football matches were threatened, theatre performances cancelled, and even the Irish clergy themselves severely rebuked for questioning a religious mission that appeared less pastoral and more juridical in the face it presented to the faithful. Inevitable, these excesses were to provoke a reaction, but throughout this decade and into the next, there remained the lingering conviction that authoritative suppression must always be available to correct any deviant behavior which might threaten the stability of society.

In 1954 the Censorship Board examined 1,217 books and banned 1034, or approximately twenty a week about which, it will be remembered, three members had to be in agreement and not more than one member in opposition. What had brought about such Herculean labors? One explanation may be that it was part of that Catholic activism mentioned above. Another may be attributed to the fact that the Chairman for the decade 1946–1956 was a Roman Catholic priest whose archbishop was in the vanguard of the opposition by the Church to the proposed State intervention into maternity care. Another factor was that from 1949 onwards there was no Protestant or University representative. However, the composition of the Board offers only a partial explanation. As has been seen, *The Bell* had mounted a reasoned assessment of the principles and pitfalls of censorship, no doubt in the expectation that the new Act with its Appeal Board could be relied upon to avoid the indiscretions of the past. Whatever the justification for this optimism, the 1948 annual report of the Board took pains to advert to the fact that its bannings were not being taken seriously and that books lingered on in shops and circulating libraries long after their dismissal from literary awareness had been decreed. To which *The Irish Times* rather ungraciously responded,

There may be a few people who will be disposed to join in the Board's lament: there are many who will not care about the matter at all; and there are many who will be sufficiently ungrateful to the Board to be pleased by the contretemps... The Board confirms, in its Report, that pressure of work has compelled it to leave 'a considerable number of formal complaints' in abeyance. This admission underlines the fact that what might be called the system of secondary censorship – operated by self-appointed Catos with a delicate palate for 'smut'– is a worse enemy of the people than the Board itself.[1]

These Catos are not unique to Ireland. Every librarian in every land

[1] Editorial, *The Irish Times*, October 5, 1948, p. 3.

must pay special regard to the local mores. No bookseller or newsagent wishes to provoke the unwanted attentions and interests of policemen about their premises. There are always library users and library committees who for different reasons choose to exercise an additional vigilance over the community's reading. Clergymen who are persuaded of the baneful effects of unguided reading have found it incumbent upon themselves to protest at the open access to particular items. When one comes to examine the Catholic Press for corroboration of these random and normal attempts at unofficial censorship, there is however a total absence of comment on its Irish manifestation, at least in the more serious journals. Among the more middlebrow, comment varies. A somewhat xenophobic and culturally protectionist journal, *The Leader*, which too often had made common cause with the extreme bigotry of the *Irish Rosary* and the *Catholic Bulletin* already alluded to, rather surprisingly took the Board to task in general for its failure to take into careful consideration 'the literary, artistic, scientific or historical merit'[1] of a book before banning, and in particular for its 'excess of zeal' in banning the report of the British Royal Commission on Population, a 'serious and important contribution to the study of social problems.'[2] *The Standard*, another Catholic weekly, while anxious to prevent the spread of objectionable periodicals and birth control literature also went to some lengths in affirming that it did not share the 'when in doubt, ban' approach, traditionally associated with the orthodox Catholic viewpoint. As for the other journals, there was, either as a reflex action to *Irish Times* liberalism or in response to some English comment on the Board's idiosyncrasies, an apposite invocation of traditional Irish values, a condemnation of wooly-headed liberal and senseless criticism that objected to the public being safeguarded from publications that pandered to unchastity, and a demand that novels be free from sympathy for, or incitement towards, sexual sin. Despite the unchanging quality of these strictures over thirty years, Catholic periodicals like the *Irish Rosary* did not devote to a consideration of the problem the space they had been wont to in the past. Now and again they would attribute venality to those who attacked the Censorship Board. In the campaigns against Indecent Literature in the late fifties, they would nail their colors to the mast. But generally, with the Board's productivity, there were little grounds for exhortation, and defensive journalism in support of the Board could leave too many loose ends and begged questions that could have uncomfortable reverberations.

What kept the censorship question alive as a violation of a civic right was the ferment of ideas that new political combinations had called into

---

[1] Editorial, *The Leader*, Vol. 94, No. 15, July 16, 1949.
[2] ibid., Vol. 94, No. 23, November 5, 1949.

being, even though each and every one of their constituents would have béen reluctant to admit that their efforts to have a political platform that distinguished them from their predecessors, were in any way responsible. The vehicle for the anti-censorship point of view of all parties and group-ings was of course *The Irish Times*. Unremittingly it sustained an attack on the aberrations of the Board, and in so doing by some inverted logic may have, by the plausibility of its case, provoked the Board to greater vigilance and redoubled efforts, safe in a conviction shared by many diehard patriots of the period, that if *The Irish Times* were against a prin-ciple, then there must be a lot to be said in its favor. Whatever the merits or demerits of such an attitude, it is still of interest to chronicle the vicis-situdes of the Board and the reactions of a growing number of liberal thinkers on the topic who no doubt found certain of their actions all the more incongruous, given the evolving political situation.

Probably the most indefatigable, the most percipient, the most tren-chant and most acidulous letter writing on the excesses of censorship was that of Seán O'Faoláin. His reasoning was the reasoning that was used thirty years later to overthrow a banning by the Censorship Board in the Supreme Court. He argued that a principle was being violated by which every Irish citizen was entitled to claim the 'protection of the ordinary Court of Law against any interference with his right by the executive au-thority of the State.'[1] The 1946 Act became operative in February 1948 and already by August he complained of 'another coup d'âne in defense of Irish innocence'[2] by the Board. And as for being unbanned by the Ap-peal Board, he asked, what gratitude should a publicly slandered writer have for a system that bans him or her one year, and revokes its decision the following. The following year he attacked librarians who arrogated to themselves the right to supplement the Board's activities. By this time, however, the Board itself had decided that it was opportune to go on the offensive and from now on the correspondence was to be sustained by its own momentum. This was the year, it should be recalled, that witnessed the inability of the Taoiseach and the President of the State to enter a Pro-testant Cathedral to pay homage to the remains of a previous incumbent of the latter's office. The liberal book lover did well to utter his *'absit omen.'*

Support for the idea of censorship, even indirect support, was not a fre-quent item in *The Irish Times*, then or now. One attempt to call a halt to the onward march of the Liberal Ethic was made by a university professor of philosophy who chose to see in the unbanning by the Appeal Board of the aforementioned British Government Report on Population, an invi-

---

[1] Seán O'Faoláin, Letter, *Irish Times*, January 28, 1948, p. 3.
[2] Seán O'Faoláin, Letter, *Irish Times*, January 3, 1948, p. 4.

tation to the Irish people 'to enjoy the benefits of contraceptive advice.'[1] This analysis set off another series of exchanges in which the nature of a religion was challenged which claimed to be based 'on transcending love (but) finds all too commonly its expression in uncharitable and misinformed attacks upon any who dare to hold differing views.'[2] The writer of course could be ignored. Despite the fact that his father had been murdered by the British, he was an agnostic and a product of Trinity. His name however was to reappear in another context. The correspondence about the Liberal Ethic, as it came to be called, dragged on, but even the most determined supporters of the Catholic viewpoint appear, by the absence of supporting letters, to have been made to feel uncomfortable by the increasingly evident irrationality of the Board's original decision, and by the quibbling and tendentious defense of it that followed. However, *The Irish Times* was selling 36,000 copies out of a total daily sale of all newspapers that reached 400,000, and any erosion of the Board's authority was in consequence likely to be, among the nonreading majority, a matter of some indifference. However, it no longer was safe to dismiss liberals as abortionists, loose-living sexual maniacs and pleasure-seeking monsters of depravity when these same liberals were all too disposed, and too able, to disprove their accusers in a public forum, and at times with greater Christian tolerance and decorum than was shown by their prosecutors. If the Coalition then in power could contain many different points of view and still function to some purpose as an alternative government, it was surely in keeping with the times that the dialogue of contrasting views on censorship – and other moral problems – should proceed, unhindered and unconfused by personal invective.

Of course *The Irish Times* had all the best tunes, and indeed some illustrious names to play them. One that was particularly interesting was a local judge (and a minor poet) who described in what purported to be a book review the *Register of Prohibited Publications*, 1950, as deserving 'a considerable circulation outside this country (where, after all, its value is largely negative) since it might be considered by some foreigners as a concise index to modern literature ... a roll call of the famous, all entitled to wear in their buttonhole a little green ribbon-o.'[3] This gay little effusion provoked a member of the Opposition to ask the Minister for Justice what action he intended to take. No doubt with all the severity and solemnity at his command, the Minister replied that while 'there can be no two opinions about the impropriety of members of the judiciary ridiculing the members of a statutory body, the more so if the latter are acting under powers which the former may have to enforce,' he still felt that a single

[1] *Irish Times* Report, January 24, 1950, p. 3.
[2] O. Sheehy Skeffington, Letter, *The Irish Times*, January 26, 1950, p. 5.
[3] Donagh McDonagh, 'Names and Numbers', *The Irish Times*, November 1, 1952, p. 6.

publication did not 'warrant the justice's removal from office in accordance with the procedure prescribed by Article 35 of the Constitution.'[1] However, even the anti-censorship lobby did not lack allies, unsolicited and unapproved, whose scatter-gun tactics diminished rather than enhanced their case. Paul Blanshard was so obviously a man of preconceptions about the Catholic Church and censorship that their apparent current identity of purpose was bound to provoke in him an analysis that was based on truths and half-truths, some fact and not a little *argumentum ad hominem*. Inevitably his overkill brought about a defensive backlash, and so inspired the traditional patriotic appeal to support the Church under attack that the force of his incontrovertible findings was dissipated. When however he stated that 'Irish Catholics are not permitted under canon law to read' his books he was very close to outdoing the Censorship Board in inanity.[2]

During these years, the Secretary, on the instructions of the Board, maintained a high profile in the national press. Whether Blanshard was being discredited, or Sheehy-Skeffington rebutted, the correspondence was conducted with a certain freedom of vocabulary and imagery that did not sit too easily with those accustomed to the formal jargon used in Civil Service communications. Language that 'verged on the bad tempered, the truculent and obstreperous'[3] was hardly appropriate for any communication emanating from a statutory body, but when that body was 'charged with a task which involved their defining the extent of the most precious liberties' then it became to some almost offensive. When the Board consistently repaid *The Irish Times*' criticisms with this currency, it therefore achieved a prominence in the public consciousness which drew from the tone of its invective a decreasing confidence in the validity of its judgments. In the meantime, it persuaded nobody of its powers of dispassionate appraisal by rounding on the paper for 'its slavish worship of everything British and its ill-concealed hatred of all things Irish.'[4]

In 1950, 410 books had been banned, a figure which represented 61% of all those examined; in 1951, 539 books had been banned, or 75%; in 1952, 640 books had been banned or 76%; in 1953, 766 books had been banned or 75%; and in 1954, 1034 books were banned or 85% of all those submitted, formally, informally, or investigated on the Board's own initiative, the ratio being 2:17:1. In the same year the Appeal Board issued revocation orders for 59 books, and dismissed applications for 4; in 1955, the number of revocation orders was 58 with 11 dismissals, and in 1956, 42

[1] Deputy Boland, *Dáil Debates*, vol. 135, col. 1159, 10 December, 1952.
[2] Paul Blanshard, *The Irish and Catholic Power*, p. 115.
[3] B. Chubb, Letter, *The Irish Times*, June 3, 1954, p. 5.
[4] B. McMahon, pp Office of Censorship of Publications, Letter, *The Irish Times*, July 12, 1954, p. 5.

and 15. The number of periodicals prohibited for 1954 was 77 and 91% of those examined. These data[1] were not to be surpassed. Ten years later the number of books banned was 317 or 67%, a figure that was a few points above the average for the forties. This year of 1954 was an election year. The coalition was to form a government for the second time. The previous government had not been able to dispel the economic and psychological gloom and doom, and this new government was not to do any better, standing as it did for increased taxation, decreased social welfare expenditure and unqualified conformity with Church thinking that had also characterized the previous administration but had been at a more discreet and limited level. The Board's ebullience in this year may therefore be put down to a flooding of the market with easily identifiable pornography, to the productivity of the Customs Officials, or, most likely of all, to a certain confidence that it had acquired, either because it felt, in this sea of political uncertainty, that it represented high moral standards, or as a result of forays into the media that it had won a backing from sections of the public who shared its views and were more likely to look to them for guidance.

Seán O'Faoláin addressed a meeting in Trinity College in February of 1956 which was reported in two half-columns of *The Irish Times*. He pointed out that censorship in Ireland had always failed to demonstrate discrimination in its decisions, either because of the minds of the Censors, or because of the inadequacy of the legal definition of indecency or obscenity. Cockburn's solution had been that these terms meant anything likely to corrupt susceptible minds to which O'Faoláin replied that 'People whose minds were open to such influences might have erotic, orgiastic tendencies at the sight of the petrol pump.'[2] He felt that the Irish Censorship Act had controlled the spread of pornography, but that banning without affording the writer the opportunity to present his point of view together with the insistence of an all-Catholic Board on its own quite out-of-date standards had resulted in its adoption of an evangelical role that fostered ignorance in the name of protecting innocence. Two nights later, the Chairman of the Publications Board, Very Rev. J. Deery, in a lecture given to the Dublin Institute of Catholic Sociology, said by way of rebuttal that the basis for censorship was the natural law which was the Divine Law as it was written and imprinted on every individual conscience. 'One page of a book could be more dangerous than fifty in another if it took the form of an attack on the Catholic Faith.' The works of most modern writers, the lecturer continued, made a laughing stock of purity. The Irish people, he felt, far from resenting censorship, were anxious to

---

[1] M. Adams, *Censorship: the Irish Experience*, pp. 119ff.
[2] Report, *The Irish Times*, February 24, 1956, p. 6.

be guided. He disputed the assertion that a book would be banned on the strength of one extract. That had never happened except 'when the offensive passage was extremely long and dirty. One such passage had run to twenty pages and it had been the worst in his experience.'[1] So much for dialogue.

Father Deery had been a member of the Board since 1945 and its Chairman since 1946. While there is nothing in the Act to indicate this office should be vested with any authority over and above that which all members possessed, it would be normal if his position, and the respect easily accorded a priest at this time, exercised some influence on the thinking of the other members. There had been various resignations from the Board down through its history, usually over the manner in which the banning process was conducted (93 books at one meeting was enough to disillusion one member). When it is further remembered that from 1949 on, all members were Catholics – some with reputations as activists – it can be assumed that his views reflected reasonably accurately the Board's when it banned books in the numbers indicated. At all events his lecture was regarded as being sufficient corroboration of the Protestant Church of Ireland's claim that his Board's approach was patently confessional.

A meeting of the Irish Association of Civil Liberties was held in support of a petition that had been sent to the Government asking for a commission to investigate the workings of the Board.[2] The Government of course declined to have anything to do with such a politically thankless cause, but did, when the occasion presented itself, replace retiring members with appointees who were either moderates or of a different religious persuasion to the majority faith. The impounding of *The Observer* in the spring of the same year by an unidentified agent on the grounds that it contained an article on family planning occasioned in the public enough disquiet to warrant some brake being put on any proclivity to excessive ardor in the discovery of putative dangers to Catholic morals. No doubt too they had in mind Ó'Faoláin's article in which he had quoted Judge Learned Hand's observation, 'if there is not abstract definition ... should not the word obscene be allowed to indicate the present critical point at which a community may have arrived here and now.'[3] Such was the practice in 'pagan Italy, or wicked Britain, or corrupt France or decadent America' where 'the now famous world story of the superhuman purity and chastity and goodness of the Irish people'[4] was believed with an intensity in inverse proportion to the distance from their hypothesized occurrence.

O'Faoláin of course was not the only Irish literary figure to run foul of

[1] Report, *The Irish Times*, February 25, 1956, p. 4.
[2] Report, *The Irish Times*, March 29, 1956, p. 9.
[3] Quoted in Seán O'Faoláin's 'Indecent or Obscene,' *The Irish Times*, March 1, 1956, p. 7.
[4] *The Irish Times*, ibid., p. 7.

the censorship official or unofficial. In a long letter to *The Irish Times* O'Casey informed the Editor how program notes he had been asked to write by the Irish Arts Council for a production of 'Juno "at Cambridge" ' had had chunks cut out of it, and how single copies of one of his books en route to friends in Ireland had been seized by the Customs. It was all very well, he continued, to talk about more study or more criteria which might help the Board to assess obscenity, when everyone knew that obscenity was only what the mind thought was obscene, and that in Ireland seemed to be exclusively connected with sex. 'But sex laughs at cleric and censor. When it comes, a physiological upsurge, the robin sports a redder breast, the lapwing gets himself another crest, a livelier iris changes on the dove, and dodging into secret places go the lover and his lass.'[1]

It is perhaps fitting that this ten years' review of public opinion of censorship should close with the resignation of the chairman, a Professor Pigott[2] who had succeeded Fr. Deery. The Minister's nominees of the previous year had demonstrated an unwillingness to ban works which were not pornographic. An impasse had been arrived at, since by the Act two dissentient voices were able to frustrate a decision to ban. This difference of opinion had virtually resulted in a cessation of the Board's activities. The Minister did not feel justified to act on the Chairman's request that the lately appointed minority censors should be asked to resign. Eventually, since Professor Pigott remained adamant in his refusal to convene a meeting, his resignation was sought, tendered and accepted. An editorial of the same date in *The Irish Times* criticized 'The foolish and humiliating Act, which is probably without parallel in any democratic country.' Though it still remained on the Statute Book the writer took heart from the fact that the Minister had given due notice by his attitude that it should be administered in conformity with its spirit and interest, and as such was to be made 'acceptable in the process to normally intelligent people.'[3] The inevitably flurry of letters followed where the contrasting options for censorship as being based on moral or on literary criteria were reviewed and statements adduced in support of the protagonists' points of view. Even to the defenders of the Board as it operated in its halcyon days in the fifties, much of what was now affirmed with such desperate and well-meaning intensity must have appeared to border on futility. The politicians for their part were about to launch forth on a new economic departure for which a hidden, introspective, socially-closed, morally subservient Ireland would play no useful part. Better than the articulators of public opinion, they were to discover the means to resolve the problem of the contending parties. Besides, being realists, they were

[1] Seán O'Casey, Letter, *The Irish Times*, May 18, 1957, p. 7.
[2] Report, *The Irish Times*, December 6, 1957, p. 5.
[3] Editorial, *The Irish Times*, December 6, 1957, p. 7.

aware of what was involved. The highest conceivable sale of any cloth-bound novel at that time in Ireland was 750 copies. A contemporary history or biography might reach a figure of 1,500. Only the lives of the saints or books on churchmen or Irish political figures ever exceeded that figure, and none went above 4,000. Paperbacks might sell a little better, but again 5,000 was a ceiling figure.[1] These statistics probably reassured the members of the Oireachtas that the book-buying public in Ireland was more vociferous than numerous. The brouhaha that broke out occasionally in the columns of *The Irish Times* should not be allowed to build on its sense of its own importance. The moral fanatic and the starry-eyed liberal were equally dangerous if their disputes were to lead people to begin to doubt the reliability of other forms of communication on which depended, for example, the electoral process.

Much attention has been paid in this survey of newspaper opinion of censorship to *The Irish Times*. The reason lies in the fact that the other two national dailies, while by no means professedly confessional in outlook, were in effect typical of what might be described as a Catholic Press, one of them devoting, even by Irish standards, an excessive amount of space to Church affairs, the other faced with the choice of recording opposition or withholding approval, usually, but not always, chose to be silent. The former, the *Irish Independent*, carried, for example, a full account of Professor Pigott's resignation and quoted *in extenso* from his explanation. In the same month, editorializing on a monster rally of 20,000 schoolgirls against the dangers to purity inherent in evil literature, it warned of the 'many foul books' on sale in Dublin, called for greater vigilance by clergy and religious organizations, and demanded of the government a drastic reform of the censorship code which would 'remove a growing menace to the youth of the country.'[2] It went on to report how the Catholic Bishops, following the lead of their brother Archbishop of Dublin, had issued a stern admonition to those who sold indecent books or periodicals that they thereby incurred grave mortal sin. The campaign was then reported nationwide with booksellers joining in for the very practical reason that a clear-cut censorship usually meant to them an avoidance of loss of profit. The *Irish Independent* next printed another editorial, New Curb on Evil Literature, and warned its readers that despite legislation and despite the precautions that have been taken, 'some of the most objectionable output originating in Britain and the United States does penetrate to Ireland.'[3] Approaches to the responsible Minister were however met with bland assurances that the Board was now functioning perfectly, and when those dissatisfied persisted, they were firmly told that

---

[1] Michael Campbell, 'Books and the Irish', *The Irish Times*, March 14, 1959, p. 6.
[2] Editorial, *Irish Independent*, December 31, 1957, p. 6.
[3] Editorial, *Irish Independent*, March 31, 1958, p. 8.

there was no need in the Government's view to change the law on obscene publications since the powers of the Censorship Board were quite adequate. The Minister promptly and discreetly encouraged its members and the Customs Officials to use these to control the importation and sale of obvious pornography, and the campaign, whatever its marginal credibility as a national manifestation of a sense of outraged proprieties, came to an unnoticed end.

Reviewing the participants in this long and often acrimonious debate it is clear that *The Irish Times* in the decade that had intervened between the coming into law of the 1946 Act in 1948 and the resignation of Professor Pigott had maintained a critical appraisal of the Censorship Board's conduct of its affairs and had made its columns available to its readers in order that they could make known their opinions. The Board, for its part, could claim that it had endeavored to maintain a rigorous interpretation of the Acts in the interests of morality, stretching from Magennis through Deery to Pigott.

On the creative literary side, the period of remonstration which had witnessed the first assault by the writers on the quality of the Board's decisions was continued in the fifties with less success but with all the greater indignation at the aesthetic condemnation and spiritual disavowal which a banning by fellow Irishmen represented. There were those who remained convinced that the Church's objections were mainly directed at the disreputable Sunday newspapers and periodicals that continued to flood the country from time to time, and once access to these had been curtailed, the custodianship of the morals of the book-reading public would assume quantitatively less significance. This assessment was accurate, as has been seen, and would probably have endured had it not been for the combination of a growing national urge to explore an alternative consciousness, and a contemporaneous movement to resist it by positing the dangers to morals such non-national influences represented. *The Irish Times'* contribution therefore was crucial. None of the more serious ecclesiastical reviews wished for obvious reasons to become involved. The less serious either ignored the problem, or merely reacted to what they saw as excessive criticism of the Board, or dutifully came in behind the bishops whenever their support appeared to be indicated. The Censorship Board at times seemed to be incubating an unavowed death wish. Its decisions, their defense and the rough-and-tumble polemics of letters to editors, its negative verdict on books universally acclaimed, all betrayed an unconscious urge, it would seem, to challenge the probity and legitimacy of its own existence in the same way as it challenged that of the books and periodicals it condemned.

CHAPTER 6

REDEFINITION OF CENSORSHIP

Gradually the momentum for change in the function and direction of censorship builds as Ireland begins to reshape its economic future. The rationale that will restore man as the arbiter of what he may allow himself to read and see will come paradoxically from the same pontifical university that had educated the bishops who had showed themselves reluctant to trust their flocks with the responsibility of their own consciences. New broadcasting legislation will be introduced to cope with the advent of television and already the limitations on freedom of expression possible on a public service medium of communication begin to appear. Just as successive governments will make quite plain these restraints, the late sixties will see the introduction of Censorship Bills that will do away with the excesses of moral protectionism in literature and films. A new definition of moral, if not political, freedom is to emerge.

The achievement of *The Irish Times* in keeping the issue of censorship before the public should not be understood as being the sole explanation for the emergence of the new thinking on the topic that was now to ensue. Within the Church itself there was a slowly increasing concern during the fifties at the direction the Board was taking and at the indefensibility of some of its judgments. Yeats had protested in 1928 that the definition of indecent as being construed to include 'calculated to excite sexual passion' must be sacrilegious to a Thomist who believed (as Yeats did) that *anima rationalis est tota in toto corpore et tota in qualibet parte corporis.* This liberalizing theology of St. Thomas had arrested the Platonism of Byzantium that had produced 'saints with thought-tortured faces and bodies that were but a framework to sustain the patterns and colors of their clothes.' In its place there came 'an art of the body, an especial glory of the Catholic Church' which inspired Giotto, and overnight changed the likeness of the Virgin from that of a sour ascetic to that of a woman so natural nobody complained when Andrea del Sarto chose for his model his wife, or Raphael his mistress, and represented her with all the patience of his 'sexual person.'[1]

In the second year of *The Furrow* (1951), a Catholic intellectual periodical, a Father Finnegan[2] suggested that film as a medium of communication had different messages for different receivers, and that what might appear to one critic as an attack on society's institutions might to another be a spiritual revelation of the artificial barriers that impede the Christian communion of men. Gradually the custom began to take hold for journals of this calibre to provide their readers with an analysis of the output of the electronic media in addition to the book reviews that formed part of its traditional offering. Thanks to an article which had appeared in *The Bell* some six years earlier,[3] cinema enthusiasts had grown more and more dissatisfied with the unsophisticated grading system adopted for certification purposes, the more so as new films were beginning to enter the country from mainland Europe where neither the trade-sponsored Hayes office nor the British Board of Film Censors guidelines were applicable.

The next-evaluation of film censorship followed on the heels of a reprint of an article by an American Jesuit which had appeared in *Books on Trial*. Murray argued that censorship was fundamentally a political device for self-preservation. Constraints were inevitable in the interests of freedom. What distinguishes traffic lights from communication control is that 'in this field religious, moral, intellectual and emotional values come into play.'[4] Literature by its nature as an artifact intended to appeal to the 'anima rationalis' in all its corporeal envelope either enlarges or diminishes. When it chooses expressly to be socially corruptive, the question arises as to when and how should the state organize preventive measures, and what norms are to be given to those agencies entrusted with the task of imposing these limitations. Social freedoms have multiple, interlocking consequences for which human logic is inadequate if not dangerous. Is society therefore helpless? No, 'it can decide on the general orientation it wishes to give to its particular solution'[5] of the activity deemed to be antisocial. In the United States a constitutional decision has come down in favor of freedom in the domain of communications, not on the basis of philosophic rationalism but as the conclusion of a political pragmatism that conceived this answer as being the only means of handling a concrete social reality, the complexity of which was and would be obvious

[1] W.B. Yeats, 'The Censorship and St. Thomas Aquinas', in *Uncollected Prose* by W.B. Yeats, ed., J. P. Frayne, C. Johnson, and M. Yeats, p. 479.

[2] C.S. Finnegan, 'A Note on Film Censorship', *The Furrow* 2:11 (Nov. 1951).

[3] Rex Mac Giolla, 'How your films are censored', *The Bell* 10:5 (August 1945).

[4] John Courtney Murray, 'Censorship and Literature', *The Furrow* 7:11 (November 1956), p. 680.

[5] *The Furrow*, ibid., p. 683.

with changes in times, in circumstances and in manners. What Murray
was saying implied a belief that man would use freedom in a responsible
manner. The Irish government had decided that he could not be trusted to
do so. American law pursues the post factum transgressor: Irish law takes
his thought into preventative detention.

Given the differences in stance, on what basis should censorship be put
into effect? The process should be founded on the norms of good jurisprudence. The purpose of law is to maintain only that morality which is
necessary for the functioning of the social order. A law must pay regard to
what St. Thomas calls its own 'possibility,' i.e. its acceptance and enforceability. Laws do not bring about moral uplift. Their 'performance' rat-
ing is in measure determined by the consent they command. The greater
the consensus in a pluralist society, the less appropriate coercive and
punitive censorship becomes. In the last analysis, even good censorship
becomes socially redundant if there are no good books. Even conceding
the doctrine of prior restraint which the Irish have written into their Constitution, Murray's analysis must have appeared as a reasoned response to
the outrages on intellectual standards (and even common sense) which
were being perpetrated in the belief that Catholic morality needed to be
protected to be preserved. In Ireland censorship had become the political
actualization of the sexual morality of the Ten Commandments. It was
the legal reification of an institutionally imposed value system presented
as an unchanging and unchangeable manifestation of the natural law.
However, it is an historical truism that constraints on freedom have unpredictable repercussions on the overall quality of life, and that laws are
limited by their inbuilt punitiveness as a focus for moral regeneration.
The internal contradictions of censorship themselves are sufficient to ensure the emergence of a countervailing need for freedom.

Meehan contributed to the analysis by asking frankly whether it would
not be time to say that whatever encomia the Irish Church might have
won in the English-speaking Catholic world in the nineteenth, and so far
in the twentieth century, it would be hard to disprove the accusation levelled against it of intellectual apathy. Equipped vocationally, pastorally
and practically, it was probably not surprising that 'Intellectual pursuits in
the traditional sense, cultural pursuits, the humanities, literature, the arts
and so on – all this, I suppose, seemed a luxury which the Irish could ill afford.'[1] The result was that 'Catholic truth is not being propagated at the
levels where it is likely to have a real effect in intellectual circles outside
the Church.' These thoughts were not published by some avant-garde lay
Catholic reformer, but by a professor of classics in the pontifical university of Maynooth. His demand that one should discover where one stood

[1] Denis Meehan, 'An Essay in Self-Criticism', *The Furrow* 8:4 (April 1957), p. 213.

at least in relation to censorship before deciding where next to go was developed by a fellow cleric who was the first to provide a balanced and well-argued view which would fruitfully engage the mind of a thinking Catholic who was unhappy with blanket condemnations and appeals to virtue substituting for reasoned discourse.

Professor Peter Connolly was involved with film criticism for some five years before he spoke of the censorship of publications. During that time, he wrote one article on film censorship in which he asserted that while its total rejection in favor of absolute freedom of presentation and discussion would be unacceptable in an Irish society, 'when so many are nominally educated but really semi-illiterate,' particularly in the media, this protectionism should not constitute the whole of the Church's task. Irish society for all that it was homogeneous with an almost universal agreement on ultimate moral principles was yet diversified enough, and likely to grow more so in changing world conditions, 'that the application of moral principles must vary with the circumstance.' More and more it should be the charge of the Church,

to train the elite and mature Catholic core towards a confident balance of freedom and responsibility, of moral theology and artistic judgment, of conscience and sensibility; a body capable of forming its own judgments, willing to apply the interior sanction, and allow discussion to correct false emphasis.'[1]

The vogue, Connolly goes on to say, is for expert witnesses on questions of censorship, or a balance of interests between lay and religious, or the institutionalization of, and accommodation for, the tension between the Pelagian and the Manichee supposed to control the affective drive of man. How much better if censors would find within themselves, in harmonious blend, capacities for moral sanity, technical know-how and critical articulacy!

Connolly's article on literary censorship as a follow-on of Murray's article was more profound and detailed. He defined ecclesiastical censorship which was binding on all religious, and then examined the concepts of freedom and authority on which it was based. In the first place, knowledge is good and intellectual enquiry is a virtue. Second, this intellectual freedom to pursue knowledge is good only when it is not at the expense of man's other powers. The interaction and interpenetration of the will, the intellect and the affections must constitute the functioning of inner freedom. Reason proposes the good, but reason must act in conformity with the natural law. Its rightness will depend on how well it orders its affective life. Mastery of this art, which leads on to right reason (and hence true freedom), is not acquired without guidance that may in certain cases take the form of limiting access to knowledge. What causes scandal in this pro-

---

[1] Peter R. Connolly, 'Censorship', *Christus Rex* 13 (1954), p. 154.

cedure is 'when all the stress is laid on the training of will and character, and little or none on intellectual curiosity and the maturing and refining of the affections themselves.' The Church when it censors books does so with a view to promoting the salvation of souls. Its sanctions run only so far as the moral consciences of its members are prepared to accept its authority. Derogations are always available on production of evidence of need and competency to read with that intellectual freedom which the Church defines alone as being real. Obscenity to be obscenity must mean by this explication a 'positive, conscious or avowed attention to teach obscenity defending it by argument, promoting it by persuasion, justifying or vindicating'[1] it as presented.

In a 92% Catholic country like Ireland what need is there of further state control of access to literature deemed unsuitable? Connolly replied that 'the Church ought not to compromise her moral authority with the compulsions of the civil law nor ought the State intrude into the private moral life,'[2] but should limit itself to dealing with crimes and misdemeanors that affect the community. Sin and error are part of the fabric of human life, and if God can tolerate their existence, so should man. Hence the repression of evil, while a duty, is not an absolute norm of action, indeed its tolerance may be necessary to promote the greater good. That conclusion should not be understood, Connolly was quick to add, as an argument for the exclusion of the State in matters which do have a moral coefficient. Even if it is not possible to make man good by law, that same law can help him from becoming evil, or evil to the extent that he contributes to evil for others. In deciding how far and in what manner the state should intervene, the enjoyment of individual freedoms must therefore be balanced against the general rights of the community. In this view freedom of expression was not therefore an absolute but was delimited by the actualization or potentiality of other rights. In such circumstances the reader had greater freedom of access to the expression than the writer had in its articulation or the publisher in its distribution. Censorship in Ireland was preventive and prohibitive. No private individual was guilty of a criminal act if he were to read a banned book. It might be confiscated but there punitive action ends. Censorship was not to be vindicated in the courts unless those involved were proven to have been guilty of breaking the law for reasons of financial profit. What was adjudged as falling within the scope of censorship would depend on the denotation of terms as understood by the contemporary community which must seek to regulate the functioning of its codes, rituals, manners and customs in the interests of the harmonious coexistence of its members. The young must surely be

---

[1] Connolly, 'Censorship', p. 155.
[2] ibid., p. 165.

protected but not to the point of denying them all intellectual and imaginative liberty or of failing to allow experience to be opportunely commensurate with maturation. Literature has a right to the vocabulary by
which it creates its particular reality. Depending on its purpose, a medical
textbook or a journal intime, each has its own repertoire of terms which
are to be judged by the context in which they are found.

   What can the State Censor hope to achieve, Connolly asks, confronted
with the task of serving the literate mass and the educated elite? First o
all, accept that censorship systems are by their negative mode of operation defective. Evil will remain after the last book, periodical or film has
been consumed in flames. There is no proof of a causal relationship between the vilest pornography and criminal action. The Catholic Church
may believe there is, but there is no clear-cut evidence that will relieve
him, as an official in a non-confessional state, of the need to calculate the
moral and psychological probabilities for evil of a book in light of its possible impact among the various cultural groups which might read it. The act
of the censor is a political act, and success extends no further than the cor-
rectness of the last decision. If he bases his judgements on the intention of
the writer as it reveals itself in the totality of his work, then at least there
will be consistency in the pattern of verdicts returned. If ever law, however, and a fortiori censorship, chooses to ignore intent, then miscar-
riages of justice will ensue, and the public will be confronted with the intolerable absurdities of books being banned on the basis of single sen-
tences, as the Chairman of the Censorship Board had announced in the
Senate debate of 1942. The distinction that must be drawn
is not between books which could corrupt and those which could not, but between
books which have no other purpose except to corrupt and books which can claim
that corruptive elements were at least not the main purpose of their composition.[1]

   It was incumbent, in Connolly's view, on the Irish censor of publications to discover the intention of the author (whom so far he never had
consulted) and the intention of the work itself (which he manifestly was
neglecting to do by allowing his judgment to be determined by the impact
of a passage or passages). His function was not to provide a verdict on its
worth as literature or even determine that it was literature. His question
to himself had to be '(1) whether the fiction before him is serious in the limited sense of not being pornographic and (2) whether there is a serious
literary intention which offsets or controls incidental indecency.'[2] Of
course there would be differences of opinion in answering these questions
so long as people remain persuaded theirs was an age of decline or were
confused as to the differences between a prevailing code of taste, decency

---

[1] Connolly, 'Censorship', p. 168.
[2] ibid., p. 170.

and reticence and what is in reality a code of morality. Censorship through time has walked with a laggard gait, a jaundiced eye, and a general air of battle-scarred wariness, as if for ever avoiding mines. The serious author will always be accident-prone if he is going to pursue his inventive bent beyond the traditional markers of conventional decorum. But for whatever lapses he is to be held accountable he should be left to his peers and to the purchasing public. To Connolly, to ban him is like concealng the name of a street which might lead someone somewhere or at the very least tell the literary wayfarer something about his current coordinates. 'Society should not be bereft of the salutary criticism of some of its own most passionately aware menbers.'[1] Literary bans are never effective. Those who are to be deprived are articulate and resourceful enough to circumvent them. But the act of banning itself bring in its train a distortion in the critique, a foreshortening of the view, and a clouding of the atmosphere that robs a new literary artifact of evenhanded justice which its author is owed, and not the *succès de scandale* which he is allotted.

Connolly was to return to this theme. His formula however remained the same. Look at the film, the book, the object, he apostrophized, and see it for what its creator intended it to be, and what the viewer or reader is likely to receive by way of a message. Disregard polemics about the virtue or vices of censorship which by now are *vieux jeu*. No one any longer need 'bury one's head in the sand, or on the other hand, sacrifice one jot of moral principle.' What Connolly achieved was to create a climate of opinion in which individual fallibility became an honest failing and intrusive authoritarianism a suspect virtue. He still would retain censorship, but as he was careful to point out, so too would the liberals.

It is injudicious to pinpoint any one piece of writing as being pivotal in changing the nation's direction of thinking. The Englishman, Mr. St. John Stevas, a Catholic intellectual and later a Conservative Minister in the British Government, had published *Obscenity and the Law* which contained a very critical chapter on Irish censorship. A Jesuit priest[2] also contributed to another Catholic intellectual journal a thought-provoking essay on the value to the Christian of making a personal judgment on what within a given framework might appear as indecent and obscene, but could also be understood as part of that reality which included concentration camps and atom bombs. And of course there was a change in the mood of the country (which will be noted) but even accepting all these influences, Connolly's article must be seen as fundamental in bridging that gap between the frustrated editorials and letter-writers in *The Irish Times* and the considerable number of people in a conservative country

---

[1] Peter Connolly, 'Turbulent Priests', *Hibernia*, 28:2 (February 1964), p. 9.
[2] John C. Kelly, 'The Modern Novels and Christian Values', *Doctrine and Life* 11:11 (Nov. 1961), p. 565

who genuinely felt themselves to be surrendering to a certain religious anomie as their personal sense of natural law was being offended by the very Act of parliament that was claimed to embody it. It was an authoritative voice, arguing dispassionately, with a sense of humor to keep the principles to be digested within the bounds of proportion, and gently persuasive in a way that might convince even the most censorious to turn again in hope to see what next might be said of the human condition. Whatever the dimensions of the impact of this article, whatever the influence of concomitant events, within ten years, as will be seen, censorship of films and books was so liberalized and the Church so freed of its garrison mentality that dialogue became a reality when most it was needed to cope with changes in Christian thinking, infinitely more disturbing to the Catholic mind than the *Tailor* or *Laws of Life*.

What did happen in the sixties? Ireland got a pragmatic leader who altered the priorities so that economic progress came out on top, and the idyll of a poor but contented Irish-speaking people nowhere. The economy from now on was to occupy the immediate, middle and far ground of everybody's attention. It was to be planned, and if predictions involved risks, then risks must be taken if taking them was the only road to expansion. The commercial banks were pressured into diverting their sterling assets into national investment. To their horror, whereas in the past balanced budgets and balance of payments took precedence in all fiscal thinking, now money was spent to make money as export industries were encouraged, foreign firms were attracted by generous tax rebates and public bodies established to provide and coordinate the data necessary for the comprehensive planning in which all were to share. [1] In a certain measure they did. National output increased, purchasing power rose, unemployment fell, the flood of emigration died to a trickle, and investment and savings increased. New housing, more consumer goods, wide and dispersed ownership of motorcars, and an opportunity to gratify those recreative needs that in themselves contributed to the general welfare. There were gaps of course in this parade of national resurgence. Education, health, housing and agriculture would have to wait to the seventies. Against even these blemishes, there was however the evidence of a wave of hope which a young American President could conjure up, the overspill of which was to reach Irish shores. There was too an old gentleman in Rome, whose pontificate was to open windows, to raise the Catholic laity to adult status, to dispense with tradition-clogged ceremonial, to propose a new spirit of criticism and to dare to invite his 500 million flock to take on the personal responsibility for their own spiritual redemption.

[1] F. S. L. Lyons, *Ireland since the Famine*, p. 619.

For the Catholic Church in Ireland, change too had come inexorably. On the plus side it could count on loyalty, a continued identification with the common people as opposed to the moneyed and landed classes, a body of religious who daily gave proof of a high sense of personal commitment and probity of conduct, and a jealously guarded distance separating it from all political organs of government and parties.[1] Against these qualities was a distrust of statism, matched only by too uncritical an acceptance of encyclical thinking on the organization of the body politic, a paternalism that rewarded conformity, a reluctance to accept some empirical findings of the human and biological sciences, an excessive dedication to the preservation of the rights of property, and a failure to curb the invective of those who attributed to the so-called enemies of religion an inordinate malevolence out of all proportion to the extent of their public disagreement with church practice or principle. Professor Connolly had pointed the way out of the dilemma for the 10% who read. For the remainder, there was another medium of communication, cheaper, more pervasive, minimally demanding of the personality, and so inexpensive that it was to be available even to the poorest. What role would the Church play once Ireland had established television as basic to its social intercourse and the arbitration of its values?

The problem of censorship now shifts from the printed to the electronic media. As has been noted, in the first few decades of radio the Director of Broadcasting had delegated powers which were so limited that in effect he was unauthorized to spend even the smallest amount of money for upkeep without prior sanction. In 1953 the Minister for Posts and Telegraphs appointed a Comhairle Radio Éireann of five persons to advise him in a part-time capacity on the conduct of the broadcasting service. From that time on Radio Éireann had in general terms been free to manage its own affairs and to spend the moneys allocated for broadcasting purposes.

In the meantime television had been making rapid strides in Britain and it soon became a matter of national policy to provide an Irish service that would reflect Irish culture and assure the continuance of the Irish identity. Since in other Western European countries the tendency (by no means unanimous) had been to establish broadcasting as an autonomous public service with the broadcasting authority acting as a trustee for the national interest, subject only to such powers of ultimate control as the government concerned had seen fit to retain, the Irish Government had decided to adopt the same model with suitable local modifications. One of these was that the two services – sound and television – would be under the same authority, and that they should be complementary rather than com-

[1] Garret Fitzgerald, 'Seeking a National Purpose', *Studies* 53 (1964), p. 347

petitive. The Government announced in 1959 that it intended to bring in a Bill proposing to establish an Authority which would be entrusted with the tasks as outlined. As regards censorship, the Minister said:

It is the Government's wish that the Authority should act as its own censor, recognizing the absolute importance of safeguarding truth and of preserving intact the moral integrity of our people.[1]

In addition however the Minister would take powers to provide that certain announcements would be broadcast on his authority and, in addition, to order that certain matters should not be broadcast as being of a detrimental character to the general public interest. He continued:

I do not imagine it will be necessary to use this power to prevent the broadcast of morally objectionable programs and I trust that the occasion will not arise to use this power at all. But circumstances may arise in which it will be very important; for instance the broadcast of a particular program or kind of program could be very embarrassing in our relations with another country or countries. While it may be argued that a responsible Authority would cooperate in these matters, the final say could not be left entirely to the Authority.[2]

Debates in both houses of the Oireachtas were protracted, the major portion of the time not being devoted to Section 31 about which the Minister spoke above, but about another section, 'which provided that any member of the Authority who had any interest in any concern with which the Authority proposed to make a contract, or any interest in any contract which the Authority proposed to make, should disclose this interest and take no part in any deliberation or decision of the Authority.'[3] When various speakers did address their minds to Section 31, they were worried about the wrong level of censorship, 'the armchair pietistic lay censorship,' 'the namby-pamby silly type.' Comparison with the British Broadcasting Act showed great similarities between the Acts, but members were anxious to go further. If the Authority were obliged to make, or to refrain from making, an announcement, it should have the duty and not just the option (as in Britain) to so inform the public.

When the Bill went to the Committee Stage, the Minister adverted to the fact that the broadcasting service was a monopoly State service, and that far from the Minister's 'seeking this power to suppress the free expression of opinion or to suppress opinion in any way, the Minister and the Government must take into consideration the public interest.'[4] It could happen that such a monopoly authority when it came to broadcast a program or a statement might not be in possession of information available to the Government but not available immediately to the public which

[1] Deputy Hilliard, *Senate Debates*, vol. 52, col. 20, January 20, 1960.
[2] ibid., vol.52, col. 22.
[3] Maurice Gorham, *Forty Years of Irish Broadcasting*, p. 303.
[4] Deputy Hilliard, *Senate Debates*, vol. 52, col. 52, 10 February, 1960.

could cast a totally different complexion on what was being transmitted. Some members while recognizing the appositeness of this subsection (1) of Section 31 still maintained that to order the Authority to refrain from broadcasting a directive would leave any Minister with the residual powers of a dictator. In addition, they argued, if he did take that power, the problem could well become one of why he had not used it on a particular occasion, rather than why he had, so that any member of the Oireachtas at any time could accuse him of failing to carry out the duties implicit in the power he now sought.[1] Another member pointed out that it was not the exercise of the power that concerned him, but that any Government could, with this section writ large in the Statute Book, get the Authority to broadcast along the lines it wanted by discussion, by suggestion, or by a mere inflexion of the voice over the telephone. The Minister who appears to have enjoyed the confidence of both Houses of the Oireachtas pleaded that he sought no more and no less than the authority conferred upon the Postmaster-General in Britain which had apparently worked quite successfully. The amendment proposing the deletion of the subsection was withdrawn.

Generally the Government's proposals were welcomed. Due recognition was made of the attempt that had been made to incorporate that which was valuable in the BBC experience and in the development of British legislation setting up the Independent Television Authority. *The Leader* considered, 'as regards freedom we find that the Act is drafted liberally ... The Minister reserves the right of limited intervention.'[2] If the Government had been hesitant in the past, not only because of the problems of economic feasibility confronting any self-supporting broadcasting service but also because of the changes that might be rung on Irish attitudes and cultural notions, then the Bill which the Oireachtas was eventually to pass into law did not appear to suffer from their misgivings. In final proof thereof it is worthy of note that the Government did accept the point made in debate: the Authority, if directed by the Minister in relation to a broadcast, no longer needed to have his consent before making an announcement to that effect.

Television in Ireland had been long awaited. The eastern seaboard had ready access to programs beamed from British stations, leaving the South and West avid to acquire this additional dimension to home entertainment and to experience for themselves that instant visual awareness and sense of theatre claimed on its behalf. A Television Commission had been set up prior to the Act and its findings had been discussed with that same passionate intensity that explains the limited unanimity of the Report it-

[1] Deputy Hayes, *Senate Debates*, vol. 52, col. 535, February 10, 1960.
[2] Editorial, *The Leader*, Vol. 60, No. 2, January 30, 1960, p. 3.

self. When the attractiveness of radio was investigated, it was discovered that for the period 7:00 – 10:00 p.m., during which 53–62% of sets were switched on, less than 10% remained tuned to the Irish station.[1] The explanation was attributed to the preference listeners had for light music variety and news bulletins. The writing on the wall was therefore clear for the new service. If Education, Enlightenment and Entertainment were the three big E's by which program planning was to be guided, the Irish, like the British, the French or any other European people, wished the order reversed in terms of output.

Perhaps it was a manifestation of this determination in the early sixties to direct their own lives that explains the fate of one amendment in the Senate debates which, except for the omission of 'indecent' and 'obscene,' was in direct lineage with the thinking enshrined in the Censorship Acts. The proposal was that the Broadcasting Authority would ensure

that nothing is included in the programs which offends good taste or decency or is likely to encourage or incite to crime or to lead to disorder or to be offensive to public feeling or which contains any offensive representation of, or reference to, a living person.[2]

During the course of the debate, reference was made to the obligation laid down in the Constitution which prohibited the use of the organs of public opinion 'to undermine public order or morality,' the existence of a similar provision in Britain, and the need to present an Ireland free of those distortions and disorders that cater for 'the mentally disturbed' and 'the enemies of the State.' The arguments for and against censorship were joined. The debate lasted forty minutes before the question was put. The last speaker summed up the point of view of those who defeated the proposal when he said that the Authority must be allowed to decide for themselves what was right or wrong. Unlike books and films, television had apparently been declared of age prior to its coming into existence.

The bishops issued a statement some months before the inauguration of the service. What it contained was perfectly in keeping with their pastoral responsibilities. It was everywhere accepted they said, that 'the normal vigilance exercised by public authorities over public entertainment (was) not sufficient in the case of television and that special standards should apply to it.'[3] This observation was not taken to mean any lack of confidence in the Broadcasting Authority. What was intended was to recall to parents their duty to protect their children from being exposed to

[1] Garret Fitzgerald, 'Radio Listenership and the TV problem', *University Review* 2:5 (1959), p. 43.
[2] Senator O'Quigly, *Senate Debates*, vol. 52, col. 429, February 4, 1960.
[3] The Bishops of Ireland, Statement on Television, *The Furrow* 12:11 (November 1961), p. 696.

programs which were plainly unsuitable. In the same issue the question of the advisability of television censorship is argued.[1] To the writer, the proven responsible record of broadcasting, the composition of the Authority, the impromptu nature of some TV material, the advantages of a wait-and-see policy, the value of public opinion as a brake on license, all seemed to be good reasons for endorsing the point of view that had been carried in the Senate, namely, to allow the Authority to discharge its responsibilities laid down in the Act. This willingness to accept life in more than its sanitized version appears to be confirmed by the Vatican II Decree on the Media which stated that 'the narration of moral evil, or its description or representation can serve men to recognize evil and extol good' provided of course that viewers 'try to understand what they see ... and learn to form right judgments by consultation.'[2]

An opportunity presented itself in 1965 and in 1966 during the debates in the Dáil and Senate on the passage of an Amendment Bill to review the operation of the Broadcasting Authority over the previous four years. The Minister was quite matter-of-fact. He still retained the power of intervention in 'a small number of matters in which it (was) important that the public interest should be safeguarded.'[3] In the speeches that followed for the next 2½ hours no member of either side of the House adverted to this part of his introductory statement. Replying to the debate that same day, he again referred to his power to 'issue a directive to compel Telefís Éireann to take off a particular program.' But he said, as Minister, while he did have a keen interest in the success of the medium, he could assure the Dáil that he would not contemplate interfering unless the Authority had failed over a protracted period to live up its obligations. That was to be the last reference to his power of veto. In the Senate there was some reaction. Objection was taken to the fact that existing policies in relation to the restoration of the Irish language could not be discussed or alternatives advanced in their place. Ministerial influence on program content, other than that emanating from the office of the responsible Minister, was alleged,[4] but there was no specific instance cited and here as in the Dáil the matter was not pursued.

This omission is explainable only by the general euphoria surrounding the discussion of the Amendment Act. Deputies and Senators competed with one another in eulogizing the service, congratulating it for all sorts of different reasons, and forecasting a bright and rosy future for this native industry of which the Irish people had every reason to feel proud. Perhaps

[1] Bernard T. Smyth, 'Irish Television', *The Furrow* 12:11 (November 1961).
[2] Promulgated by Pope Paul VI, Vatican II Decree on the Media, *Christus Rex* 19:1 (January 1965), pp. 56–57.
[3] Deputy Brennan, *Dáil Debates*, vol. 220, vol. 536, February 1965.
[4] Senator Fitzgerald, *Senate Debates*, vol. 63, col. 1428, 16 February 1966.

it was due to the fact that there had been no overt use by the Government of its power; perhaps it was the result of having been conditioned to accept censorship almost since the foundation of the State; or perhaps the country was riding a wave of economic buoyancy and did not wish to become involved in the inequity of a right not exercised. Perhaps the liberals really believed that it was a reserve power to be used only in an emergency and that it would obsolesce in time.

How wrong they were they discovered when in that same year the Taoiseach, Seán Lemass, was asked whether he had made suggestions to RTÉ that certain news items should be changed or deleted and that certain individuals should not be allowed to broadcast. The reply was frank, explicit and unambiguous. In so far as the Government has overall responsibility for the conduct of its affairs, the Taoiseach said, it

rejects the view that Radio Telefís Éireann should be, either generally or in regard to its current affairs and news programs, completely independent of Government supervision. As a public institution supported by public funds and operating under statute, it has the duty, while maintaining impartiality between political parties, to present programs which inform the public regarding current affairs, to sustain public respect for the institutions of Government and, where appropriate, to assist public understanding of the polices enshrined in legislation enacted by the Oireachtas. The Government will take such action by way of making representations or otherwise as may be necessary to ensure that Radio Telefís Éireann does not deviate from the due performance of this duty.[1]

The Opposition now proceeded to question each of the Government Ministers in turn about the extent of their relations with the Broadcasting service. Each referred the questioner to the Taoiseach's reply though some effort was made to blur the sharp edges of its authoritarianism by pointing out that no written directive had as yet ever been transmitted to the Director. One minister admitted that he had complained orally to a news editor that a statement he had given in all good faith to the House was repeated in the evening news only to be followed by a statement from another source flatly contradicting everything he had said. Having raised the hare, the Opposition drew back.

Lemass' statement was deliberate and reflected the thinking of the time of any Minister questioned about the performance of a semi-state body, created by the will of the Government to provide a service, advantageous to the people. However, RTÉ differed from the national airline, the national peat industry, the national electricity grid, and others in that its operations brought it within the ambit of constitutional guarantees. While the Government had the right to ensure that it did not 'undermine public order or morality or the authority of the State', that did not exclude criti-

[1] Deputy Lemass, *Dáil Debates*, vol. 224, col. 1046, 12 October 1966.

cism of legislation, even when passed into law, and, still less, include interference by Ministers with matters relating to editorial judgment.

Perhaps most significant of all was the description of RTÉ as an 'instrument of public policy,' a function that is not found in the wording of the Act which set it up. Subsequent events were however to demonstrate that the Government did mean to exercise its control to the full. A proposal by the Broadcasting Authority to send a television team to North Vietnam was withdrawn on the grounds that it would be assumed that they were going with the approval of the Government. Another team had travelled as far as Lisbon on its way to Biafra when it too was recalled. As the Minister concerned said, 'It would be wise for semi-state bodies, when they went outside their formal function across the line of international relations, to consult the Department of External Affairs.'[1] No need to issue a directive: as forecast, the existence of Section 31 was sufficient.

A communication agency had been set up, endowed ostensibly with almost total freedom to go about its normal business of reporting and informing, only to find itself kept on a leash that would eventually make it consider every time before it produced a particular program, whether it would not find itself in conflict with some Departmental policy and whether the end-product would justify the confrontation. Either it had the right as any news-gathering agency had to present a first-hand impression of how it read a situation, or it submitted for approval its projects before broadcasting them. To most people it was perfectly clear,

that when the Oireachtas passed the Broadcasting Authority Act it was not intending to provide a service in which the only material in broadcasting programs would be material which the Government thought would be harmless to its policies on general governmental matters (as distinct from the security of the State and organs of the Constitution).[2]

Perhaps, but the promise that the power to control broadcasts would be used only 'in most exceptional circumstances, and I am sure no Minister would try to abuse it'[3] was on the evidence beginning to sound quite hollow. The issues so far had fallen outside the scope of section 31 of the 1960 Broadcasting Act and might be explained as being due to differences in approach between the Minister, influenced by political considerations, and the reporter anxious to break new ground in pursuit of a newsworthy item. It remained to be seen what would happen when the Minister would be presented with a *fait accompli*. Either he accepted freedom of expression with its potentially dangerous consequences for a small country or he acted to prevent any future recurrence. In which case he would be obliged to come before the Dáil and defend prior restraint, never a comfortable

[1] Deputy Aiken, *Dáil Debates*, vol. 227, col. 1664, 13 April 1967.
[2] J.M. Kelly, 'The Constitutional Position of RTÉ', p. 209.
[3] Deputy Hilliard, *Dáil Debates*, vol. 179, col. 761, 26 February 1960.

chore in a parliamentary democracy, but preferable to tolerating a semi-state agency's claim that the country had a right to hear that which the Government did not at that time think it should.

The Press in Ireland during this period was not inhibited in what it wished to print, except indirectly. Fr. Devane who had been active in endeavoring to restrain the importation of British Dailies and Sundays had made one final appeal in 1950 to try to get the Government of the day to restrict their entry into Ireland on the economic grounds that Irish newspapers and periodicals were denied admission going in the opposite direction. He instanced the fact that in 1948 Ireland had imported 4 million dailies, 17 million Sunday papers and 19½ million periodicals for a population of under 3 million. When he complained that 'No people can be said to be mentally free who live under the dominance of an alien Press to the extent that we do,'[1] he was reechoing a complaint that had been part of Irish political thinking since before independence. Political and economic liberty had been achieved but as long as Ireland remained under the intellectual influence that this importation of newspapers represented, there would be no opportunity to emancipate the spirit, the only sure means of reconstructing a society in keeping with the Irish ethos.

For the inhabitants of the country with their experience of censorship, the situation must have seemed (if they had thought of it) somewhat bizarre. What they learned of the outside world, given the slender resources of Irish newspapers, they learnt through the grace and favor of Britain, which obviously tailored the news to suit its own requirements. Now it was proposed to tax them beyond the purse of the average newspaper reader, an effective form of censorship. However there were further grounds for concern. Thanks to 'The Paper Wall ... erected by Britain, through whom alone the world would get a picture of Ireland,'[2] the country would be represented by a newspaper service which it was proposed to censor. Fr. Devane's proposals were not accepted but they did have the unintended result of alerting the Government to the control over reporting affairs inside and outside the country which the British possessed. Seán MacBride was to try to correct this in- and out-censorship when he set up the Irish News Agency in 1950. It lasted eight years, and with its demise there disappeared the opportunity of building up a reputation and a clientele that would have provided an alternative to the unilateral, if not censored, reporting that was to create confusion for a world which wished to understand what was happening in Northern Ireland. Distrust on the part of journalists who saw their stringer earnings de-

[1] R.S. Devane, S.J., 'The Imported Press', Letter to *The Irish Press*, April 30, 1949, p. 8.
[2] Douglas Gageby, 'The Media 1945 – 70' in J.J. Lee (ed.), *Ireland 1945–70*, p. 129.

crease, failure to set up the organization on a commercial basis, but above all the same bureaucratic controls on quality and content that had dogged and were to dog (if from a discreet distance) the activities of RTÉ, were enough to undermine the confidence of those who believed in its existence. As the sixties wore on, the national dailies grew less identified with a political party and closer to *The Irish Times* which was always ready to demonstrate its independence of view. It was a time of consensus politics, and consensus politics does its own censoring. Ideologies become blurred and unorthodoxies anachronistic. The political reporter moves out and the theater critic moves in. It was however to be a lull before the storm that was to break in the north, the reverberations of which are still sounding.

Halfway through the sixties it is worthwhile to look back a moment at the course the country had taken since independence. The old class structure had disappeared. A literary revival had accompanied and survived the physical force movement. Industry had been encouraged. Emigration till the decade in question had continued. Politics had only recently escaped from the simplicities of competing variants of nationalism. The parish priest was still the school manager, the chairman of the Education Committee, the President of the branch of the Gaelic Athletic Association, in short the social leader. Till 1950, Ireland retrenched, moving slowly from *laissez-faire* policies through agrarian idealism to survival and, to complete the cycle, ended up back again in stagnancy, uncertainty and stasis. After a brief interlude of radical republicanism that saw Ireland totally isolated, everybody became republican. A difference over maternity care brought about so total a submission of the State to the Church that, paradoxically, neither would ever allow another such confrontation to develop. The political pendulum swung, not from right to left, or vice versa, but from tweedledum to tweedledee. And censorship in these political doldrums, as has been seen, reached its apogee.

There next emerged the politics of economic growth, social welfare, cosmopolitanism, urbanism and the consumer society. Everywhere there were signs that forces were on the move. Even rural Ireland, where depopulation had been accelerating, knew about change. Now in 1962 there was television to bury for ever the concept of a cultural Sinn Féin and the notion that the island-fortress was proof against external events. It was no longer possible to lock out the world:

No greater barrier had ever been imposed upon any attempt at either moral censorship or cultural discrimination against foreign influences than the sheer inability of the native television to produce enough material to fill its own schedules.[1]

Enough remained after the laundered importations of 'sitcom,' serials,

---

[1] David Thornley, 'Ireland: The End of an Era?', *Studies* 53 (1964) p. 13.

chat shows and documentaries to make the Irish people aware that this politically controlled medium was sufficiently potent and pervasive to render the most benign, the most tolerant and the most liberal censorship irrelevant and inoperative. Slowly the idea began to percolate among the Irish that morality was more than a list of sexual taboos, that the State had no obligations to further the Church's teaching, and that while their political naïveté, caught as it was in the aspic of their inherited loyalties, was matched only by the unintellectuality of their religion, there was no statement, no position, no slogan and no doctrine that would not sooner or later be challenged by someone.

How then did the censorship of books and films fare in the second half of the sixties? Despite the turn for the better that followed the departure of Professor Pigott, and the more tolerant attitude adopted by a Board that the Minister had taken care to see was like-minded, the irritant continued. Various journals up and down the country found the need to protest, usually provoked by some egregious decision taken for no discernible reason. *The Kilkenny Magazine* demanded that the banning of Frank O'Connor's translation of Bryan Merriman's *Midnight Court* be revoked 'for the honor of a dead Irish poet who wrote, as a poet should, from his experience and his vision; and for the honor of his translator, a living Irish writer who had recreated the dead poet's words in a language of which he is acknowledged to be a master.'[1] The 'living Irish writer' himself was still anything but mollified when the ban on the *Midnight Court* was lifted, since a few weeks later he was to be found addressing a meeting of the College Historical Society in Trinity College and relating with bitter pathos his personal experience with the Tailor and Anstey, described, he reminds his audience, in the Irish Senate as 'a dirty old man' and his 'moron' of a wife.

As a result that kind old couple who had offered their simple hospitality to students from all over Ireland were boycotted. I am not exaggerating. I was there with them one night when a branch of a tree was driven between the wall and the latch so we were imprisoned. Three priests appeared at their little cottage one day and forced that dying old man to go on his knees at his own hearth and burn the only copy he had of his own book.[2]

Finally there was one brave effort to assess the value that might lie in a censorship that was not underpinned by a morality based on an infallible interpretation of a specially revealed natural law. The artist, the theory went, would claim that his work could not be immoral, since art and immorality are incompatible. Whatever his feelings may be when the moralist tells him in fact his work is immoral, they are probably matched

---

[1] The Editor, 'To Our Readers', *The Kilkenny Magazine*, No. 5. (Aut.-Win. 1961), p. 7.
[2] Frank O'Connor, 'On Censorship', *The Dubliner* 2 (March 1962), p. 44.

by those of the moralist who is told by the critic that a piece of blatant pornography is a work of art and therefore beyond reproach. Why not admit
that art can tend to corrupt and still remain art? Suppose artistry is only
part of the equation between the reader and the book. Dickens can be
read for the story he tells, for the sociological insights into his times as well
as for the aesthetic pleasures he gives as a literary craftsman. Certainly,
educated adults will read for aesthetic enjoyment in an ideal situation but
as Synge proved with *The Playboy*,

in spite of the perfectly innocent intentions of the author, and without any depravity or bad faith on their part, certain sections of society cannot adopt an aesthetic
attitude to certain works.[1]

There might, the author concluded, be something to be said for grading
books in the same manner as films, depending on maturation. There was
certainly no justification for keeping any book sequestered from
everyone.

While it did not resolve, and indeed did not attempt to resolve, the institution of censorship as distinct from the principles that might justify or
explain its retention, the essay, by its reasoned approach and temperate
tone, is indicative that the days of the language of offended susceptibilities, replacing logical argument, had disappeared. Yeats, Æ, O'Faoláin, O'Casey, and countless others had spoken of their personal grief –
Irish sales of their works never amounted to more than a pittance – at
being condemned in their own country without right of appearance to defend their slandered works. Their protests, considered as being in the line
of business, were ignored until cumulatively the injustice and the violence
being done to the creative impulse had prompted Connolly's magisterial
refutation of the inanities that had characterized the administration of
censorship since Ireland had turned in on itself in the forties. Connolly
had broken through the veneer of a morality from which individual responsibility had been banished and had asserted the need for personal accountability in art. Barrett was part of the dialectic that Connolly had
begun. There would have been further theses if the Government had not
stepped in and made it difficult to sustain the search for a solution by taking away the problem, or at least enough of it to remind the Irish reader
that it no longer was one.

The Minister for Justice introduced his Censorship of Publications Bill
(1967) to a Dáil that was not unaware of the consequences of its deliberations some forty years earlier. The Bill was intended to limit to twenty
years (later amended to twelve) the life of any prohibition on any book
that had been banned on the grounds that it was obscene or indecent, and,
further, to allow an appeal to be taken at any time against a banning and

[1] Cyril Barret, 'Censorship', *Studies* 53 (1964), p. 155.

not just in the year following the making of the prohibition. The debates in the Dáil and in the Senate passed off without rancor, deputies and senators being at one in congratulating themselves on their adult and sophisticated approach to the legislation that contrasted sharply with the tartuffeism of their predecessors. The Minister informed the Senate that thanks 'to a board that had common sense, a board who reflects the best of the current opinions of the day and the best of the current attitudes and views'[1] in 1963, the number of books banned was 442; in 1964, 353; in 1965, 288; and in 1966, 158. At the same time, while the Bill went through the Oireachtas rapidly and with appreciation on all sides for its promoter, two of the more senior members of the episcopal bench had announced that instead of mitigation, the censorship laws should be made more rigorous in order that the Irish people be protected from those who neither accepted nor practiced the Christian moral law. Twenty-five years earlier, one of these bishops had stopped social welfare legislation, occasioned the resignation of a Minister and was responsible for imprinting in the Irish mind a benchmark for Church-State relations. This time the Government stood firm and the Bill passed, thereby probably providing more relief to embarrassed clerics than to lay bibliophiles.

There remained films. What Connolly had begun, Kelly continued by providing thoughtful and informative analysis of films, some of which had been refused licenses by the Censor. The message he conveyed mirrored what enlightened Church thought was saying about literature. Sex was good and noble as an attractive force between persons; it was only immoral when it became *égoïsme à deux*. The moral value of a film should depend on the film maker's approach, Kelly claimed. His work must be seen in its entirety and not judged on a few erotic scenes. What shocks or disgusts need not be immoral, and 'The film maker should not stop making films in which sexual matters are treated properly merely because some people in the audiences, because of their own bad dispositions, may make some improper use of his film.'[2]

The censorship of films had not attracted the same hostile reaction as had the censorship of publications. Films, unlike books, were not released and then recalled. The procedures were business-like and in any year in the fifties when as many as 80% of books were banned, never fewer than 80% of films were passed, admittedly 20% of which had been cut. No information has ever been made available as to the reasons why films are banned or indeed for over a long period what their titles were. Whether the Censor, as a paid state official, ever sought guidance from psychologists, sociologists or educationalists, remains a secret. Around

[1] Deputy Lenihan, *Senate Debates*, vol. 63, col. 474, 14 June 1967.
[2] John C. Kelly, 'The Morality of Films', *The Furrow* 12:7 (July 1961), p. 23.

1964, the number of films banned or mutilated began to attract considerable adverse comment. The same Minister for Justice who was to pilot the amending legislation for publications took advantage of the ending of the term of office for the Appeal Board to replace them with a new and more liberal-minded team with Fr. Kelly as their chairman. Immediately there was a 500% increase in the number of successful appeals. The real innovation however was the introduction of certificates in 1965 for limited viewing, that is, for people who had attained a certain age. Hitherto the Appeal Board had decided that if a film were not suitable for even the most juvenile audience, then it might not be shown publicly to any audience in Ireland. All that was required now was liberal legislation of the kind that had released so many books into the literary market. In 1970, a Censorship of Films (Amendment) Bill was introduced which allowed for the re-submission of films banned prior to 1965 (when limited viewing was introduced) and for the re-submission of a film at any time seven years or more after the date of a censorship exclusion order. The Bill was nodded through within the space of an hour, and one more limitation on the right of access to the enjoyment of human creativity was removed.

Was censorship dead? Certainly those who had fulminated against the *News of the World* in their Lenten Pastorals, who had stopped trains to burn English newspapers, who had organized vigilance committees, had written letters to the papers, and had conducted investigations of circulating libraries – they would have had no doubt that all their good work had been undone. The censorship movement had begun with a raid on weekly Sunday newspapers and periodicals which even in Britain were considered objectionable but were much more intolerable in a country whose moral formation had been determined by sexual forces of which neither their pastors nor they themselves were totally aware.

Ireland had become a nation of small land proprietors a generation after the Famine. The holdings were so small that it was possible to sustain only one family from what they yielded. Accordingly, all brothers and most girls had the choice of either emigrating or remaining in celibate service to the father, and then to the eldest son after his death. An ideology had in the course of time to be invented to explain both the dispersal and the bondage. The family was transmogrified in a century from being a harsh, aggressive, scheming, materialist human unit (which in an agrarian society of eight million, straddled for the most part by absentee or incompetent landlords, it could well have been) into a loving and mutually supportive grouping whose goodness was matched only by its adherence to Church teaching: those off-loaded into the coffin ships bound for American became romanticized exiles; and those who remained at home were inducted into the mysteries of inviolate womanhood whose virginity 'ensured that inheritance patterns would not be spoiled by untimely 'accidents' occurring due to the delayed age of marriage.''[1] Hence concentration on sexual morality transcended all other virtues to the extent that the idealized total repression of the procreative urge made other moralities of such subsidiary significance that drunkenness and violence were elevated to the weakness of a good man. But the ideology had to be actualized. The celibate state had to become heroic: the fallen creature an object of shame and rejection. Love was decarnalized in the Madonna; the priest in the family represented social advance, and honor was duly paid to him as one who had elected to go into the trenches to guarantee the smooth working of primogeniture. The young men then who burnt the English Sunday newspapers were lighting a candle to their ideal self, an ideal that was more·the product of superimposed socio-economic forces than the outcome of personal convictions.

Between 1930 and 1968, a total of 6,116 books was banned, all of which would now eventually become available, with the exception of some 90 which dealt with birth control. The role of the family had been restored by handing back the deciding of what was appropriate reading for the young. Attention began to drift from the morality of sex to the morality of violence, from woman as mother and housekeeper to woman as woman. Values were no longer to be urged as justifying protective measures but were notions to be acquired or rejected as the outcome of a positive and personal act of volition. Catholics discovered they were Christians, and as Christians shared a consensual position which still admitted alternative views of what was of enduring worth. The Church itself began to redefine its mission, the layman began to assume responsibilities for his own private and public morality which he now came to realize involved a highly personal and individual range of choices. Was censorship dead? No, not by any means! Rarely outrageous, often dormant, usually conservative, never adventurous, its decisions, however, were more in keeping with the changing, moral temperament of the people. The Irish were less liberal than the British or the Americans, but the days when moral decisions could be preempted in broad swathes on their behalf were gone.

---

[1] J.J. Lee, *Continuity and Change in Ireland, 1945–70*, p. 169.

CHAPTER 7

THE MORALITY OF CENSORSHIP

The development of democratic institutions and civil rights in the West owes much to the Millian conceptualization of liberty. How its insistence on the responsibility of the citizen for his actions came to be matched by the affirmation of rights which inhere in the consciences of those who seek the Kingdom of God is an intellectual phenomenon of the third quarter of the 20th century. As English jurisprudence debated the relationship between positive law and Christian morality, theologians in the Catholic church in Ireland redefined the bases on which personal conduct might be determined. That the natural law is no longer an absolute is evidenced by their willingness, and by that of the Irish courts, to look to what is understood contemporaneously to be justice before ruling on the nature of fundamental rights. The influence of British thinking on the moral role of the media serves to stress the differences which may arise when personal independence is at variance with society's need for consensus. The impact of new thinking on the constitutive elements of morality will be tested by reviewing the operation of the Censorship Board in the seventies, and by the experiences of County Librarians with the book-reading public. The conclusion would appear to be that the choice of literature henceforward will be determined by the individual, making in this experience, as in others, a free and independent judgment.

According to Mill the only justification for interfering with the liberty of the individual

is to prevent harm to others. His own good, either physical or moral, is not a sufficient warrant. He cannot rightfully be compelled to do or forbear because it will be better for him to do so, because it will make him happier, because, in the opinion of others, to do so would be wise or even right... The only part of the conduct of anyone for which he is amenable to society is that part which concerns others. In the part which merely concerns himself, his independence is, of right, absolute.[1]

In this utilitarian calculus paternalism does not necessarily work because the harm it does outweighs the good. Mill does not satisfactorily demonstrate the first assertion to be true in all circumstances and his argument, therefore, depends for its validity on the second. Like all enlightened philosophers Mill believed that the clear and vivid apprehension of the truth is essential to happiness. Freedom of thought and discussion are required as means to that end. Inhibition of the spontaneous development of the individual, except in cases where it is necessary to prevent harm to others, may do good but will most certainly have, sooner or later, worse consequences for the general welfare.

Suppose the state were able to secure for its citizens a greater good than that which was achievable by them on their own, and did this without adverse interference with the individual, would not the manipulation of freedom be justified on grounds of utility? The rejection of this proposition implies not only that individual liberty is intrinsically desirable but also that its value is greater than the conjunction of all other 'goods', each of which is intrinsically desirable, too, in itself. Now, if liberty is valuable as a means to happiness, so too are health, virtue and others which, it may be conceded, are as much ends in themselves as is liberty. The problem then arises for Mill how to order these ends–means should they be in conflict. Why should liberty 'weigh more heavily in the scales of moral choice than health?'[2] Happiness which is the congeries of these desirables is not an empirically definable absolute of universal applicability. Mill does not, therefore, provide a ranking order of values that will resolve the problems of choice. Moreover, no plausible ordering theory is evident to justify a higher place being assigned to liberty than to health, or virtue, or the other desirables encountered in a pluralist society.

Mill argued that liberty and the liberal society are justified because of their utility. In the absence of priorities, each one must judge where his own interests lie provided that their pursuit does not harm his fellow man. Information is essential to this activity, and any suppression of it presupposes a claim by the suppressor to infallible knowledge of its falsity. When the act of suppression is coercive as in censorship, the moral worth of action is diminished since people act from fear rather than from conviction. Any such coercive act subtracts from the respect that is due to man as a free rational being.

There are difficulties in these statements which justify reservations. No

[1] J.S. Mill, 'On Liberty', in *Utilitarianism, Liberty and Representative Government* (New York: Everyman, 1951), p. 95–6.
[2] James Bogen and Daniel M. Farrell, 'Freedom and Happiness in Mill's Defense of Liberty', *Philosophical Quarterly* 28 (1978), p. 337.

empirical evidence is available to support the conclusion that liberty is conducive to truth: *a priori* arguments, yes, facts, no. Conclusions in scientific journals, for example, are handicapped by the measure in which they deviate in their formulation from orthodox method. Likewise, freedom of speech cannot be argued as an indefeasible right in all circumstances, as emergent nations and nations at war will attest. If liberty then is reversible or contingent, can it be claimed as being indispensable in the pursuit of happiness?

Mill himself was not totally convinced of the efficacy of the argument that each is the best judge of his own interests. If it were true as a universal generalization, the need for the existence of a state disappears. History would become a chronicle of the actions of competing egomaniacs, and regulatory institutions, like the law, would be supererogatory. This view claims for man a sufficiency which the social contract belies. Even where the particularity of the situation leaves the individual in the position of being the only judge, there are problems in distinguishing self-regarding from other-regarding actions.

Suppression, it has been said, is based on the supposition of infallibility. Conversely, tolerance is grounded on the lack of certainty with which beliefs are held. Pre-Vatican II Catholic Ireland saw the Church as the authoritative custodian of moral truth and as such, tolerance of error was unjustifiable. More important, however, is the fallacious identification of suppression with infallibility. Successive Irish governments have not granted the IRA access to the media on what was never claimed to be more than a strong conviction that what might be said, while it could be true or false, would certainly be harmful. If intolerance in their view leads to suppression of the good, tolerance may also lead to commission of the evil. The probabilities must be weighed in considering the impact of the message in the situation. If this approach is adopted, there will be a derogation from the liberalism of the society in question, which Irish goverments were prepared to pay as the price for the functioning of the State.

The argument that coercion robs actions of avoidance of their moral worth is patently untrue. Refraining from crime is not due alone to fear of consequences. Indeed, fear may not even be a consideration in the decision not to perform an evil deed. Even right actions done from fear are moral in their consequences as would be the case for bookshops which refused to deal with censored publications. Further, the coerciveness of censorship 'can educate public opinion and inculcate a moral concern about important activities about which the ordinary person is morally insensitive,'[1] as may also be seen in legislation dealing with drunken driving. If the worth of the conversion to sobriety is morally questionable by

[1] H.J. McCloskey, 'Some Arguments for a Liberal Society', *Philosophy* 43 (1968) p. 35.

virtue of the nature of its inducement, e.g., the fear of losing one's driving license, would a true tolerance be rejected because of its being the outcome of brainwashing or subliminal techniques?

In discussing the intrinsic value of liberty, Mill sees the freedom of self-determination as being an invitation to self-development. Man is not enjoying true liberty when he stultifies its gift by the dissipation or atrophying of his talents. In his activity man must face the paradox that the liberty he seeks in order to achieve his fullest self-realization is surrounded by restrictive codes which rationally he cannot challenge (for example, the prohibition of heroin consumption) but which square uneasily with a liberal society defined in the abstract.

One of the recurrent themes in the protest literature about Irish censorship was that the deprivation of access to films and books involved a reduction in respect for man as an autonomous human being. But are there circumstances when the duty to respect persons may be subordinated to other demands? Obviously vaccination, compulsory education, social welfare participation, obligation to vote in some countries, all involve some legalized breach of this duty. The acts themselves may be translated as mutilation, brainwashing, regimentation and conscription, and may, out of context, appear repugnant to accepted notions of what constitutes a liberal society. They are coercive, as is the forceful restraint imposed on an individual driven mad with grief, or the suspension of a life-support system when the march towards death is irreversible, and pain the wayfarer's only companion.

Censorship is paternalistic. It has pretensions to infallibility, whereas its normal performance shows it to be inefficient and ungenerous. Its premiss is a universal and absolute good, recognizable by all. The reality is different, and the more the person coerced feels there is dissonance between the legislated good and the personal good, the less he will feel respect for himself as a person. Obviously the intensity of this conviction will be in inverse proportion to the credibility of the legislative or judicial act that interferes with the free exercise of his liberty. In short, respect for persons may entail acts of disrespect in the interests of ensuring a good, like health or happiness, deemed more important than respect.

Finally, there is in a liberal society the assumption that freedom is coterminous with respect for human rights. Liberty is defined in terms of rights, which, as they appear in the Irish Constitution, are generally circumscribed. If a right is instituted on utilitarian grounds, it may always be overridden in the presence of a greater good. If it is accorded as a function of social recognition, then its existence is predicated on the society where one lives. If, however, a right is characterized as a moral entitlement which may lead to evil, then it is only valuable and real as long as that choice exists. In this view, since what is true cannot be known infallibly then the right exists to pursue knowledge and act as a result as one thinks one should. But does a right exist simply because of a belief in its necessity? One has the right to pursue undisturbed one's conviction about the flatness of the earth since such a belief will not harm others. On the other hand, one does not have the right to murder simply by believing that one has the right to do as one pleases. The State has not the right to prosecute the first: it does have the right to pursue the second since one's right has been expunged by the nature of its use. The utilitarian arguments in favor of liberty are two-way; the empirical arguments either conceal the need for coercion in support of morality or fail to point out that the full enjoyment of liberty may be overtaken by other considerations; and the theoretical arguments re-emphasize what obtains in all cases, namely, that the justification of liberty is relative to the society in which it is to be enjoyed.

Mill's influence on the development of English jurisprudence persists. One hundred years after the publication of his essay *On Liberty*, the Wolfenden *Committee on Prostitution and Homosexual Offenses* was to say in Section 61 of its Report: 'There must remain a realm of private morality and immorality which is, in brief and crude terms, not the law's business,' an opinion reflected in a recommendation contained in an American draft Model Penal Code which stated that 'there is the fundamental question of the protection to which every individual is entitled against state interference in his personal affairs when he is not hurting others.'[1] Lord Devlin, on the other hand, a judge, a member of the House of Lords and a distinguished writer on criminal law who was identified with many humane enterprises, took issue with these statements in his book, *The Enforcement of Morals*, in which he said that it was just as much the duty of the law to suppress vice as it was to suppress treason. The questions that arise from the differences in these views are: Can the law be invoked to punish conduct that is regarded as immoral? Is the enforcement of morality itself moral? Is immorality criminal? Which morality is to be enforced, a utilitarian morality that punishes only activities which are harmful or a morality which reflects the rules and standards of behavior of society themselves inspired by the natural law?

Mill protested with considerable determination against the paternalism of the law. His was an age that affirmed by its works the efficacy of calculative reason. Today there are grounds for more modesty. No longer would there be much antipathy to restrictions being placed on the sale of drugs. At the same time, Mill, if he had known then as much psychology of deviance as is known today, might well have muted his antagonisms, at least to the extent of protecting the victim against himself. This modified pater-

---

[1] Quoted in H.L.A. Hart, *Law, Liberty and Morality* (London: OUP, 1967), p. 15.

nalism would have been preferable, to his way of thinking, to legal moralisms whose purpose was to make of law the enforcement of a moral principle.

Ireland, for many reasons of geography, history and political development, has, it is generally recognized, a morality that is more widely and deeply shared among its citizens than in other countries. That morality, such as it is, represents a meaningful system of values by which the Irish regulate their existence and seek to understand it. Hence whilst the reader of evil literature in the second quarter of the century in the privacy of his own home gave offense to none, yet his action still threatened one of the moral principles on which his society was based. His conduct could be construed as an offense against society as a whole, and that society was entitled to use the law to safeguard its moral existence. Unfortunately, Lord Devlin and the Irish bishops, who would have justified censorship on the grounds that a shared morality is essential to the cohesion of society, do not demonstrate as an empirical fact how exactly the private reading of evil literature jeopardizes society's well-being. The omission is perhaps explicable by their conception of morality as a seamless robe in which sexual morality is one of many strands that include murder, theft, treason and arson. This view that sees general hostility to society in reading evil literature no doubt explains the intensity of the invective that accompanied some of the campaigns in Ireland. What further intensified feelings was the tendency to identify Irish society with its morality, so that any change in the latter (which would inevitably be for the worse) would be interpreted as the destruction of the former. Sexual morality was to be the guarantor of the immutability of the community, the litmus test for the strength of its moral convictions. Hence the private act of reading evil literature is treason against the stability of the collective mind.

On what grounds should infractions of a code be punished? Fear of punishment is appropriate for restraining those who would harm others, but how does it induce one to abstain from an act which may deviate from accepted morality but does not harm the public? Is conformity to the letter of the law, where there is neither victim nor violence, worth pursuing? Was this another piece in the ritualism of Catholicism at the time? There are other questions that might be asked to discover the thinking behind the banning of books. Whatever avenues of investigation are followed, they would all, however, arrive at the imponderables. Was the Censorship of Publications Act, with its threat of legal punishment, introduced in order to sustain the voluntary practice of morality? Did the values that emerged justify the cost in human degradation which the banned authors claimed to have experienced? How far should the State endeavor by its laws to influence or determine the moral code?

In analyzing the society to which these questions relate, it is incumbent on the observer to recognize certain basic discriminations. The social morality of Ireland recognizes universals like individual freedom, safety of life, rights of property and others. In the past, the Church has argued their importance in the preservation of society. Today it might argue their necessity for the personality and identity of the individual in the anomie of the modern world. Second, the spirit and practice of an accepted social morality has been a cohesive force in a small country where an imposed legal system was at times alien to the national sentiments. What created the problem, as has been said, was that its conservation was pursued with a determination that excluded all possibility of change, as if moral attitudes in Ireland would be altered irremediably by any one gesture to adapt to new criteria. Then, unfortunately opposing points of view were locked by statutory legislation into fixed positions with the result that,

The use of legal punishment to freeze into immobility the morality dominant at a particular time in a society's existence may possibly succeed, but even where it does, it contributes nothing to the survival of the animating spirit and formal values of social morality and may do much harm to them.[1]

Moral conservatism which rejects any change thus becomes a religious value in itself and as such justifies legal enforcement. No natural law was adduced to support this proposition, at least in relation to censorship. Instead there was an authoritarian assertion that the preservation of morality was to be achieved along negative and repressive guidelines, criticism of which was to be regarded as subversive. Catholics accustomed to accepting dogmatic assertions did not challenge in sufficient numbers, and with a loud enough voice, the adequacy of an assertion that offered admonition in place of evidence. The inevitable result when law is invoked to sustain the moral status quo at any time in a nation's history is the arrest of the renewal process which gives social institutions their value. If Ireland however spent the first forty years of independence in moral inertia, this moral indifference cannot be laid at the door of Mill's doctrine of liberty. If he disapproved of social pressures such as moral blame and threats to the nonconformist, he was also at pains to point out that human beings must help each other to distinguish the better from the worse and encourage one's fellow man to choose the former and avoid the latter.

A long debate ensued between Lord Devlin and Professor H.L.A. Hart in which the former contended that 'society may use the law to preserve morality in the same way as it uses it to safeguard anything else that is essential to its existence,'[2] and the latter who maintained, in cases where laws are correctly interpreted to enforce morality, that man was not forced to choose between jettisoning them or assenting to the princi-

[1] H.L.A. Hart, *Law, Liberty and Morality*, p. 72.
[2] Patrick Devlin, *The Enforcement of Morals* (London: OUP, 1965), p. 52.

ple that the criminal law might be used for that purpose. There were other explanations for the existence in laws of rules governing morality which took infractions out of the domain of criminality and brought them within the concern of a paternalistic state. Basically what Devlin was presupposing was that the whole of European morality was based on Christian belief. For Hart, there was 'a morality of "universal values" whose acceptance is a necessary condition of viability of any society, and a morality of personal ideals which are essentially a matter of individual choice and are not susceptible of rational discussion.'[1]

Of course these two points of view did not exhaust all the possible accounts that might explain the existence of morality as a force in society. Christian thinkers, for their part, maintained that the whole of morality was contained in the natural law whose teaching was intelligible to the human reason. The Roman Catholic would add that revelation would be a practical necessity for the Christian who wished to make his discovery free of error. Obviously, in Ireland, moral questions could not be determined without reference to the majority church's views. How had thinking about the natural law progressed in Ireland?

With the exception of the work of men like John Scotus and Bishop Berkeley, philosophical thinking in Ireland has been limited in its impact. Whatever other explanation is valid, certainly an at times abrasive and alien presence did not contribute to that stability and continuity which encourage speculative thought to take root. The invader may have been responsible for the Irish interest in ideas rather than facts, but it was an interest that was not to be made amenable to systematization. The harsh reality of expropriation may be responsible for the deep disillusionment and disenchantment with reality that made, for example, the two old people in Synge's *The Well of the Saints* desire to return to the Kingdom of the Blind or Samuel Beckett's *Murphy* to opt for the lunatic asylum. 'One feels the lack of a synthesizing philosophy of life: one misses a realization of the anguish of the modern consciousness' in Irish letters where one might have looked for philosophical thought. One found instead 'a virginal neutrality in this world of warring ideas.'[2]

Roman Catholic neo-Thomism can hardly be said to have been an energizing force among Irish intellectuals in the first half of the twentieth century but it is among them that must be sought the response to the Johannine challenges to the content of traditional morality from which Ireland could not be preserved by its bishops. Watson asks what content has the term 'natural law.' Historically it was used to signify what we would un-

[1] Basil Mitchell, *Law, Morality, and Religion in a Secular Society* (London: OUP, 1970), p. 104.
[2] Arland Ussher, 'The Contemporary Thought of Ireland' *Dublin Magazine*, July-Sept 1947, p. 26.

derstand by morality. The early Greek church believed that the terms 'right' and 'wrong' could be used as meaningfully in the province of action as the terms 'false' and 'true' are used in the province of knowledge,[1] but not with the minuteness or normativeness which the term *law* suggests. Daly quotes from the encyclical of Pope John, *Pacem in Terris*, 'By the natural law every human being has the right to freedom in searching for truth ... and he has the right to be informed truthfully about public events. The natural law also gives man the right to share in the benefits of culture.'[2] Masterson explains that 'When St. Thomas speaks of natural law he is referring primarily, not to man's needs and tendencies, but rather to the truths of life which reason discovers through reflection upon these needs and tendencies.'[3] Being a rational creature, man is guided not by what he can do but rather by what he must do in order to do good and avoid evil. Man by reflecting on his own nature discovers what he must do for himself and to others. The complexity of existence will demand periodic reassessment, not of the moral truths his reason has proposed, but of the changing cultural circumstances in which they are intended to operate. Anyone who reflects rationally can discover natural law ethics. A Christian illumined by his faith will find however in the natural law greater reasonableness and coherence.

The latter end of the sixties was a period when the communications gap between the teaching and the learning Church began to cause obvious disquiet. There was no free flow of information, no central office for the clearing of reports, and certainly no open debate. The *Irish Independent*, the daily closest to Church thinking, drew the bishops' attention in an editorial to the fact that 'If they wish to influence public opinion they, too, must say what they think. Otherwise events may pass them out ... few people would wish the opinions of the Church authorities to be denied a full and respectful hearing. But how can one hear those who do not speak?'[4] The appeal to close ranks and wait for the message did not sit too easily on the minds of those who were being told 'by a tide of irresponsible journalists' that this learning Church was no longer composed of the laity alone, no more than the teaching Church was confined to the hierarchy. There were vague stirrings across the world that the exercise of authority would no longer be accepted as its own justification, that people cared less for its authenticity as the source of eternal truths, and more and more for the rightness of what it enjoined. Initiatives came in every size and shape, and from the most unexpected sources.

[1] Gerard Watson, 'The Early History of "Natural Law" ', *Irish Theological Quarterly* 33 (1966), pp. 65–74.
[2] Cahal B. Daly, 'Natural Law Morality Today' *Christus Rex* 19:3 (1965), p. 154.
[3] Patrick Masterson, 'Natural Law Today' *Doctrine and Life* 16:2 (1966), p. 61.
[4] Editorial, *Irish Independent*, September 21, 1967, p. 8.

Then in 1968 McGrath began to criticize the Emperor's clothes. *Humanae Vitae* was then a subject for debate, though practice since has made its findings more and more irrelevant. Was the natural law theory valid?[1] McGrath asked, pointing to the deficiencies of the philosophical defense of the encyclical position in particular and to the inadequacy of scholasticism as a basis for Catholic thought in general. Passing from these considerations, he then turns to what he deems to be a more serious objection to natural law theory, namely that of legalism which he defines as a system in which principles are more important than persons, and in which rules take precedence over the people to whom they apply. Absolute moral principles based on natural law must not jostle with Christian love for standing room. McGrath rejects human nature as the norm of morality because of the ambiguity of the term, its reduction to ethical voluntarism and its temporal limitations as the product of a different age. He does not suggest that natural law should be abandoned as a theory, provided that the term law be shorn of its verifiability/falsifiability associations and that the inappropriate notion of a code of conduct imposed from outside, complete with sanctions for violations, be dropped. Since 'what natural law theory says in essence, is that there are objectively true moral principles which follow from the sort of being man is'[2] morality should be derived from his personality and not from his nature. Actions are good if they are compatible with the dignity of the person in respect of whose rights man lays out for himself his moral code as a Christian.

McGrath had now placed man in all his individuality at the center of the universe. He had given him back possession of himself with all the insecurity, the uncertainty and the problematic that self-accountability entails. He would not be without rudimentary charts. Formulations like the Ten Commandments will point out the general directions, but they and other precepts are cardinal points when what a man may need is a street map. Morality is however much more than following directions. It 'is a way of becoming, a way of development. We do not see sin, then, simply as crossing a line. Sin is a failure that bit more in the situation in which we are.'[3] Crowe argued that natural law fails as a dynamic, existing reality for the realization of the rational self if it fails to accept the genuine insights of situationism and that 'the subject matter of moral judgments is a shifting

---

[1] Patrick McGrath, 'Natural Law Ethics – Has it a Future?' *The Furrow* 19:3 (1968) p. 202.
[2] Patrick McGrath, 'Natural Law Ethics – Has it a Future?', p. 208.
[3] Enda McDonagh, 'An Approach to Morality' *The Furrow* 19:6 (1968) p. 316.

terrain, incapable of sustaining the firm and universal certitudes one seeks in speculative affairs.'[1]

If a new personal moral consciousness were to develop in Ireland, then it would emerge as a result of facing up squarely to problems to which answers from the majority Church were felt to be either uninformed or unformulated. In respect of censorship, as will be seen, little now appeared in relation to literature or periodicals by way of guidance. This did not mean that the subject as an exercise in personal decision-making disappeared completely from Irish awareness. From the inception of the state, traffic in newspapers and journals had been with exceptions unimpeded, British radio and television were available to at least one-third of the population, and movement across the Irish Sea remained the most frequent route for those seeking an alternative to life at home, whatever the length of the sojourn. The fact that the British had a different religious history, had incubated and fostered the liberal ethic, enjoyed a continuity and width of experience of which Ireland itself was a part, were not serious handicaps to the Irish wish to evolve its own frame of moral meaning. Society in Britain was like a laboratory in which experiments were being conducted in a simultaneity, profusion and variety that would be impossible in an island of three million inhabitants. Its location, however, did not preclude the intelligent observation of what was happening, nor did it preempt alternative assessments of the experiences to those drawn by the participants.

The Irish therefore might not have known about the court case that resulted in a guilty verdict being brought in against the publisher of the *Ladies' Street Directory*; they certainly knew of the exculpation of *Lady Chatterley's Lover*, *Fanny Hill* and *Last Exit to Brooklyn*. They may not have read the American Commission's *Statement on Violence in Television Entertainment* but they would have been fully apprised that a multiple sex murderer had in his possession when arrested works of pornography. When the English *Times* reported that the Church of England's Board of Social Responsibility wanted to curb the sale of obscene books it described the Church's proposal as 'a kind of arrogance to expect that the law should, in so private a matter, be framed by the restraints which a Christian puts on himself in his choice of reading.' The appositeness of the observation would have been equally patent to the Irish reader.

Explanations of the introduction of the Censorship of Publications Act, 1929, have attributed its immediate cause to English Sunday newspapers, its remote cause to a combination of fears that attacks on the government, on symbols of authority and on the Church's version of sexual mores,

---

[1] M.B. Crowe, 'Natural Law Theory Today: Some Materials for the Reassessment' *Irish Ecclesiastical Record* 109 (1968), p. 378.

would bring about social chaos and disorder. Of these, sexuality, its power and pleasures, represented the greatest disruptive force since on the basis of the relevant attitudes that were formed depended in any competitive economy (so it was believed) attitudes to work, to thrift, to order and to good living. When Irishmen read in the *New Statesman*[1] that the England of the Beatles was reliving its experience of the twenties – the decade from which they were absent – inevitably interest arose as to the nature of the experience, *mutatis mutandis*. The British of course had passed two Obscene Publications Acts in 1959 and in 1964. In them obscenity was defined as that which 'tends to deprave and corrupt persons who are likely, having regard to all relevant circumstances, to read, see or hear the matter contained or embodied in it.' The defense available was to prove 'that publication of the article in question is justified as being for the public good' and hence *Last Exit to Brooklyn*, 'admittedly and intentionally disgusting' has successfully pleaded its right to existence on the grounds that the very degradation it portrayed was a summons to society to eradicate its causes. The British who favored some form of censorship were obviously unhappy with its present version and therefore found it worthwhile to try to devise a formulation that would correspond to their needs. At stake is our own hard-won privacy – the kernel of individuality. Every man is unique. The Smithism of Smith is precisely the part of him which he could not borrow, which he cannot bestow, which he must keep undefiled. Its guardian angel is the right to secrecy, the right to an utterly private life. Çivilisation is the pretence that such privacy exists.[2]

The Do-It-Yourself Irish moralist would no doubt have been in full agreement.

Interest in pornography as an aspect of social deviancy was very much alive in England in 1972. Fryer wrote that censorship was dead and pornography doomed, and attributed the change to a morally pluralist society which refused to have imposed on it one set of morals to the exclusion of all others. Since Fielding, writers in English literature had been 'unable to acknowledge the realities of the sexual impulse, unable to print the demotic words for sex organs and sexual activity, unable to portray sexual activity as a part of life.'[3] This attitude had of course been responsible for a specialized hard-core pornography which in effect was the reverse side of censorship, two faces of the same coin. Closer to the Irish experience was Figes' quotation of George Mangakis, describing from a Greek cell, how his gaolers first confiscated his writings and then returned them.

[1] Richard Hoggart, 'Controls and Shocks', *New Statesman*, 13 June 1969, p. 837.
[2] C.H. Rolph, 'The Literary Censorship in Britain', *British Book News*, July 1969, p. 498.
[3] Peter Fryer, 'The death of censorship', *Times Literary Supplement*, February 18, 1972, p. 195.

'They want to make you see your thoughts through their eyes and control them yourself from their point of view.'[1]

Inevitably there had to be a reaction. Lord Longford was an Irish peer, co-author of a biography of de Valera, champion of prison reform and a Minister of State in a previous Labour Government. Mary Whitehouse, housewife and mother, was general secretary of the National Viewers and Listeners Association. David Holbrook, an Oxford don, author and poet, was a veteran campaigner against pornography principally on the quite plausible grounds that vested interests were undermining public attitudes to their commercial advantages. Labour, Conservative and Liberal, these three would represent the spectrum of political opinion found in Ireland, each urging his case independently of any religious affiliation. Longford's influence was made felt through a report by an unofficial (i.e., not established by the British Government) committee on pornography in which there were factual details of the quantity and quality of pornography, recommendations for amending the Obscene Publications Acts, and arguments on analogical grounds for not abandoning the presumption of a causal relationship between pornography and crime, sexual deviancy and other social and personal disorders. The editorial in *The Times* was relevant to the Irish situation with its history of demands on the government to intervene by campaigners against evil literature.

They are simply asking too much of the law, which can neither create nor prevent the disintegration of an enlightened conscience. And in the absence of an enlightened public conscience it is no good asking the law to check the manifold and profitable expressions of licentiousness. That way the law is made to be either absurd or tyrannical.[2]

What would always be needed was the protection of minors and the prohibition of the display of indecent or suggestive materials, but the adult must be left with the right to take his own moral decisions.

Mary Whitehouse is a product of that same reaction to the extremes of the permissive sixties that ushered Margaret Thatcher onto the political stage. She spoke for the Christian faith and against gratuitous sex and violence. She campaigned against a world where 'Morality was stood on its head: rationality and compassion were discarded; truth was converted into perfidy and love into a mockery.'[3] She fought against misrepresentation of her standards which were not censorial in the traditional sense of that word: she stood for the decency of the ordinary man with a job, anxious to ensure a stability in his private and public relationships that would allow him to enjoy his pleasure without embarassment. What she suc-

[1] Quoted by Eva Figes, 'Enemies of the People' *New Humanist* 88 (1972), p. 210.
[2] Editorial, *The Times*, September, 2, 1972, p. 15.
[3] Mary Whitehouse, 'Inverted Censorship that turned morality on its head', *The Times*, February 4, 1974, p. 12.

ceeded in doing was creating a presence that sought and obtained participation, access and dialogue in the formulation of the norms of public entertainment, to which she was not a whit abashed to contribute her particular brand of grundyism.

Holbrook is, like Whitehouse, dedicated to the eradication of what appears to both as license masquerading as exploration of the human personality. His objection to pornography was based on his conviction that it induced distress, feelings of aggression and fear, destroyed the disinterestedness of interpersonal sexual relationships and led to a sense of emotional inadequacy which found relief only in manifestations of hate. Holbrook's solution would have been familiar. A new social psychology, the reinvigoration of institutions so that works which offend public taste can be discussed, the alerting of public opinion as Lord Longford had done, but

we also need to make our Law and our courts capable of effectively deciding where the line shall be drawn, and how the impulse to harm others through culture shall be restrained.[1]

without of course impeding the artist as he follows his muse down the labyrinthine ways where human behavior in all of its variety of forms is wont to tread. These names continue to impinge on the consciousness of the Irish, particularly that of Mrs. Whitehouse. Their traditional duality of approach permitted on the one hand an opportunity to express an intellectual (if not a sniggering) contempt for someone who resented what she considered exploitation of the young by the media, and, on the other, to privately confess to an unavowed sense of relief that someone was doing something about pornography in a language that all could understand and none was given the opportunity to ignore.

Two television personalities who happen also to be outstanding academics dedicated to the interpretation of the role of the media will serve to open and close this decade's selection of those of whom the media-conscious Irish would have been aware in their search for non-national views on the morality of censorship. The first is Jonathan Miller and the occasion in 1971 was the sixth annual lecture for the Thank-Offering to Britain Fund under the aegis of the prestigious British Academy. He begins by pointing out that inconsistencies and self-contradictions are not the exclusive prerogative of the pro-censorship lobby. Moral judgments are always problematical and moral discourse rarely 'expands steadily towards a fixed circumference of axiomatic certainty.'[2] While principles play their part in all moral decisions, one will be deemed subsidiary to another and the result to the hostile eye will be interpreted as

[1] David Holbrook, '...so that evil things may be done with a clear conscience', *Books*, Summer 1972, No. 8, p. 12.

[2] Jonathan Miller, *Censorship and the Limits of Permission* (London: OUP 1971), p. 4.

expedient equivocation. Principles do not emerge like branches from a tree trunk, but rather bear on one another like the stress-bearing parts of a cantilever bridge 'carrying the weight of conflicting interests across the span of relevant concern.'[3]

Censorship, according to Miller, is defended by its exponents on three grounds: the moral principle, the prudential principle which claimed that pornography was socially harmful, and finally the argument that literature even if neither immoral nor harmful may still be offensive. Lord Chief Justice Stephen's solution had been to the effect that the function of the law was to prosecute vice and promote virtue. Vice would be determined by public revulsion, resulting in a kind of an emotional populism urging the law to take action. Unfortunately, the punishment that follows on the administration of law, far from enforcing morality, may create a new dimension of immorality. Murder, for example, is heinous in itself, certainly, but it is that much more so because murderers are hanged. Devlin, as has been seen, took up Stephens' argument and would condemn any practice that violated the morality by which a society is held together that would otherwise disintegrate. Hart, it will be recalled, had challenged the notion of a shared morality as a seamless garment. Miller now disputed the essentiality of regulative morality as a social control. What raises society above a pre-civilization Hobbesian level is its constitutive rules which provide it with an identity just as much as the restrictions which are intended to preserve it. At all events condemnation of literature on the grounds that it offends current moral susceptibilities presupposes these to be optimal, a verdict that is rarely returned by a wide-eyed posterity.

What would have been particularly salient to the Irish mind were the psychological insights into morality that Miller provided. In the first place innocence, moral pupilship and spiritual dependency are attributes of the situation if the role of the teacher is to be justified. Defining a child as a schoolchild allows the teacher to make a lot of dispositions that effectively control what it does and thinks. Second (and this would refer particularly to critical turning points in a nation's history, such as the immediate post-independence era in Ireland or the political confusion of Weimar), excessive emphasis is placed on the maintenance of certain symbolic social actions free of moral pollution. Authority, be it of the State, the Church or the institution is conceived to be in or out of jeopardy depending on the public response to particularistic definitions of moral norms in everyday life. What troubled the bishops, for example, after the British presence had been removed as a guarantee against anarchy, was that Irish civil disturbance would continue even though the Civil War had come to an end

[1] ibid. p. 6.

and that the whole moral fabric of the nation would be rent in consequence. They decided that the only corrective action available to them was
to create a moral standard, to advocate a morality of literature, since to
attack the living standard or the morality of violence would embroil them
even further than they cared to go at that time in domestic politics. As a
social pollutant, English Sunday newspapers were much less grievous in
their moral consequences than assassinations, police harassment, gom-
beenism and job discrimination, but they did represent a suitable target
for a religious crusade. Their source was suspect, their customers were
drawn from all political groupings and they provided a focus for the drive
on the alleged moral corruption that would have a spin-off effect hopefully on the other activities of society. The Church was asserting its magis-
terium in this new independent Ireland which had acquired powers of
self-government that had not been anticipated by the bishops or even the
parliamentarians. They were to redefine matters of faith and morals so
that they became co-extensive with the parameters of the encyclicals.
Public morality and natural law were blank cheques on the face of which
the amount drawable on the Irish people might be entered in the specie
which the circumstances demanded.

Miller, Whitehouse, Longford, Holbrook and others provided evidence throughout the seventies of endeavors to come to grips with the
problems of handling literature and media products in the interest of society. In 1979 the Report of the Committee on Obscenity and Film Censorship, under the chairmanship of Bernard Williams, was published. It recommended that 'The printed word should be neither restricted nor prohibited since its nature makes it neither immediately offensive nor capable of involving the harms we identify, and because of its importance in
conveying ideas.'[1] The Committee had accepted Mill's dictum that no
conduct should be forbidden by law unless it could be shown to harm
someone. Did breaches of prevailing morality constitute harm? The extreme liberal view denied the relevance of morality that did not offend the
harm condition. A contrary opinion would however reject the narrow-
ness of this approach on the grounds that what is of serious moral concern
cannot be appropriately assessed exclusively on such a limited basis. Society operates on a moral consensus, and where that consensus is
threatened, the meaningfulness of the understandings people have of,
and use with, one another becomes endangered. What of an act that is not
harmful to others but is morally disapproved of by a majority of the citizens? Lord Devlin had argued that such an act which is not discouraged by
the law ends up a harmful act. In a society, however, with a different

[1] *Report of the Committee on Obscenity and Film Censorship*. London, November 1979, p.
40, Cmnd. 7772.

moral register (or in the same society where disapproval shifts over time), it is possible that no harm might follow, as witnessed, for example, by the different social attitudes toward the act of procreation. In this view moral opinion does not override the harm condition. Lord Mansfield's 1774 dictum, 'Whatever is *contra bonos mores et decorum* the principles of our laws prohibit, and the King's Court as the general censor and guardian of the public morals is bound to restrain and punish' would appear therefore coercive, sacrificing, as it would, the freedom of personal choice on the altar of moral homogeneity.

In their deliberations the Committee were obviously influenced by Mill and his arguments in favor of the fundamentality of the freedom of expression. While accepting the ongoing relevance of his reasons, they were however less than persuaded of the totality of his case. They accepted that truth would emerge by a process of natural selection in the free market of ideas as the good won acceptance and evil was rejected, but expressed reservations that every medium of communication could be legitimately regarded as a means to ensure the survival of truth. They instanced the rejection of pornography by the United States Supreme Court on the grounds that it lacked communicative content. They were not persuaded of the reality of Locke's 'Truth certainly would do well enough if she were left to fend for herself.' They pointed out that Gresham's Law has also its application in modern culture, particularly when the sponsors behind the modern media command very unequal resources. 'If everyone talks at once, truth will not prevail and falsehood indeed may prevail, if powerful agencies can gain an undue hold on the market.'[1] However, despite its limitations, the marketplace model remained for the Committee the most suitable solution. No one could predict in which direction society would develop, but for any rational understanding of the process, freedom of expression was not only a contributory instrument but also an integral element.

To those who were persuaded that moral truths were unchanging and unchangeable, the Committee replied that their essence was not being called into question, only their application and interpretation in light of what discoveries in historiography, anthropology, and indeed theology have revealed. In addition, and the point would have particular significance in Irish awareness, mankind shares a living space in which proliferate sets of moral certainties, all sincerely held. People do not simply mirror beliefs, they live by them, and the evolving religious consciousness to be truly the œuvre of the human personality demands freedom to express itself. While public morality should not be offended, neither should the present be a determinant of the moral perceptions of tomorrow. What is

---

[1] *Report of the Committee on Obscenity*, p. 55.

the alternative to free expression? Censorship is patently and inherently defective. Its operation involves the violation of rights which brings in its train its own harms. And yet if drugs are restricted, why not books? Disregarding the lack of agreement surrounding the 'effects' of the experience, the Committee argued that the question of what constituted moral harm must always at the very least leave room for a personal decision. The Irish Censorship Board in deciding what was the intent behind the author's writing had entered a judgment on its potential harm that had preempted just this possibility. Its morality had recognized only its own subsets. The actualization of its authority had robbed the individual of his moral identity.

This posited fundamentality of individual responsibility in the area of morality by the Williams Committee matches the assertion of its functionality and pivotalness in the domain of censorship that had been expressed by contemporary developments in theological thinking in Ireland. Obviously there were teleological differences. Obviously there was a greater sense of immediacy, both political and personal, in the consequences for the Irish way of life that were to emerge as the new thinking was assimilated and applied. Irish customs and conventions became less rule-bound as Church practice itself came to emphasize meaning rather than form. Without prescriptive formulae to order their existence, it behoved all to think out their own redemption. In the course of his deliberations Williams had offered to the Irish mind, as had Miller, Longford and others, the materials and method for its thinking on censorship. The concept of public morality and the notion of natural law would come from elsewhere. What made their activation necessary were questions like contraception, abortion and divorce which became legal and political issues at this time. Like censorship they were part of that patchwork quilt of an unsecured pluralism which the Irish were eyeing speculatively as circumstances proceeded to strip them of the counterpane of comfortable and unthinking orthodoxy. Mill had been in no doubt in the English context that some first principle was necessary to justify human behavior on a rational basis, if only to enable man to choose between conflicting moral precepts. 'There must be some standard by which to determine the goodness or badness, absolute or comparative, of ends or objects of desire. And whatever that standard is there can be but one...'[1] History had demonstrated that human existence must come to an agreement as to what is the minimum content of some fundamental law that would enhance the prospectives of collective survival. Finnis describes this natural law as being composed of 'a set of basic practical principles which indicate the basic forms of human flourishing as goods to be pursued and realized, and

[1] J.S. Mill, *A System of Logic: Ratiocinative and Inductive* (London: RKP, 1961), vii, xii, 7.

which are in one way or another used by everyone who considers what to do, however unsound his conclusions.'[1] In addition there were certain procedures in reasoned thinking to be followed so as to make possible the generation of certain moral standards. Some of these standards have a particular importancé in that they lay down what is not permissible in interpersonal relations, for example, violence to one's neighbor, or violation of a sexual taboo. Second, they cannot be abrogated deliberately. Third, they only measure voluntary acts, and lastly they must appeal in themselves as being good for the community. This social morality is the product of a social experience over time. Hart was to distinguish between what the nineteenth century Utilitarians had described as positive morality, 'the morality actually accepted and shared by a given social group'[2] from what he called critical morality which sought to

exhibit and lay bare the value assumptions implicit in positive morality, to reassess these and render them coherent and thus to develop critical principles by reference to which we can appraise and reorient our ordinary day-to-day judgments and standards of judgment.[3]

So much for English society, its attitude to censorship and the thinking on which it relied. At the end of 1976 it was generally accepted that after the exoneration of the publisher of *Inside Linda Lovelace* there would never be another prosecution for an obscene publication. Three years later the Williams report substituted the objective test of what people found to be offensive for the subjective test of what had appeared to be obscene or thought likely to corrupt. How did Ireland compare in 1983 with Britain which would be generally recognized as containing a permissive society? Had the momentum of the sixties been sustained? Had there emerged a different understanding of private and public morality, of the coexistence of Church and State, and of the relationship between law and morality about which Devlin and Hart had disputed? If there were new definitions, did censorship reflect the interaction of a traditional positive morality and the new critical morality that was presaged by the thinking of the sixties? Do the measures of tolerance for cultural artifacts approximate despite differences in their moral point of departure? A review of the evidence will provide grounds for postulating certain tentative conclusions.

The willingness to examine morality as a functioning of the human psyche independent of religious considerations did indeed gather momentum in the seventies. How man was to live was an insoluble enigma unless the problem comprehended the integrated questions of who was man and what was living. Morality was to come more and more

[1] J.M. Finnis, *Natural Law and Natural Rights* (New York: OUP, 1980), p. 23.
[2] H.L.A. Hart, *Law, Liberty and Morality*, p. 20.
[3] Neil McCormack, *H.L.A. Hart* (London: Arnold, 1981), p. 50.

to be understood as being centered in the individual and not as an imposed programme for living drawn up by an institutionalized Church. Morality was autonomous, a human response to choices that satisfied an innate need for personal consistency, corresponded with an appropriation of values derived from the community experience, and was continually being readjusted as understanding of the situation and the players deepened. The difference between man and the rest of creation was the obligation imposed on him to regulate for himself that which differentiated him, call it mind, soul, or whatever from other living things. The backdrop to the action was the Judaeo-Christian tradition; the props were the environment; the weight of possessions, the onus of responsibilities, and the characters on the stage were those for and with whom man elaborated his self-directions, his dialogue, his 'business.' The end of the play was always to be rewritten according to the actors' reinterpretation of the message. There were no ready-made answers, nowhere to go for solutions except to oneself. Morality was not a demonstrable Euclidean theorem. 'It is filtered through a sensitivity to the demands of the human spirit and through an appeal to the experience of men and to the demands, even, of a particular culture. But this is difficult. It calls for imagination and vision.'[1]

It is perhaps appropriate to recall how far thinking had progressed by 1972 on the question of the nature of the relationships between Church and State. It was no longer a matter to be decided by what the Constitution contained, repealed or omitted, but addressed the larger and more free-ranging problem of the relationship between religious belief and civic life. Confessional beliefs after Vatican II recognized the need for individual freedoms. Civic existence was not to be predicated on any Christian absolutes. The right to believe carried as a supplement the right to disbelieve. 'Christians who look either to the State or to political pressure groups for security of tenure on a way of life which is in serious need of reform are simply compromising the gospel they profess to serve.'[2] The notion of pre-Vatican II that the State should underwrite the Church's conception of the moral law has been replaced by the community's aspiration to live according to the Gospel, whatever the political setting it found itself in. If there were concurrence of civil and moral law, they were not thereby identical. The Church should reject the State's identification of itself as an agent of the Gospel. On the contrary, the greater the approach to the secular state, the greater the approach to the Christian religion, since that religion can only flourish where the freedom of the receiver is matched by the freedom of the message-bringer. In Ireland, the limita-

[1] Vincent McNamara, 'Justifying Moral Positions' *The Furrow* 29:9 (Sept. 1978), p. 566.
[2] Gabriel Daly, 'Church and State', *Doctrine and Life* 23:5 (1973) p. 244.

tions of received answers have been made progressively more obvious as new questions revealed terrain to be explored.

If Church and State were to separate, this independence would give the Christian the freedom to act out his religious life without the obligation to seek to impose his political will. He could act in accordance with the secular standards implied in his public life, while he behaved in conformity with his religious convictions in his private. Nor would there be a need for those with whom he dealt to fear that these secular standards were a threat to Christian morality. The Christian had no exclusive insight into what it meant to be human in the highest sense. There would inevitably be overlap, and when the consensus did not reflect the Christian bias, the Christian supplied the deficiencies from his own spiritual convictions. He could disapprove of divorce, therefore, for personal reasons, but he had no right to have his conclusions made into a law prohibiting it for others.

The Church should declare that it was no longer prepared to act as the conscience of the State, since consciences were often placed in the difficult position of having to decide what was the higher good or worse evil. It could therefore safely distance God when it so wished from political expediency. It should not shackle Him to the smaller pragmatisms. It was to be left free to sound the tocsin and to advertise what it found contradicted its message. The Church in Ireland should accept Aristotle's suggestion that the virtues of the good citizen are not the same as those of the good man. Maybe its message would not be received in the same reverential silence, but there would be no confusion and suspicion as to the intention and motive behind its sending. When contrasted with what had been the nature of thinking on morality, opinion over the decade continued to reflect the development and enlargement of the Catholic personality.

As Ireland industrialized, the individual began to lead a more private existence. 'The primary public institutions no longer significantly contribute to the formation of individual consciousness and personality, despite the massive control'[1] they had available to them. Cast back on his own resources he built his own scheme of significant values by which to measure his response to society. Of course he accepted many taken-for-granted explanations, depending on the level of his interest and education. The intrusion of the modern state also acted as a restraint on his freedom to create a world to his fancy. However, everywhere, at least in the Western democracies, he heard cried aloud the primacy of the individual and the ideal of pluralism as an interpersonal lubricant to ensure that society functions in a spirit of tolerance. Paradoxically, institutionalized religion,

[1] T. Luckmann, 'The Invisible Religion' in *The Problem of Religion in Modern Society*, (New York: Macmillan), p. 97.

which had been compared with Marxism because they were both alleged to desire the reformulation of the environment in order to bring about the millennium, was now attacked by the latter for its demand that man elaborate his own meanings, drawing as he might on the revealed truths to which he could subscribe. The Christian, in a sense, had been cast loose, and his Church was at long last recognizing the rights of conscience of those who differ from it in its explanation to him of what his role might be. Religion had become a matter of self-identification. Faith was a free act.

In this new religious climate, socialization took on a very different aspect. Indoctrination was out: thinking at some risk was in. Conformity was meaningless: personal affirmation alone was satisfying. Each was to reconstruct his world view. While all had drawing rights on the past, none was doomed to be its apologist. Whatever new institutions were to emerge, they must stand on their own worth, and not claim some outcropping of Christianity as a legitimating basis. No longer were human arrangements to repel assault by identifying attacks on them as attacks on established religion. No exclusivity, no absolutes, no my-God-right-or-wrong as opposed to your God. Pluralism was to mean respect, and the means whereby that respect would be seen and recognized would never emerge if there was an obligation to make that respect subservient to ideas that were now felt to be inert. New cultural forms must be sought that reflected the emancipation of the spirit from the onus of heritage and tradition if their weight prevented man from raising his head to look beyond what his eyes could see. 'Irish culture is being recreated, not according to any set of prefabricated rules but in the general directions established by influential figures and groups – but allowing far greater personal latitude than would be found in any culture in the past.'[1]

British culture on the other hand is heterogeneous, its population around 55 million, its ethnic composition drawing on all the nations of the Commonwealth, its religious history that of an Established Church anxious to ensure the maintenance of its privileges as well as profess its particular view of Christianity. In the circumstances no clear, widely accepted definition of public morality was perhaps to be expected. In the Republic of Ireland with its three million inhabitants, 92% of whom belonged to one denomination, some authoritative statement should have been expressed in the normal course of events given the spiritual questions Catholics were more and more beginning to ask. According to the Survey of Religious Practices[2] already mentioned, while 85% agreed that missing Mass on Sundays was always wrong, questions on premarital relations, contraceptives, self-interest, desertion and divorce were very far

[1] Donal Dorr, 'Change and the Irish identity', *Doctrine and Life* 24:1 (1974), p. 15.
[2] Research and Development Unit, *Moral Values of Catholics in the Irish Republic* quoted in *The Furrow*, 38–42.

from sharing that measure of unanimity. Public morality, it will be remembered, serves in the Irish Constitution as an overriding condition to
the enjoyment of personal rights, and as such its interpretation would be
crucial. Ryan traced the history of the Church as its role was interpreted
by its bishops since World War II. Some views were obviously the product
of pre-Vatican II thinking. One bishop declared in 1955 that the bishops
'were the final arbiters of right and wrong in political matters.'[1] On the
matter of possible contraception legislation, some twenty years later, that
opinion did not appear to have changed. Legislators were to be denied authority by some members of the episcopal bench to act according to their
own best judgements. The moral rights of the majority in this view were
entitled to be respected even to the detriment of the minority. On a proposal to introduce divorce the archbishop of Dublin, in 1976, suggested in
effect that 'even if the State is not bound to enshrine the Catholic moral
law in legislation, Catholics may be still bound to reject civil laws which
seem contrary to their moral code.'[2] These opinions underline what might
have been expected in a Church whose leaders maintain a high profile in
the society to which they minister. What represents, of course, the official view of the Irish hierarchy which has been pursued consistently ever
since and reiterated in 1976, 1978 and 1983 was expressed in a statement
in 1973, 'There are many things which the Catholic Church holds to be
morally wrong and no one has ever suggested, least of all the Church herself, that they should be prohibited by the State.' In Irish society there are
other evils than contraception or divorce. Violence, injustice, poverty
and corruption all demand to be assessed at the bar of public morality.
The judgment that will be entered, according to Ryan, will be 'the critical
collective consciousness of the people of God'[3] making known the response a Christian conscience deems appropriate.

There is enough critical written analysis around this period to make this
statement assume a reality it might not have possessed in more authoritarian times. Many believed that human understanding was quite capable of
distinguishing between the questions, 'How am *I* to live and act?' and
'How are *we* to organize our lives together?' The individual was competent in the areas of public and private *morality* to the extent that he
realized that the answer to the question of what constituted the common
good must inevitably involve all the participants and must therefore take
into account needs and situations. MacNamara in writing on this problem
began by quoting paragraph 13 of the Vatican Council *Declaration on Religious Liberty* to the effect that 'a person may not be constrained to do

[1] Liam Ryan, 'Church and Politics, The Last Twenty-Six Years,' *The Furrow* 30:1 (1979), p. 10.
[2] ibid., p. 13.
[3] ibid., p. 14.

what his conscience forbids, or, on the other hand, be prevented from doing what conscience demands."[1] The question that arose from consideration of proposals to legislate for contraception, divorce and other social changes was to determine to what extent could this freedom of conscience be reconciled with what public morality requires. Who was to decide what constituted public morality? McNamara replied that the body politic, reflecting as it does the collective wisdom of society; prepared 'to look beyond the immediate wishes of the public and base (its) policy on principles and values which the public do indeed share;'[2] and ready to listen to informed opinion, it alone was capable of deciding what the requirements of public morality were. At all events no consideration of public morality could ever justify legislation enacted at the behest of the Catholic Church. Which structures and practices, what attitudes and social beliefs are to be endorsed or rejected 'by the State in its laws or other activities remains a continuing problem for the members of that society and their political representatives.'[3]

Garrett Fitzgerald addressed his mind to the problem confronting the state of how 'to determine the extent to which the laws of a State should endeavor to influence or determine its moral climate,' and of how to distinguish 'that which is in all circumstances ... unlawful from that which is morally repugnant.'[4] The state of course could not and did not reflect the morality of any church, but if politicians were to have some criteria, they needed to hear something more from competent religious authorities than the rehearsal of the 'domino theory' which seemed to put censorship and abortion on the same consequential level of moral criminality. What he was saying was of course being echoed from within the Church. McDonagh had criticized the Church for 'conveying the impression that authoritative statements are a substitute for reasonable discussion.'[5] Kirby criticized Catholicism for its 'lack of any intellectual element' and held the bishops responsible that 'the self-image of the Irish Church (is) defined by its actual role in Irish society rather than by any critical theological reflection on what that role should be, that its only response to criticism is to seek to perpetuate what was.'[6] O'Sullivan complained that the Irish 'model of Christianity was the product of a theology which viewed the environment in which people lived as extrinsic to being human

---

[1] Published in *Studies*, Spring/Summer, 1978, p. 24.
[2] Kevin McNamara, 'Church and State', *Doctrine and Life* 29 (1979) , p. 142.
[3] Enda McDonagh, 'The Believing Community and the Political Community', *The Maynooth Review* (Dec. 1978), p. 67.
[4] Garrett Fitzgerald, 'The Politician as a Christian', *The Furrow* 29:1 (1978), p. 13.
[5] Enda McDonagh, 'Church, State and Morality', *The Furrow* 27:6 (1976), p. 326.
[6] Peadar M. Kirby, 'The Irish Church: Shifting Sands', *Doctrine and Life* 28:10 (1977), p. 31.

and so outside the sphere of personal salvation."[1] O'Mahony warned that the State, while professing pluralism, could be in effect confessional so that 'the distinct danger exists of exercising moral and religious imperialism, on the paternalistic principle that "we know best, we have it on divine authority".'[2]

This review of Irish thought on the definition of public morality and the function of the state in relation to its observance has been drawn almost exclusively from practicing philosophers and theologians most of whom are academics in the pontifical university of Maynooth or at one of the major seminaries. Taking their departure from a moral principle based on Christian love they arrived at the beginning of the eighties at a point reached by Hart and others who had drawn on Mill's utilitarian ethics. Both schools would now concur in doubting whether it was the function of the State to proscribe vice since the pursuit of the good life involved values of privacy, freedom, independence and the protection of the conscientious rights of others. On both sides of the Irish sea there are those who understood that to compel man to be moral was in itself an immorality if the conduct to be imposed violated his right to the free exercise of his will. Whatever the springs that promoted the revision of the traditional relationship of natural law and morality that had sufficed for the garrison church, they would not suffice for the pilgrim church in Ireland. It would need an informed mind among its faithful if it were to counter the open societies obtaining in Britain and America whence would come challenges to religion, ethical relativism and new definitions of sexuality. What these writers sought to achieve was to interiorize Christian belief, and this, they realized, would be possible only if instead of authority and sanctions, there were commitment and understanding. In placing man at the center of the moral dilemma they were reaffirming his right not to be forced to do what his belief forbade as a solution to his problem, and at the same time that he should not be prevented from doing what his belief permitted. They were saying what Jefferson had said, that God's intention for each man that he should think for himself should be respected. They were saying also what Pope John had said when he asserted that man's right to religious freedom resided not in his subjective disposition but in his very being. From now on he who would curtail man's freedom must incur the dangerous and difficult onus of proof that awaits any afflicted with the hubris of presumptive omniscience. In the meantime, The Church had taken up a position near-identical with the best of secular thinking on human rights and especially on the right of human freedom. So it is, after all

[1] Michael O'Sullivan, 'Freedom for Irish Christianity', *The Furrow* 33:3 (1982), p. 153.
[2] Brendan O'Mahony, 'Medical Ethics in the Pluralist State – a Catholic View', Report in *The Irish Times*, 4 May 1982.

the tribulations of the revolutionary age, civil jurisprudence and Church teaching today share the same ground.[1]

No one imagined for one instant that the tyranny of the majority was over. The state since its inception had no alternative morality or theology by which it might test its comprehension of that which it professed. It had been so preoccupied with existing that it did not think to question the existence it was so busily defending. There had been up until now no informed, intellectual appraisal of Catholic action within the Church. Now that this freedom was recognized as the only means to achieve renewal, the minimalism of the ecclesiastical establishment would grow progressively less tenable. It now appeared that there had come about distinct changes in the climate of public opinion with regard to the semi-confessional state and to its laws on censorship, contraception and the civil status of religion. The state had responded to the particularism of contraception. Could the Church in its turn avoid the wider issue of personal freedom that, as in liberal England, was regarded as basic to the act of conscious commitment? Given the circumstances there did not appear to be much choice. In the absence of such commitment, and on the basis of a continuing reliance on the socially imposed observance of a ritualized and moralized religion, the decline in its practice would continue, particularly among young parents where the consequences would be reiterative. What these writers were saying was that a society that had turned in on itself for almost fifty years, that had never been taught an intellectual self-reliance or the intellectuality of being a Christian, that had been fed too long on idealisms which bred narrow isolationism and claustrophobic introversion, was now intent on exploiting its new freedom by examining the non-Irish and non-Catholic world to see how others were coping with the problems and pleasures of self-discovery. Censorship was a symbol of the incarceration of the spirit they were no longer prepared to tolerate. Censorship as a social detergent, as a sanitizer in channels so overloaded with messages that filtering systems have become indispensable, and as a bulwark against importunate intrusion, yes, such a form of censorship was tolerable. But where the human spirit roamed in search of that which answered to its creative need to express its vision, no one would henceforward be barred access.

Ireland in its ambivalent relationship with Britain had rejected the latter's moral definition of man at the same time as it accepted for its political institutions the emergence of a countervailing force in the protest against a permissiveness and explicitness that matched what Steiner called an 'assault upon privacy'[2] with a deterioration in quality. The possible danger in

[1] Louis McRedmond, 'Not to be coerced', *Studies* 67 (1978), p. 38.
[2] See John Sutherland, *Offensive Literature, Recensorship in Britain, 1960–82* (London: Function Books, 1982).

Ireland was that 'Years of pawky censorship seem to have left people with the confused and contrary notions, first of all that Big Brother knows best, and then that when one flies in the face of what Big Brother is acknowledged to want, that is presumably being at long last liberated.'[1] Alternatively, there was the emancipation that followed on recognition of the independence of the human spirit in its choice of action. This freedom to which the theologian had pointed would remove the need to tilt at the Establishment's windmills. Standards would evolve as the public came to realize they mattered.

The proposition sustained above has argued that post-Vatican II theology has redefined man as the epicentre of a morality which emphasized free expression and individual rights. It also sought to accommodate the Thomist philosophy wherein the good of the citizen was subsumed in the common good of the community. As has been shown, there had been protests at the practice of blanket references to this overall good in defense of laws which undermined human rights, and a determined affirmation that the justice which the Irish Constitution invokes, only holds good whenever individual freedom is fully respected. What might be claimed now was by restoring man as critical to the functioning of society, any wrong done to him was being done to the community. In effect, natural law was to have an inbuilt governor in the actuality of the liberal critique.

If a harmonization of the relationship between the individual and the State is possible, under the conditions outlined, should the law of the land in Ireland which according to the Preamble to the Constitution is understood to embody the law of God, be similarly subject to a liberal overrider that sees any impairment to individual freedom as a derogation from man's inherent rights which precede, and are independent of, the Constitution itself? If such provision be made, then 'the traditional Catholic insistence on an objective moral law which applies to all men and which a legal system must seek to embody is a stumbling block.'[2]

To a certain extent Ireland, in coming to terms with the problem of resolving this difficulty, was rehearsing the Devlin–Hart controversy which, it will be remembered, contrasted the enforceability of a shared morality and the wrongfulness of imposing any particular moral point of view on society. The liberal view and the Thomist view of natural law therefore differ in that the former sees the state as an institutional mechanism that enables the social contract to function, and the latter sees it, at the very least, as enabling God's writ to run. Each will therefore understand differently the relationship of law and morality. The first regards them as distinct, the second considers that the function of law is to give effect to, or

---

[1] Bruce Stewart, 'The Censorship Debate', *Month* 13 Jan 1980, p. 7.
[2] Edmund Grace, 'Human Rights and the Constitution: A Role for Irish Catholicism', *Doctrine and Life* 29:8 (1979), p. 498.

reflect, morality. The first considers the validity of any law to lie with the people, the second that it derives from justice. On what is this justice to be based? The Preamble to the Constitution declares the desire of the Irish people to be

to promote the common good with due observance of Prudence, Justice and Charity, so that the dignity and freedom of the individual may be assured, true social order attained, the unity of our country restored and concord established with other nations,

but how to determine these virtues is not indicated. To say that justice should be rooted in natural law raises problems. As McGrath has pointed out, deriving moral values from the consideration of man's nature is determined by a priori philosophical conclusions. The McGee case[1] (in which the rights to marital privacy in relation to contraceptives had been upheld) had, in the opinion of the Supreme Court, shown the existence of rights in natural law over which the state has no authority. How to reconcile this view with the view advanced by the Catholic Church that the natural law in fact condemned artificial means of preventing conception led to only one conclusion that one version of natural law was preferred to others. Thus the attitude of those entrusted with interpreting the Constitution would appear to indicate a recognition of the place of natural law in arriving at their decisions. Whose interpretation for what occasion was a question which would always remain problematic since Thomist and other theories of natural law inevitably differ as to what is 'self-evident,' 'objective' and 'reasonable'.

Successive Supreme Court decisions seem to be moving away from the philosophical doctrine of natural law to a view of natural rights as 'those which are contingent on various natural facts, events or relations, but the validity and justification of which is derived from some independent, constitutional, legal or moral source.'[2] Whatever they were, they would include rights held equally, rights derived from a metaphysical definition of justice, and rights of the weak against the strong. Now in deciding which right is to prevail, bearing in mind rights unspecified in the Constitution but which the Constitution recognizes, what guidance is available if natural law is felt to be defective as to its agreed premiss or in the consistency of its application? Walsh J. said in the McGee decision,

In a pluralist society such as ours, the Courts cannot as a matter of constitutional law be asked to choose between the differing views, where they exist, of experts on the interpretation by the different religious denominations of either the nature or extent of these natural rights as they are to be found in the natural law. The same considerations apply also to the question of ascertaining the nature and

[1] *McGee* v. *Attorney General* (1974) I.R. 284.
[2] D.M. Clarke, 'The Role of Natural Law in Irish Constitutional Law', *The Irish Jurist* 17 (1982), p. 211.

extent of the duties which flow from natural law ... In this country it falls finally upon the judges to interpret the Constitution and in doing so to determine, where necessary, the rights which are superior or antecedent to positive law or which are imprescriptible or inalienable.[1]

It would appear that the nature-of-man version of natural law is being replaced by a nature-of-justice approach which is shaped by contemporary, rather by Thomistic, philosophy. In this view justice is not objectively discoverable and its subjective interpretation in a democratic society is deemed not to be tolerable. Instead, justice is seen as the product of historical conditions, as undergoing evolution in the light of changing circumstances, and as representing to a certain measure what thinking men and women at any point in time are prepared to ratify.

Justice is a human creation rather than an invention; or, it is an invention in the sense of making something new but not in the sense of finding something already there.[2]

The courts in this view have the task of passing judgment on human behavior, not on the basis of any particular natural law theory arising from a theory of the nature of man, and still less by what any one judge may think, but on the grounds of constitutionally affirmed values corroborated, explored and clarified by whatever international standard of justice is deemed appropriate, whether it be the U.S. Supreme Court or the United Nations' Declaration of Rights. The Irish people gave themselves a Constitution which derived from justice. Therefore any case at issue in an Irish court must ultimately evaluate the application of all laws against the requirements of this justice. What these are, had always appeared so self-evident that no theory has so far been advanced to account for them in Irish law. Hence, as has been pointed out, the provision, for example, of *audi alteram partem* was disregarded with impunity by the Censorship of Publications Board, that is, until the Family Planning case which in itself constituted a significant milestone in the history of Irish censorship.

What had happened was that the Irish Family Planning Association had published in 1971 a booklet (entitled Family Planning) outlining various methods of conception prevention, all of which it recommended should only be used after medical advice had been sought. The *Iris Oifigiúil* on December 3rd, 1976 carried a notice for the first time to the effect that it had been banned in all of its editions not on the grounds that it was 'advocating the unnatural prevention of conception' as forbidden by the 1929 and 1946 Acts, but for the reason that it was 'indecent or obscene.' Since the Appeal Board was without a chairman and lacked a quorum, the Association brought an action in the High Court challenging the validity of

---

[1] *McGee* v. *Attorney General*. I.R. 284 at p. 318.
[2] D. M. Clarke, 'The Role of Natural Law', p. 218.

the Prohibition Order on the grounds that the Censorship of Publications Board had disregarded the requirements of natural or constitutional justice by its failure to communicate with it or provide it with an opportunity to make representations on behalf of the work in question. The trial judge found on its behalf on the grounds that the Censorship Board had failed to exercise its powers 'fairly and judicially in accordance with the principles of natural justice'[1] by its failure to notify the Association.

When the decision was appealed to the Supreme Court, the verdict of the lower court was upheld though the grounds were varied in that the obligation to communicate with the producers of a book was declared to be not mandatory but discretionary. It would, in the Chief Justice's view, be impractical to require of the Board that it do so 'Where the publication is clearly indecent or obscene,' or 'Where the editor, author or publisher cannot be traced or contacted, or where to attempt to do so would lead to undue delay.' He contributed, in addition, the following *obiter dictum* about the Censorship Act:

The Act of 1946, being a post-Constitution statute, is presumed to be constitutional. As has been pointed out by the Court on previous occasions, this presumption of constitutionality carries with it the subsequent presumption that powers of a discretionary nature conferred by such a statute are not intended to be arbitrary powers, and are only exercisable in a constitutional manner.[2]

Justice Kenny added in a separate concurring judgment.

A discretion to do something, given to any body exercising limited functions of a judicial nature, involves the idea that they may or may not do something. There are, however, cases in which a given discretion can be exercised in one way only if justice is to be done. If such a discretion is not so exercised, the High Court may intervene and reverse the decision.[3].

From these statements it would appear that constitutionality and justice are one and the same thing, or, alternatively, that rights guaranteed under the constitution are to be interpreted under the prevailing notion of what constitutes justice. Bearing in mind the intention of the Constitution to assure the dignity and freedom of the individual, 'The judges must, therefore, as best they can from their training and their experience interpret these rights in accordance with their ideas of prudence, justice and charity.'[4] Presuming that any conception of human right must require it be informed by a moral sense, on what morality will the interpretation be based?

There are other questions which the Supreme Court left unanswered

---

[1] *The Irish Family Planning Association Limited and Joan M. Wilson, Plaintiffs* v. *Patrick Noel Ryan and others.* (1976 No. 5622P) The Irish Reports, 1979.

[2] ibid., pp. 313, 314.

[3] ibid., p. 319.

[4] *McGee* v. *Attorney General* (1974) I.R. 284, at p. 319.

and which in the interests of clarification it was deemed proper to seek whatever operational solution existed by addressing them to the Chairman of the Censorship Board. In a private interview he was asked how he and his Board defined 'indecent' and 'obscene.' The reply was that they didn't, and that any attempt to confine their meanings within a static formula would defeat the current approach to censorship. Safeguards lay in their procedures. Any one of the criteria, literary, artistic or historic merit, general tenor, audience anticipated, etc., would be sufficient if proved applicable to ensure favorable consideration. If two members dissented to a prohibition order, the book was automatically released. If only one person dissented, deliberations were suspended and the publisher invited to make representations, which might include a personal appearance. If after all these precautions had been taken and a recommendation adopted that a book should be prohibited, then the definition of 'indecent' and 'obscene' as two moral and social constructs must be presumed to have been exhaustively explored in relation to the work in question. In the author's interest, this *modus operandi* seemed preferable to evaluating it against a fixed conceptualization which might not have envisioned the work in question.

Did the Board feel obliged to communicate with those responsible for the production of a book, the prohibition of which was being considered? The reply was that in natural justice it would be impossible to do otherwise, provided, of course, that the book in question had any sort of pretension to be taken as something worth reading, and was not an obvious and blatant attempt to cater for the psychologically disturbed or socially alienated. The Board offered any publisher who wished to come forward (and sales in Ireland were so small that very few to date had availed of the Board's invitation) the opportunity of explaining what was the purpose and intent of the work in question and why he or she thought that a *prima facie* case for prohibition should be set aside. The Board were conscious of the constitutional guarantees of freedom of expression and rights of property vested in the book. These were additional considerations any one of which if unanimously agreed was sufficient to make publication possible on condition, as before, that the Board were convinced that the underlying purpose was communication and not titillation.

Was the Board aware that it was exercising a function that belonged appropriately to the judiciary in the final analysis? The chairman's reply was quite explicit. The Irish system of law rested on the right of appeal to a superior court provided the conditions for making the appeal were satisfied. If the Board through some frailty of procedure had given grounds for believing that natural justice had been denied, then the injured party must be encouraged to take his plea to the court of higher jurisdiction. At the same time it must be remembered in the economics of justice and equity, the people through its elected governments and Constitution had made certain dispositions as to how alleged infractions of its laws should be adjudged, and these decisions, provided the procedures were as good as human contrivance could make them, were not to be lightly set aside. Was the Board aware of the Chief Justice's words that prudence, justice and charity could change as society changes and should be interpreted accordingly? Of course, every censor should have Shelley's *Ozymandias* by his side. Man has no permanent perspective, and every act of creation lives only the span of his attention. Right and wrong can be the product of circumstances, can be, but are not so necessarily. Periodic visits to the basement of the Censorship's office reminded everybody of the travesties of justice which their predecessors had perpetrated, but the undeniable exaggerations in the past could not be rationally held to obligate some form of compensatory liberalization in the present that would be at variance with their good judgment. The perversion of the communicative act, as the U.S. Supreme Court had pointed out, will always leave certain media products subject to close scrutiny. Finally, the Chairman was asked, Did he consider as a constitutional lawyer that the Censorship Acts were constitutionally valid? The answer was slow and measured, and the words presumably weighed and chosen with care. 'Yes, they would pass muster on the grounds of public order and morality, and in the interests of the common good.' With these *obiter dicta* in mind it is now appropriate to look at how the Censorship Board functions.

According to Ann Bristow's description of three years ago,

A visit to the Republic of Ireland Censorship Board in its beautiful but shabby Georgian offices in Dublin's Upper Pembroke Street is a strange experience. The mood is gentle and apologetic: there are friendly cups of tea. The atmosphere is one of doubt and paralysis.[1]

Tempora mutantur, nos et mutamur in illis. Today's experience is one of quiet efficiency that can be no means be described as apologetic and self-effacing. A public service is being offered, part of which is to provide any information that is humanly possible to provide. What does emerge from the data collected is the change in terms of 'output' over the period in question. In the first quinquennium 1969–1974, 1176 books were prohibited, an average of 235 a year. In the second quinquennium, the Board was not active for the year 1978. The number of books prohibited was therefore smaller and stood at the figure of 550, an average of 137. In the last quinquennium the number of books prohibited was as follows: 1979, 111; 1980, 74; 1981, 108; 1982, 39; and 1983, 26, giving a total of 358 and an average of 71. The total number of books prohibited therefore was 2084, of which 93.95% had been brought to the attention of the Censors

[1] Ann Bristow, 'Dublin's Book Banners', *Index on Censorship* 10:2 (1981), p. 29.

by the Customs, and 5.81% by members of the public. The number of books submitted for judgment was 2926 so that the prohibition figure of 2084 represents 71.22% of the total (See Appendix 1).

The operations of the Board do not appear to have attracted much notice in the media. In November 1972 employees of Drogheda Printers, Ltd., were fined for publishing a booklet called *Freedom Struggle for the Provisional IRA*. 'All copies of the booklet were ordered to be forfeited and the metal type used for its production was to be melted down.'[1] This action was of course taken under the Offenses Against the State Act. Broderick complained about the banning of the book of a fellow-author (Lee Dunne) and its subsequent confirmation by the Appeal Board. While he admitted, 'Of recent years, this iniquitous law has not been much employed ... it still remains on the statute books; and over the past forty years it has been used to brand the work of practically every well known Irish writer of merit.'[2] Given the preference of Irish readers for Irish authors, the financial loss to someone who wished to work out of Ireland could be quite considerable.

The trial of the Linda Lovelace book in Britain provoked so much publicity that an *Irish Times* editorial complained that its circulation would be further improved by the undoubted corrective action that the Irish Censorship Board would take with the 'wretched book' that ought to be 'left in indecent obscurity.'[3] Cullen writes in the same year on the banning of his novel '*Astra and Flandrix* which resulted in his having dishonor without profit in one's own country.'[4] In 1977 the British feminine magazine *Spare Rib* was banned, and, in 1978, *The Grapevine*, another thoughtful if somewhat unorthodox periodical, was withdrawn after a visit by an inspector of police. *Hibernia* published a leader on 'The Moral Custodians' in which it chastised the Board for its undeniable failure to 'be possessed of at least a modicum of common sense'[5] which they seemed to have lacked in banning the Family Planning booklet. It also drew attention to the seizure of publications by the Customs, a form of censorship they considered 'the most arbitrary of all.' But apart from a report of Lord Longford's comments on Irish censorship in *The Irish Times* of the same year, the suspension of the Board's activities is matched understandably by their disappearance from media awareness.

An article in the English *Bookseller* did not consider the respite anything more than an accidental victory for liberal opinion. It felt many banned titles which appeared on the censored list in the past had been ex-

[1] Report in *Index*, Vol. 2, No. 4, p. iii.
[2] John Broderick, 'The Labelling of Lee Dunne', *Hibernia*, 11 May 1973, p. 11.
[3] Editorial, *The Irish Times*, February 2, 1976, p. 9.
[4] Séamas Cullen, 'On Being Banned', *Hibernia*, 17 Dec. 1976, p. 10.
[5] Leader, *Hibernia*, p. 3.

pendable and went on to give as the opinion of the trade in Ireland 'that the list itself in recent times should have been banned since the titles given could have stimulated the innocent to consider exotic variations, hitherto unknown.'[1] This view of a growing tolerance combined with a determina̓-tion to weed out what was obviously devoid of literary or artistic merit seems to have been shared by Adams, whose insight into the workings of Irish censorship has been freely drawn upon in these pages. 'Of the 2900 books banned for indecency in 1967–1980 I, as a publisher, *au fait* with the trade press, would have heard of the authors in perhaps a hundred cases. Lee Dunne is conspicuous for being Irish.'[2] Adams went on to wonder why there had been no adverse comment on the workings of the Board during the current decade. Were they examining enough books? Had they frightened off the Customs? Could it be possible that Irish censorship was being successful when there were no complaints? The only other item on the restriction of sales of print media came in a report in *The Irish Times* which presented a somewhat ambivalent attitude to pornography that had emerged as a result of a feminist seminar in Dublin.[3] Was censor-ship of books therefore about to disappear from Irish awareness? Did grassroots reaction reflect this change of attitude? A useful indicator as a response to this question would come from an analysis of librarians' ex-periences in the period under study.

No research has ever been carried out in relation to the censorship of books in public libraries in Ireland. This, in today's world, might well ap-pear surprising, but in a country which desperately lacked social amenities, the provision of books outside the metropolitan area would have come low down in the list of priorities, and hence a national scrutiny of their use was a matter that could be postponed. While the country was literate, it had to wait almost fifty years before it could lay claim to a gen-eral standard of education that would make reading an essential element in a person's formation. Whatever their rate of usage, however, books did exist, and for a considerable period of time after independence the public supply was to be supplemented by circulating libraries. These exercised a form of unwritten control for those authors who had to bear in mind that, spread throughout the British Isles as they were, any one organization represented a considerable network of outlets. Whatever the public lib-raries might decide by way of policy in their selection of books, for the commercial variety, nothing was countenanced 'which could not be safely read aloud in the family circle.'[4] In Britain, Thompson found evidence

[1] H. Clarke, *The Bookseller*, January 1978, p. 237
[2] Michael Adams, 'Censorship of Publications' in *Morality and the Law*, D.M. Clarke (ed.), (Cork: RTÉ/Mercier, 1981).
[3] Sheila Wayman, 'Feminists divide on Censorship', *The Irish Times*, p. 7.
[4] H. H. Thompson, *Censorship in Public Libraries* (London: Bowker, 1978), p. 7.

that showed censorship to be widespread throughout the twentieth century, and it is hardly to be expected that where books did exist in Ireland, supervision of what was being offered out of the public purse would have been any less exacting. At all events the presence of clergymen on book-selection committees ensured that no work likely to disturb tender consciences would find a place on a library bookshelf in the first decade of independence. Some committees indeed went so far in their desire to copper-fasten the guarantee of irreproachableness as to place their orders only with Irish publishers who because of a commercial interest in eliminating any contentious or objectionable material would in consequence be completely reliable. All librarians are conscious of problems concerning the unrestricted access to certain classes of books. They deny their role as censors and explain that they are public servants with an obligation to respect local mores where these can be distinguished from the pretensions of cranks. Books are not banned: they are simply kept out of sight. It was not unknown therefore for intending borrowers in the thirties and forties to be subjected to a cross-examination as to motive if ever they did conquer their understandable diffidence and actually asked for them.

Conditions in libraries in independent Ireland were somewhat primitive. Reductions in public expenditure affected spending departments in the public service the most rigorously, and the County Libraries taken over from the Carnegie Trust in 1925 were somewhat short of champions both in the legislature and in local county councils. Unfortunately, too, the scheme suffered from adverse publicity right from the beginning. Lennox Robinson, the Trust's Secretary, who had authored *The Madonna of Slieve Dun* already referred to, was accused of abusing his position by peddling pornography and was eventually dismissed. The support he attracted however from the liberal ex-Ascendancy clique ensured that the affair attracted considerable attention in the media. From then on, books were slightly suspect, and libraries were considered, if they weren't watched, as being likely to turn into breeding grounds for West Britons, anarchists and anti-Christs. The wise librarian in the twenties and thirties stayed with westerns, detective novels, cheap romances, approved nineteenth century classics, Irish (but not English) Catholic authors, and a wide collection that ranged from *My Travels in Tibet* to *Life among the Eskimos*.

One librarian who did live to tell the tale of his experiences recounted how in a county town in the west of Ireland his library committee on receiving notice that dirty books were polluting the shelves of their center and branches by the thousands formed a panel of readers of fifty-two 'upright citizens capable of spotting dirt at a hundred yards.' The woman's sodality collaborated and nine specimens were handed to the parish priest who preached 'a sulphurous sermon on obscenity in the local library' the following Sunday. The matter came up at the next meeting when the local curate drew attention to the fact that 'whatever about the other books, one of them was about a bunch of male criminals on a panel settlement out in Australia, 'and not one female within a 100 miles of it.' Sensation! ... It wasn't for me, was it, to divert the course of the meeting towards the awful mysteries of a thing like experimental sodomy? As for the other eight titles, a general order was made: in all cases of doubt, the book is to be withdrawn, nem. con.'[1]

To discover what current conditions are like in Ireland today, a questionnaire (see Appendix 3) was sent to all city and county librarians in Ireland. Dublin was omitted because of the heterogeneity of a metropolitan population. Answers were received in 25 cases, giving a return of 89.29%. The number of books in all 25 libraries was 5,457,007, giving an average number of 2.39 books per head of the corresponding population. The range was between 0.71 and 4.30 (see Appendix 3). The figure 2.39 is less than the three volumes per inhabitant which was recommended by the International Federation of Library Associations (Public Libraries Section) but is higher than a crude average of 2.06 obtained by dividing the total number of volumes in the country in public libraries as listed in the *Unesco Statistical Year Book* (1977) into the population estimated from censal returns.

Nineteen of the twenty-five librarians reported withdrawing books as a result of protest from private citizens. Over the fifteen-year period, twelve reported being obliged to take such action on less than ten occasions, one reported less than twenty, five reported less than thirty and one reported thirty to fifty, all because of alleged immorality or pornography. Six reported making no withdrawals. Two librarians reported removing books less than ten times because of the intervention of ministers of religion. Three different librarians removed books less than ten times because of protests from local government employees, and two of these three also reported the same rate of withdrawals because of objections lodged by institutions, societies, etc. One librarian advised complainants of the ruling by the Library Council that,

The public are entitled to rely upon librarians for access to information and enlightenment upon every field of human experience and activity. Those who provide library services should not restrict this access except by standards which are endorsed by law,

presumably before coming to his decision. One librarian reported complaints that certain books did not portray the Irish favorably, another that a book was blasphemous. Only in one location were there complaints

---

[1] Dermot Foley, 'A Minstrel Boy with a Satchel of Books', *Irish University Review* 4:2 (1974), pp. 209–10.

based on the seditious character of a work. Still another librarian discovered that censorship took the form of book mutilation which was as-
cribed to a country-wide vigilante group. Sex, the holy name of Jesus and
any photographic or pictorial presentation of either nude or semi-nude
men or women, suffered from the attention of these moral guardians. In
one instance, a photostat supplied indicated violent anti-feminist feeling.
There was no indication recorded of protests at, or attempt to censor, violence. Two or three librarians solved the problem of what they considered
to be excessive vigilance by keeping certain volumes in an inner private
room but available for anyone who had successfully divined their existence. One librarian felt that it would be an impossible task to change
local moral standards and provided these did not become intolerable was
prepared to withdraw books alleged to be objectionable in the hope that
standards would change. The average withdrawal for libraries responding
was one book per year.

A Censorship Board whose rate of prohibition has been reduced to a
fraction of what it had been accustomed, together with a low incidence of
local banning as a result of protests in public libraries, demonstrate that
what had been a minor irritant for the majority, and an intellectual affront
for a very tiny minority, was no longer a disturbing or divisive element in
Irish society. No doubt the shift to television as a medium played its role.
No doubt British influences had easier access. The fact still remains that
moral attitudes had changed. Few knew of the intellectuals who had set
about the process of re-identifying man and his reasoned nature as the
gauge for determining public morality. They were read, however, and understood in different ways and at different levels. What they slowly in-
filtrated concerned thinking with was the realization that censorship can
be defended and attacked – on moralist and on causalistic grounds. Censorship can be justified morally not just because it brings about goodness
but because it creates an environment in which virtue need not necessarily
be the victim of vice. Censorship can be condemned also on moralist
grounds as the denial of human freedom to man to express his humanity
and develop his freedom of thought, even if the consequences in the short
term are dire. Censorship can be justified on the causalist grounds that
without restraint over what is read, the reader will behave in an anti-social
manner. Censorship can be condemned also on the causalist grounds that
so-called indecent or obscene literature has never been proven to have
the anti-social effects imputed to it, and that in fact it might well be
prophylactic. What happened in Ireland was that a moralist censorship
was built on a causalist base, neither of which had been adequately secured in theory or in fact. According to the belief that had existed, indecent or obscene literature was morally wrong because it bred anarchy in
society, attacked the family and distorted approved relationships bet-

ween the sexes. The Church helped to restore the independence of the individual in the decision-making process: the social scientists on the whole rejected the hypothesis that there was a proven causal relationship between deviancy and immoral literature. With personal judgment restored, evidence would be looked at firsthand and not through the eyes of another, no matter how authoritative. In the meantime the Censor could continue to remove the brushwood to which everybody objected and leave the public to concentrate on its attitude to the major issues – an attitude which the Board would take cognizance of as it sought to live up to the Chief Justice's admonition that rights be jealously guarded under the kaleidoscope of prudence, justice and charity 'which fall to be interpreted from time to time in accordance with prevailing ideas.'[1]

[1] Rajeev Dharan and Christie Davies, *Censorship and Obscenity* (London: Martin Robertson, 1978), p. 22.

CHAPTER 8

THE POLITICS OF CENSORSHIP

This chapter gives an account of the approaches adopted by the media to reporting news in Ireland generally and the activities of terrorists in Northern Ireland in particular. A major source of confrontation was found to lie in the dissatisfaction evinced by successive governments with the performance of the national broadcasting system which, it will be remembered, is controlled by an Act of the Oireachtas. Reporting terrorism has been recognized to be fraught with indeterminate and unpredictable consequences for the public interest. Various European countries, while conceding freedom of expression, have placed restrictions on the liberties enjoyed by the electronic media. In Ireland because of the Irish Republican Army (IRA) such restrictions have been considered essential in the interests of political stability. Control of the media is however complicated by the availability to most of the population of two non-Irish broadcast systems. Censorship has therefore to a certain extent been stultified. Even if it had not been, it is arguably a derogation from that political freedom the enjoyment of which is guaranteed the citizen by the Irish constitution and by other international declarations to which Ireland is a signatory. Moral censorship has been replaced by political censorship, but the paternalism of the censor remains.

By the 1970s, the focus for defining morality had shifted from the institution to the individual. Personal freedom replaced confessional absolutes. Unbelief became the obverse of belief as the right to decide for self was exercised within the context of personal decision. Whichever had slipped its moorings from the other, Church and State were now to navigate independently, and by different stars. The citizen, in his turn, had learnt there were many answers where before there had been only one. The age of certainties had passed, and there was now to intervene a period of discomfort and doubt when the traditional formulae associated with a religion strong on ritual could no longer predict the interaction of man and his environment. The special offers on eternity, conditional on immediate down payments of prayer and penance, were henceforth brokered with less conviction to fewer clients. When there was no magic left to believe in, the Irish were forced to see their mysteries as problems for which they were to be dependent on themselves for solutions. They were aware that they had moral choices. They had to adopt a course of action, a range of attitudes and a system of explaining their existence to themselves. In short, they were being asked to think, and being a religious people, it was appropriate they should first be asked to think about themselves in relation to a Supreme Being and in consequence about the behavior that should reflect their thoughts. Heretofore, attendance, observance, and conformity were enough to regulate how they should live in obedience to an other-worldly dimension. The time had come to make their own arrangements. Was the milieu propitious?

The Irish are historically disposed to recognizing authority. Hierarchies are acknowledged and rights are conceded to agents of standing that allow them to take arbitrary decisions which are intended to bind. Power that is concentrated in one or two figures, that is unchallenged, that is manifest, and that is itself legitimated by other forms of power is sensed as a force to be respectful to in the everyday business of living. What prevents the emergence of a totalitarian society is a personalism that mitigates relationships at different levels of the policy. This was an essential social mechanism in a colonial society which suffered from the impersonalness and remoteness of justice and equity. It was a vital support function among group members when an agricultural economy offered little above the subsistence level. It was a necessary personal input for the individual to feel that if he could do little to change his existence, he knew somebody who had the power to do so. These two guiding principles of authoritarianism and personalism were to define the parameters of his political thinking just at the moment the Church had sent him on his way to make his own spiritual destiny. He had evolved a similar system for interacting with both institutions. He did not seek that which he was entitled to on the basis of who he was. No, he sought a favor, and in return he was prepared to subscribe, to belong, to pay his dues, to inform, to give an ostentatiously unqualified commitment and to join the club for this life and, hopefully, the next.

This then was the mind-set of the average Irishman. He belonged to an organization which relieved him of the need to develop and substantiate an independent point of view. He inherited his religion and (for the most part) his politics. He felt safe that the commitment he had made to those in authority would be amply rewarded, if not tangibly, at least by the reassurance of sharing the rationale that justified those who actually did wield power. He now found himself faced with decisions about matters that were no doubt trivial in themselves but left him to face their consequences on his own. He was in the next decade to make up his mind about contraception, abortion and divorce. He was to confront such moral problems as care for the disadvantaged, nuclear disarmament and violence in the streets about which the outmoded traditional teaching of the Church had very little to offer that was relevant. He also had a problem about murder, maiming and arson outside the territory of the state which persisted in trespassing on his consciousness. He found himself reliving another cycle of communal violence at one remove. In appraising its significance, he was found to exercise that independence of mind which came in the sequel to Vatican II. He found himself dependent on data which were made available to him in print media form, free of the intermediation of his Church and State. What was obviously to make the greatest impact on him however was the immediacy of the television coverage which he might expect from the national broadcasting system.

Journalists reporting on Northern Ireland had inherited an ethic of factuality about events which occurred outside their state, were aware of the influence they exercised, and were conscious of Benda's *trahison des clercs* – of those who wrote 'in the service of states, governments and parties, neglecting the duty which education and experience placed on them to serve only justice, reason and truth.'[1] They went to Northern Ireland accepting the obligation to investigate what was happening, to facilitate the free flow of information and knowledge, and in the best Millian tradition 'to contribute their ideas as a sort of social obligation' so that society would not be deprived 'of some valuable opportunity to gain an intellectual commodity or at least to reinforce its existing ideas on a better basis as a result of debate.'[2] Unfortunately there was little enough room for the laissez-faire of reporting when the giant institutions in the field only recognized truth that had been molded to fit their pragmatic preconceptions of what was publishable. The market was not always determined therefore by the laws of supply and demand but by what the controllers of the media thought was politic. The significant question eventually for the reporter in the field would be not whether their reports or features were being revised, but at what level in the authority, and in the interest of which sector of government.

Television journalists in particular, given the nature of their medium, were to find in particular that instead of the free exchange of intellectual products, there was 'an industrial system for the manufacture and distribution of symbolic goods within the structure of a programme

---

[1] Gerard Long, 'Government and the Journalist', *Intermedia*, Vol. 4, No. 5 (1976), p. 8.
[2] Anthony Smith, 'Broadcasting – The Origins of a Conflict', *New Humanist*, Vol. 88, (1973) p. 391.

schedule."[1] In an area as small as Northern Ireland, the relationships that existed between social forces made up of the audience, the State and the economy were well documented. So, too, were their motivations which revealed not only the normal incompatibility among all three sectors but also laid bare the internal incompatibilities within each that would defy their best efforts most of the time to satisfy the statutory requirements of impartiality, balance and objectivity. Censorship, editorial control, code of practice, guidelines, whatever the discipline, all made the messenger realize that, to those entrusted with the conduct of the nation's affairs, the message was less important than its repercussions. On the other hand, perhaps more than the news media, broadcasting by its overtness assumes an ideology in addition to its functionalism – an ideology born out of the need for credibility that is made up of neutrality, objectivity, and fairness. What remains a problem for those who would subscribe to such an approach is that they, knowingly or unknowingly, run the risk of becoming a maker of events instead of a medium to relate them.

The tensions that ensued created much argument about the function of broadcasting. Was it merely to reflect, or was it, because of its powers, to use them to redress a wrong? Was it to mirror or to mold? Who was to decide what role the media should play? The obvious answer was the institutional authorities where the editorial center of broadcasting lay. Consider the problems they faced. Would the reporting of an event cause a counter-event? How did one report an illegal organization without contributing to its myth? In what manner did one balance a discussion between the victims of a bomb and the representatives of its thrower? What did one do in estimating the effects of a report when the frames of reference for the *dramatis personae* were not the same as for those of the audience? When there was no agreed center of political, intellectual, religious or national gravity, what were the referents to be used that would not betray the spectacle, that would not bemuse the spectator ?

Before attempting to answer any of these questions, it would be wise to consider the symbiosis of terrorism and the media, for one unexpected consequence of the internationalization of violence is, as Bowyer Bell says[2] that 'It has become far more alluring for the frantic few to appear on the world stage of television than remain obscure guerrillas of the bush.' Acts of terrorism are meant to impress themselves on public attention. Their dramatic significance is lodged securely in the anonymity and incidentality of the instant victim, the innocent bystanders, the chance passer-by. Terrorists are deep into sensationalism. For them the media are the indispensable carriers of their message. They know too well the ir-

[1] Nicholas Graham, 'How free is British Broadcasting?', *Index on Censorship*, May 1982, p. 27.

[2] J. Bowyer Bell, *Transnational Terror* (Washington, D.C., 1975), p. 14.

resistibility of having something newsworthy to tell. They appreciate the First Amendment, the need to know, and the moving target of what constitutes the public interest. So, too, do governments.

While terrorism is not confined to urban areas, those who employ it as a coercive modality recognize the theatrical values of a defined area for its presentation. Modern technology has added considerable increments to the vulnerability of society, particularly when that society is reasonably predictable in terms of flow, as happens in cities and towns. The days of politics by numbers is gone. A single terrorist can terminate the lives of many people; a cell can hold a large residential area to ransom.

Terrorism, as has been said, is always publicity-hungry, and television has added considerably to the immediacy and dissemination of its impact. This ability to attract the media so as to reach a worldwide audience has changed not only what the terrorist does but how he sees himself.[1] Terrorism, as a result, is aimed not at the victims but the viewers who will see it all appropriately edited on the evening news. The apocryphal protest, 'Don't shoot. We're not on prime time', catches the sense of macabre theater in which collusion displaces reality. 'Terrorism has unfortunately become a form of mass entertainment,' as Hacker[2] reported to the House of Representatives. As long as liberal democracies continue to recognize that, on balance, censorship is worse than free but responsible reporting, they are bound to find that the reporting of terrorist incidents may well have a contagion effect; that coverage may hinder effective police operations; that providing a platform for terrorist views may tend to undermine the state; that the competitive nature of news gathering is an incentive to the terrorists themselves to intensify the sensationalism of their acts; and that, as may be inferred from the quotation above, reporters often become participants in, rather than observers of, events so that their professional function of objective reporting may be impaired.

In Northern Ireland, censorship has always been employed, and was all the more effective for its informality. Since there was little hope that any of the heavily partisan newspapers might be read, never mind accepted, by a non-subscriber to their political credo, the electronic media had the opportunity to act as a forum prior to the outbreak of the troubles. How far this potential opportunity was from reality is shown by the fact that not only did the BBC Area Director control all news emanating from Northern Ireland to the United Kingdom, but he also had a veto on news originating elsewhere in the United Kingdom about Northern Ireland so that nothing was transmitted without his approval. Obviously with the prorogation of the Stormont Parliament and the assimilation of the Six

---

[1] H.H.A. Cooper, 'Terrorism and the Media', *Chitty's Law Journal*, Vol. 24, No. 7, (1976), p. 15.
[2] *Terrorism, Part I*. Washington, D.C.: Committee on Internal Security, 1974, p. 16.

Counties to the British mainland for a period of direct rule, this situation has been ameliorated. However, problems still remained. Chief of these was the recurrent problem of broadcasting journalists who wished to avail themselves of the role of their print media colleagues, but who felt themselves caught 'between the view that broadcasting should invariably create and transmit a simulated balanced model of the prevailing political scene and the view that broadcasting should now exist as a reporting tool pure and simple.'[1] Broadcasting organizations which pursue the doctrine of impartiality often find themselves playing a social part that may leave them extremely vulnerable. When further they seek objectivity where objectivity is not easily found, they may well consider that they have cut a switch to beat themselves, an activity without profit or edification.

'Fairness' of treatment in reporting in Northern Ireland for the United Kingdom and the Republic of Ireland broadcast networks is not easy to administer, without at times incurring the risk of being accused of bias. Northern Ireland is not Southern Vietnam. It connotes for the audience engagement. Be it dispassionate analysis or passionate commitment, people in the two islands are involved for many different reasons with what is happening in a small section of one of them. The contrived reality of television does nothing to reduce the tensions that inevitably follow the reporting. The personalities, the horror of the incidents, the reversal of norms, all make impossible the task of providing a format for presentation that would be reassuring in itself if only because of its predictability. There are no formulae when the nature of the elements in each event is never agreed upon by those who are called upon to discuss their interaction. There is not much communication when what is looked for is not objectivity but a reinforcement of prejudice.

The alternative to the media as a fourth estate is their absence, or merely nominal presence. According to this view, violence is overplayed, community spirit underplayed. What is needed is a better balance between the 'good' and the 'bad' that appear on the front page, perhaps even a toning down of the horror and in its stead greater emphasis on aspects of life that will create a sense, an image of normality. These opinions are often heard, are just as often refuted, and finally just as often reoccur. There were reasons why Northern Ireland would prove stony ground in which to seed illusions. First, normal life is being reported in Northern media to the Northern Irish. What made headlines is not rural electrification, a victory at football or a three-act play, but explosions, fires, maiming and death. Second, what contributed to the problem of discrimination was the failure, as has been said, of the media to contribute to the just society. This omission was not unique. Every country is remiss in

[1] Anthony Smith, 'Television Coverage of Northern Ireland', *Index*, Spring 1972, p. 20.

reporting – always for good programmatic reasons – what should be an ongoing matter of concern. The problem in Northern Ireland was that a non-political Civil Rights Movement stepped in to report what the media had failed to report, aroused the police whose overreaction brought the IRA whose presence in turn provoked the Loyalists, and so on. Third, underreporting can bring about the direct opposite of the consequences intended. All news values are relative, and a bomb a day soon appears to be unexceptional. But if that bomb goes unreported, there will always be a danger that the bomber will do more next time. If what the illegal organization states goes unreported, it may decide that stepped-up violence speaks louder and delivers a longer-echoing message. Fourth, the appearance of illegal organizations in the news is not commitment. There is no question of being impartial between right and wrong. Just as attribution alerts the viewer to the credibility of the message, the public interview of a paramilitary is the best guarantee that can be offered to the public as to the quality-of-life solution which his bombs offer.

British television producers when they came to Northern Ireland soon found that they did not always share the same frame of reference with either the Loyalist or the Nationalist populations, and to do justice to both they were obliged at times to reduce truth to its lowest common multiple of credibility. Given the nature of television it was certain that some programs would overstep the mark of 'impartiality,' 'objectivity,' 'thoroughness' or 'balance,' and when it did indeed happen, it imposed a social role on the broadcasters to define objectivity beyond the material to be presented and beyond the perspective of those most involved. The process was to leave them vulnerable to attack. The Broadcasting Authorities worried over the interpretation of their statutes which enjoined impartiality, good taste and decency, and avoidance of any program that would lead to crime and disorder or be offensive to the viewer's feelings. The Establishment in any country disposes of many means of impressing the urgency of its views, the cogency of its opinions, the disasters that await those who neglect the assessments of experts on the ground. In 1978, an Amnesty Report was banned. 'Not surprisingly, government and the Authority denied political interference. Few believed them. Anthony Smith's prophecy had been fulfilled four years ahead of its time: the institutional relationships between the broadcasting authorities and the state were now fully cemented.'[1]

It is important at this juncture to contrast this point of view on British media performance in reporting Northern Ireland with that expressed by the senior reporter for RTÉ in Belfast.

[1] Peter Taylor, 'Reporting Northern Ireland', *Index of Censorship*, Vol. 7, No. 6, (1978), p. 10.

Throughout the hunger strike crisis, the public was denied the opportunity to hear and to hear challenged directly the views of important sections of opinion regarding the most serious crisis which has arisen in these islands in recent times. The election which chose Owen Carron provided a major elected representative, who is excluded from the airwaves of RTÉ. No matter how much his views are liked or detested, over 31,000 Irish people voted that he should express them. RTÉ's inability, because of Ministerial direction, to provide a platform for those views has, in my view, seriously damaged its credibility in the North where the other media suffer no such constraints. It seems a negation of the democratic process to ban elected representatives from the airways. It is as true to say that no democracy should negate the principle of free speech as to say that no democracy can tolerate terrorism.[1]

What is the attitude of other European governments to the transmission of news, information and comment? Was the Irish television service unique in retaining for the Government the control of broadcasting as laid down by the 1976 Amendment Act Section 16 (1)? The powers to be vested in the Minister were quite explicit:

Where the Minister is of the opinion that the broadcasting of a particular matter or any matter of a particular class would be likely to promote, or incite to, crime or would tend to undermine the authority of the State, he may by order direct the Authority to refrain from broadcasting the matter or any matter of the particular class, and the Authority shall comply with the order.[2]

How widespread was this approach in the legislation governing public service broadcasting in democratic countries with which Ireland might be compared?

While differences exist among countries and among classes of communication services in Europe, in most the press is unregulated whereas the electronic media are tightly controlled, either by government or by parliament or by both. Supervision is highly centralized and there is little evidence of the public's being able to influence program content, or to determine social responsibility. In Italy a parliamentary committee ensures political independence of broadcasters and the objectivity of feature programs. In Belgium it is forbidden to broadcast programs contrary to the laws of public interest, or contrary to public order or morality in a manner that does violence to opinions of others, or which offends foreign states. In Switzerland programs are expected to defend and develop the cultural values of the country, and contribute to the spiritual, moral, religious, civic and artistic formation of the country. In Norway there is no legislation laying down either positive obligations or imposing restrictions or constraints. In Denmark, all views of a political and related nature

[1] Jim Dougal. 'The Media and the 'troubles',' *Irish Broadcasting Review* No. 13, (Spring 1982).
[2] Broadcasting Authority (Amendment) Act 1976, Section 16(1).

which are of general interest shall be heard. Care must be taken that opinions against democracy are not given in apparently political programs. There must be no sensationalized or colored reporting. The goal to strive for is a natural evaluation of what is true and essential. Program material and questions of principle concerning political broadcasting must be submitted to a Radio Council which is appointed by the Minister of Cultural Affairs. Sweden requires those responsible for broadcasting to uphold democratic values, observe balance between different opinions, afford right of reply to correct false statements, respect privacy save in cases of overriding public interest, and retain copies of all broadcasts for six months so as to provide access for those who consider themselves to have been unfairly represented. Austria requires that the opinions of legally recognized societies and institutions must be respected and that broadcasts relating to national policy must be distinguished by a high sense of responsibility. In the Netherlands, by the Broadcasting Act of March 1974, the Minister appointed 'shall be in charge of the general policy with regard to broadcasting and the resulting supervision in virtue of the provisions of this Act.' The Minister has at his disposal television time and the Prime Minister having consulted the appropriate minister may in an emergency lay down rules in respect of supervision of transmissions. In normal times control of programs was to be post-factum.

The most liberal constitution ever known in Germany was ratified in 1949. Section 1 of the Basic Law deals with basic rights and may not be altered in substance. Article 5 which guarantees freedom of opinion, information and Press in the Federal Republic of Germany declares, *inter alia*, Everyone has the right freely to express or disseminate his opinions in words, writing and images and to inform himself unhindered from generally accessible sources. Press freedom and the freedom of reporting by broadcasting and film are guaranteed. Censorship shall not take place.

The current situation would appear to belie the liberalism of these statements. Legislation has been invoked to prevent 'anti-constitutional incitement to violent activities' in such a manner as to make even descriptions of historic acts of violence illegal. France has never possessed a public service broadcasting organization of the same model as the BBC. All French governments have used the service in a partisan fashion. During the de Gaulle presidency, opposition politicians were rigorously excluded from access to the air waves, and the Pompidou and Giscard presidencies did not materially alter the situation. Close supporters continued to be appointed to key positions and control over content remained firmly in the hands of the party in government. The advent of the socialist Mitterrand was supposed to herald a new era of open broadcasting with the creation of a High Authority which like the BBC would act as a buffer between the service and the government. However since nominations to this body will remain, as in Ireland, with the government in power, 'control of the broadcasting media, an established facet of French political culture, seems destined to survive the changeover from a Right- to a Left-wing regime.'[1]

The British Broadcasting Corporation is universally recognized as providing a service that is of a quality against which other public broadcasting services might usefully be measured. From Lord Crawford's Committee onwards the concept had been sustained that a public corporation should act as a trustee for the national interest in all of its communication. It is interesting therefore to compare Clause 13(4) of its current License with Section 16(1) of the Irish Act mentioned above,

The Minister may from time to time by notice in writing require the Corporation to refrain at any specified time or at all times from sending any matter or matters of any class specified in such notice.

In addition, Clause 13(3) requires of the Corporation that it

send from all or any of the stations any announcement which (any) such Minister may request the Corporation to broadcast

and at its own expense. The right of veto exists, for all that it has not been called into play. While the right to transmit programs, not of the Corporation's but of any Minister's choosing, is limited to announcements, and whatever is deemed appropriate by any such Minister in whose opinion an emergency has arisen or continues, even so, it does present considerable scope. The fact that successive British Governments have refrained from determining what the BBC does and does not send out rests, in short, as much if not more on convention than on constitutional considerations.

The scarcity of wave frequencies, and the existence of near-monopolies therefore in the electronic media, made it inevitable that any government in the past would retain some ultimate sanctions. What renders their use additionally unnecessary now is the acceptance of certain understandings that govern the conduct of affairs. The first of these is that to be wholly believable means to be wholly independent. Governments have a need to be believed, and this general requirement comes into conflict with the need to present some aspect of policy in a manner that can be anything from a favorable gloss to blatant propaganda. Some governments have opted for credibility, and when the broadcasting is not to their political liking, they have limited their reaction to a private as opposed to a public remonstration. This need to be believed also requires internal independence. Broadcasting staff are expected not to allow personal convictions to influence, any more than they would wish governments to determine, the manner and content of their output. This impartiality has different con-

---

[1] Raymond Keehn, 'Government and Broadcasting: the 1980s', *Political Quarterly*, Vol. 5, (1982), p. 447.

sequences for those in power and for those in opposition, whatever the locus of contending forces. Governments have to cope with trouble, and the mere reporting of that trouble may constitute almost as grave a problem as the original mishap. Given that such trouble is always news, and normality is not, it must appear to those responsible that the media are operating as a temporary extension of the opposition. What ensures nonintervention is the realization that the party in power will one day be the party in opposition, and that reporting will then take on a different aspect. In the meantime, critical and detailed calling to account is one more price that those in power must be prepared to pay, whatever the institution.

The third plank on which the independence of a broadcasting organization is built derives from its public financing. The collection of a license fee and the constant need to seek parliament's approval before an increase can be granted might make alternative methods of providing more attractive, as, for example, a direct government grant. This latter solution has always been resisted in Britain and in Ireland on the grounds that direct financing with its inherent obligation to satisfy the requirements of public accountability and national economic strategy would lead inevitably to erosion of freedom of action. Indeed failure on the part of government to oversee at whatever remove the spending of public money would be tantamount to a dereliction of duty, and since every activity in communications has a price tag, there is nothing that would lie outside their area of jurisdiction. When one considers that the media exist to attract public attention, little if anything would remain uncontroversial when there existed a parliamentary means by which protest could be ventilated. Of the three columns of convention on which broadcasting autonomy reposes, independence as a guarantor of credibility, the democratic freedom to criticize whatever government is in power, the support of financial independence is the most exposed to being undermined, all the more so in that its removal and substitution by direct financing or advertising would be least likely to provoke the outcry that an attack on the other two would assuredly occasion.

The history of media performance in the years 1969–1983 in a Catholic country like Ireland belies the Vatican II Declaration on Religious Freedom that 'The truth cannot impose itself except by virtue of its own truth, and it makes its entrance into the mind quietly and with power.' In 1969 a very successful television current affairs program made a program on money-lending activities in Dublin. Grievous defects were alleged either from honest doubt as to its conclusions or from embarrassment as to the prevalence of this social practice. At all events a judicial tribunal was set up by the government not into the money-lending but into the making of the program with the result that the Broadcasting Authority was criticized for failing to take adequate precautions to corroborate and verify statements; for using illustrative shots which 'went far beyond describing what was actually witnessed and created an impression which was misleading;'[1] for the use of a concealed camera and microphone; and for creating erroneous impressions as to the rate of incidence of money-lending in Dublin, the threat of violence, and laxity by the police force in prosecuting offenders. The programs on Vietnam and Biafra had been discreetly discouraged in the sixties. This conflict had escalated into a full judicial inquiry. Events appeared to be building up to a confrontation. However, the Minister[2] for Posts and Telegraphs was still able to say in April of 1970 that no direction had ever been given by him or by his predecessor under Section 31 of the Act. At the same time, it was interesting to note that RTÉ had decided for its part not to proceed with a program on bank robberies, because the Minister for Justice had not been prepared to appear for the normal discussion that was planned to follow. The same Minister was also to reject the same year the suggestion that the national news media had been requested to publish items of news. The situation would then appear to be that if broadcasting in Ireland was going to take as its remit the reporting and analysis of events, it would remain open to discreet, informal influencing in the amount and manner which the government of the day deemed advisable to exercise. There were defects in the 1960 Act, hairline cracks at the time but which were now tending to become fissures. Irish television brought into Irish homes with some courage and an ever-improving technical competence programs on itinerancy, housing, health and many similar social concerns: it might have also presented itself as an issue whose solution like the others affected everybody. Set up to maintain and promote a culture and at the same time to be self-financing, its administration still had much to learn of 'the loosely structured interaction of human beings which is an indispensable precondition for the exercise of creativity.'[3] The next problem was how to educate the Irish people to appreciate the novelty and 'monstrosity' of television at a level above that of an undeveloped third-world country. Did they want a national megaphone for their own unthinking reassurance or did they want the opportunity to talk to one another constructively, which for a small, politically compact population was an eminently practicable proposition? The other problem of course, as has been and will be shown, lay with the government which was going to have to resist or succumb to the temptation to use the powers it had legislated for itself. The Act had indeed been drafted broadly enough to allow a very wide area of discretion to any party in power which disliked the information that was being pro-

[1] Leon Ó Broin, 'Anatomy of a program', *EBU Review*. No. 127, May 1971, p. 47.
[2] Deputy Lalor, *Dáil Debates*, Vol. 431, 30 April 1970.
[3] John Horgan, 'Irish Television's Trouble', *The Listener*, Vol. 83, no. 2128 p. 34.

vided for the electorate. Opposition deputies protested that the insidious ploy of imposing on the media the obligation to prove legally everything reported – which was what the aggregate of statutory legislation was beginning to compel – meant in effect the erosion of the right of free speech.

On June 24, 1971, the Taoiseach had indicated that it was in his view unsuitable to use a publicly funded broadcasting system to interview members of an illegal organization in a program the Authority were intending to transmit. The Director-General refused to amend the program unless requested to do so in writing, and it had subsequently been broadcast. On this occasion a Labour Opposition deputy, Conor Cruise O'Brien, and a future Minister for Posts and Telegraphs, argued that the best means of enabling the public to form an opinion of the substantiality of the IRA as a political force was to have their spokespersons interviewed, their arguments scrutinized by competent journalists and political analysts, and the extent of what they had to offer as a viable solution to the political unrest thoroughly exposed.

On October 1 of the same year a directive was sent from the government to the Broadcasting Authority to the effect that it was to

refrain from broadcasting any matter that could be calculated to promote the aims or activities of any organisation which engaged in, promotes, encourages, or advocates the attaining of any political objective by violent means.[1]

What had provoked its issuance was the misguided decision by RTÉ to broadcast a denunciation by both wings of the IRA of talks which had been held that very day between the Irish and British Prime Ministers, Messrs Lynch and Heath, immediately after a report on them had gone out on the air. As *The Irish Times* was to editorialize

There has been too much breathlessness on RTÉ. It seemed at times that a Ministerial resignation or some other sensation had to be produced, or announced as being impending, for every programme. The government, by a literal interpretation of its directive, may bring about a state of affairs where the station is not believed at all. If RTÉ has failed to exercise judgment, good direction within that organization, and even staff changes, are necessary.

Better a service which makes mistakes – grave as the result of an indiscretion seen on thousands of screens may be – than a service which people in the North, for example, will now take to be merely Mr. Lynch's mouthpiece and no longer free to tell us what is going on in our country.[2]

The Authority for its part expressed the view that it had an obligation to provide a comprehensive news and current affairs programs, which of necessity included coverage of violent events taking place in Northern Ireland and the comments of the participants. It recognized at the same

[1] Reported in *The Irish Times*, October 2, 1971, p. 1.
[2] ibid., p. 11.

time its responsibilities as a monopoly national broadcasting service, statutorily enjoined to present news and views objectively and impartially. In discharging this duty, incidental publicity might unavoidably derive from the broadcast treatment itself of events and activities. There had been difficulties in determining where the emphasis should fall, but – the Authority went on to argue – it felt that it had at all times acted in the national interest. To avoid further misunderstandings, the Minister might care to elaborate on how his directive should be interpreted. To which the Minister was to reply rather testily that the directive spoke for itself.

On October 4, journalists working for RTÉ condemned the government's action in thus invoking Section 31 of the Broadcasting Authority Act, 1960, insofar as the action would 'jeopardise freedoms which are basic to democracy and cannot fail to undermine the credibility of the service.'[1] That same evening the Taoiseach defended his government's action by claiming that television should not be used against the public's interest and especially in a way that threatened the security of the state. If it had acted otherwise it would have failed the public. He went on to intimate that undesirable propaganda, subjective views and even sensation were much more attractive than the relation of good news to some people responsible for broadcasting. The principal opposition party supported the directive, and few indeed were the voices that were raised to point out its dangers. Was RTÉ to be used as an instrument to carry out the Government's policy against the IRA? What were the consequences likely to ensue if reports were to be denied explanatory comment? Would journalists on the electronic media be inhibited by a consciousness that their role as communicator would be determined by faceless civil servants? If newspapers were to be allowed comment, why should the same liberty be denied the Broadcasting Authority? Was the present diktat the outcome of a Government–Authority relationship which had remained unbroken since the establishment of the latter and was now beginning to reveal the friction of wear and tear as the former sought to impose its will? Was RTÉ a national or a government service? How did one reconcile allowing the IRA to hold meetings and parades with a refusal to subject their claims to the cleansing power of debate?

There were other reservations expressed by a few Labour politicans. 'Acting in a manner prejudicial to the public interest' was a very portmanteau expression and capable of a wide interpretation as indeed were the words of the directive. Issuing instructions to RTÉ was not a suitable response to the IRA who should be either arrested or allowed to make their appeal for a hearing. Informed criticism was more effective than suppression. The resulting inhibitions on journalists, it was feared, would be to

[1] Reported in *The Irish Times*. October 4, 1971, p. 1.

transfer to reporting, and commentary upon, other aspects of government activity the same deference to its policies as Lemass had stated should be the norm in the sixties. If such were the case, then the government itself was conniving in destroying the impartiality and objectivity which it had made such a significant feature in its own legislation.

The problem of political censorship was still not resolved, as time was to show. The Prohibition of Forcible Entry and Occupation Act was aimed at outlawing the protest activities of Sinn Féin and suppressing their newspaper *The United Irishman*. Newspapers were approached again to reduce the measure of publicity given to extra-parliamentary groups, particularly the IRA. Douglas Gageby[1] of *The Irish Times* refused. RTÉ seemed itself to be caught in a quandary of its own making, allowing an Irish language program to carry statements from the President of Sinn Féin while denying the same opportunity to a similar current affairs program. Slowly the idea was forming that any government in power would resent discussion of politics in relation to Northern Ireland taking place outside parliamentary control. Only those who had been elected by the people, so it seemed, could be entrusted with determining how the Irish people should think, or not think, about a problem that was affecting the people who reside in the north-eastern corner of the country. This was the time when the archbishops and bishops of Ireland issued their pastoral letter, *Change in the Church*, in which they pointed out that a certain variety of acceptable reactions to the person and work of Christ was possible. Cultural forces were influencing thinking: the old certainties were going. People should question and attitudes should be challenged, even if the result is some spiritual discomfort. 'We must be prepared to suffer from the pace of change, from the extent of the questionings.'[2] Would the Government react similarly to the position it had taken up on the IRA question?

In November of 1972, the British Prime Minister visited Northern Ireland where he made an important policy statement on future developments in Northern Ireland. RTÉ decided to send a journalist to interview the IRA Chief of Staff to establish whether their point of view had been altered or modified as a result. A lengthy summary of his comments and points of view was broadcast on a current affairs program on November 19, 1972. The police next arrested the IRA Chief of Staff, searched the reporter's house, and demanded that the Director-General hand over the tape recording of the interview. Subsequently, as has been seen, the reporter was convicted for contempt of court in refusing to identify the speaker on tape and sentenced to three months' imprisonment, later reduced on appeal to a fine. The Minister ordered the Chairman to summon

---

[1] Reported in *Hibernia*, October 8, 1971, p. 9.
[2] Reported in 'The Church: A Liberal Change?', *Hibernia*, October 20, 1972, p. 4.

a meeting of the Authority which, it must be remembered, was composed of important people in the cultural life of Ireland who had been selected by the government itself because of their potential contribution to overseeing the running of the broadcasting service. The Authority dutifully met and at the end of a 10-hours discussion informed the Minister that they had done everything possible to lay down guidelines in keeping with his directive of October 1, 1971, the ambiguities in which they had often been at considerable pains to point out. Their constant aim had been to prevent the broadcasting service from being used for the advocacy of violence, and to that end, in the bewildering complexity of political, social, religious and physical aspects of the situation to be contended with in analyzing Northern Ireland affairs, they were satisfied that the RTÉ staff had shown a remarkable sense of duty and a genuine commitment to reporting impartially and accurately. The Authority admitted that in retrospect the interview with the IRA Chief of Staff had been a lapse in editorial judgment and steps had already been taken to ensure a tighter control over critical material.

The Government's reply was to dismiss the Authority out of hand. The responsible minister appeared on television to make the announcement himself and to assure his audience that his decision was what the Prime Minister later described as an exercise in democracy. The community must be protected (as they had had to be protected in the twenties, thirties, forties and fifties against evil literature). The Authority had agreed that 'the offending programme should not have been broadcast in the form in which it was done but had offered no apology, no expression of regret, no indication that they accepted responsibility and no adequate assurance for the future.'[1] One member of this government-maligned group was Professor T. W. Moody, an eminent historian of international reputation. In a letter to *The Irish Times* he observed: 'A democratic society needs to face disagreeable truths, and the best service the communications media can render at a time of grave crisis may well be to help it to do so.'[2] The danger was, as it always has been, that one of the first casualties arising from the curtailment of the freedom of expression would inevitably be truth. The Opposition reaction was to inform the electorate that the decision was a black day for free speech. The minister replied that what he had done had won general commendation, which the same Opposition party decided it too might share in when, on taking up the reins of the government after the next election, they quietly decided to continue it. Those who had misgivings felt that

The notion that mere representation of the views of such bodies necessarily pro-

---

[1] Leon Ó Broin, 'The dismissal of the Irish Broadcasting Authority', *EBU Review*, March 1973, p. 27.
[2] T.W. Moody, Letter to *The Irish Times*, 27 November 1972, p. 11.

vides an opportunity for recruiting new supporters shows a curious lack of faith in the democratic process on the part of those purporting to be its defenders. In any case what the public interest requires should not be confused at any one moment with what the Government currently considers to be in its interest.[1]

When the government went on in the following month to bring in The Offenses against the State (Amendment) Bill, 1972, which would facilitate court action against statements and meetings deemed to constitute an interference with the course of justice, it was patently clear that the right to make up its own mind was going to be denied the public just as it had been denied the right to select its own reading. As for the reporter who had reported the IRA Chief of Staff, he had been transferred to religious programmes. He was fortunate. A John Joseph Denigan, who worked for one of the national dailies, *The Irish Press*, had spent a month in gaol for refusing to divulge the sources of his information. Two journalists had been sentenced to three months in England in the Vassall spy case for the same reason and a British television reporter had been sent to prison by a High Court judge in Belfast. The forces of suppression now were dominant. Fortunately outside the Republic of Ireland there were to be heard the dull sustained rumblings of protest. These were loud enough for Irish journalists to appreciate they were not alone in their resistance.

When the new Government took office, it continued, as has been said, the directive of its predecessor while pondering what form new legislation should take, given the public unease, not so much at the erosion of the right of free speech but at the cavalier way the services of a group of highly respected citizens had been so peremptorily thrown into the discard. Till such time as the new legislation would be brought in, a form of self-censorship ensued. New guide-lines for interpreting the directive were drawn up and to avoid further conflict the part-time chairman and members of the Authority found themselves involved in the pre-transmission consultations of a prior restraint situation – an activity for which they felt themselves no doubt unqualified. Unfortunately the consequences contributed even more to inhibiting whatever initiative remained among journalists to bring events to the people. However, the new Minister, who was later to prove bitterly unyielding in his attachment to Section 31 of the 1960 Act, had done what his predecessor had always refused to do – he had agreed to resolve some of the ambiguities of his own directive. Perhaps as a journalist he had realised the impossible position in which the Authority found itself. At all events, for the first time, a responsible Minister now acknowledged that the guide lines which had been drawn to meet the requirement of the directive were satisfactory. Censorship, at least and at last, possessed a chart on which the reefs and barriers had been marked.

[1] Paul O'Higgins, 'The Irish TV sackings'. *Index*. Vol. 3. pt. 1 (1973), p. 24.

The next milestone was to be the examination of the political conscience of Ireland that accompanied the passing of the Broadcasting Authority Act (1976). As O'Faoláin and others had done in the thirties there
were voices appealing for a return to that particular brand of sanity that
should diffuse through the interstices of democratic reality. By now over
half the population who possessed television sets were receiving BBC and
ITV where, despite 'refer-up' guidelines, an alternative version of the
IRA reality was available. Was it only to be the western coast of Ireland
where, on the presumption that they could not read, people were to be
screened and protected from the call of the IRA? In the meantime the
NUJ protested, went on strike, blacked programs, led deputations, all to
no avail. It was as if successive Governments had made up their minds
that if the IRA weren't seen or heard, they would go away. *Hibernia* and
The Irish Times, and indeed all the national dailies, kept protesting
not only at the iniquity, not only at the futility, but also at the obloquy of
Section 31 that the Irish were so politically dull-witted or so ideologically
volatile that they would succumb immediately to the blandishments of the
first terrorist spokesman they heard. It was all to no purpose. All Irish
politicians seemed to view the communication medium as a cockpit of
contention: they were consequently only totally satisfied with it when
they were able to use it to gain an advantage over their adversaries.
Whether these were the IRA or whether they simply symbolized to the
elected representatives of the Oireachtas the anarchy which existed
beyond the circumference of parliamentary debate, having legislated for
control of the broadcasting service, they were not going to surrender it.
Large-scale cable television was ten years away, and maybe by that time
the problem would have been redefined or the British would adopt a more
positive role of exclusion. In the meantime, if a broadcaster overstepped
the mark by doing for example a piece on internment without trial, there
would have to be explanations. The new minister might well have said
that the Labour party did not believe that the democratic idea was served
by imposing censorship of any kind, but that was in Opposition. The responsibilities of office were such as to preclude the investment in trust
which it would be necessary to make if the journalists of RTÉ were to be
given the opportunity to expose the IRA to a detailed evaluation by the
Irish people.

The new Broadcasting Authority (Amendment) Bill was described by
the Minister as a moderate liberalization. It proposed a revision of the absolute discretion of the 1960 Act which the Minister possessed to prevent
anything being broadcast of which he did not approve. Under the new
Bill, this power was restricted by defining the area of what might be prohibited, by setting a time limit on ministerial directives and by giving the
Dáil the power to revoke them – a power which had not been used regard-

less of who was in power. Another aspect of the Bill gave greater security to the Broadcasting Authority by making it impossible for the minister to dispense with the services of one or all of the members without first tabling a parliamentary resolution.

The minister left to the end of the speech that introduced the Broadcasting Authority (Amendment) Bill consideration of his proposed powers of censorship – a word which he did not shrink from using. He asked the Senate to consider seven questions. Had a democratic state the right to pass repressive legislation? As long as the need continues to exist to protect the weak from the barbarous, the exploiter and the tyrant, 'the democratic State has to save itself on the one hand from being pushed by fear of anarchy into excess of rule and on the other hand to save itself from falling into anarchy through fear of excess of rule.'[1] The second question he posed was, had the State the right to restrict freedom of expression? Language was not confined to rational discourse and every state prohibited racial or religious incitement in its endeavor to secure peace for all its citizens. 'Words are in fact an integral part of many patterns of action. If this is accepted, the absolute distinction between words and actions is broken down, and words and action together become part of a pattern of behaviour which is and should be amenable to law.'[2] Were one to accept the force of this argument, what limitations may be placed on these rights of restraint? A restriction should only be accepted when it can be shown to be for the protection of the citizen and not for the benefit of the ruler. The minister did not allude to the question of who was to do the showing, or to whom, or by whom were decisions to be taken, or finally how the ruler could escape the responsibility of being judge and jury ultimately once he had assigned the role to himself of balancing excess of rule and anarchy.

The minister's fourth question to the Senate was, Should the state have rights in relation to broadcasting that it did not seek in relation to the press? Broadcasting is a public asset and the state in allocating its use must be responsible to its citizens to ensure that it does not endanger the public weal. In addition the Minister felt (and he was to return to this theme on many occasions in the Dáil as well as in the Senate) that

broadcasting, of all the media, both through sound and images, has by far the most immediate impact on people and situations, has by far the greatest capacity to generate emotion, and its capacities in these regards have aroused and held the fascinated attention of people interested in promoting and justifying violence, and strongly desirous of access to broadcasting for precisely these ends.[3]

The minister did not support these conclusions with any empirical evi-

[1] Deputy O'Brien, *Senate Debates*. Vol. 79, Col. 781, 12 March 1975.
[2] ibid., col. 783.
[3] ibid., col. 785.

dence, nor did he advert to the possibility of the critical independence of the viewer to whom the propaganda was pitched. The Irish in this view had become image-dominated so that the imprint on the retina produced automatically action or sentiments hostile to the general welfare. His next question was, If it be granted the state has a right to impose limitations, how far should they extend? One might have expected some development of Millian thought but here the minister limited himself to an enough-but-not-too-much argument, as if the journalist within him was rising to protest against the consequences of the politician's train of thought. Eventually, the literary man was to solve the conundrum by providing a refuge in one of Dr. Johnson's bromides. 'The danger of such unbounded liberty, and the danger of bounding it have produced a problem in the science of government, which human understanding seems hitherto unable to solve.'[1] If Dr Johnson didn't solve the problem, neither did Dr O'Brien.

The sixth question the Minister asked was, When we speak of freedom in broadcasting, whose freedom do we mean and how is it to be defended? How does one protect the broadcaster and at the same time protect the public against any abuse of which the former may be guilty? What was needed was the strengthening of existing structures whereby the Director-General of RTÉ is nominated by and responsible to an Authority which itself has been appointed by the elected government. There could usefully be introduced a classification of the relationships between broadcasting and the state so that the former's freedom and the latter's responsibility should come into sharper focus for the other. The minister did not say there would be an ongoing dialogue or how views and opinions might be mutually adjusted in the interests of the citizen. The last question he asked was, Are there special circumstances which dictate how these principles should be applied? The minister was quite sure of the response: 'In our conditions there are forces at work which tend to turn the normal sturdy sulkiness (*sic*) of the democratic citizen into something rather more disturbing.'[2] These forces were of course those subversive men of violence who were intent on the overthrow of the state. The Irish people, in the minister's view, failed to appreciate the danger to law and order they represented, how close to legitimizing terrorists history and intellectual indolence had brought public opinion, how irresponsibly some communicators had behaved in maintaining a double standard in evaluating the IRA and other illegal organizations, and how necessary it was for the future of the country as a whole that its broadcasting service would give no grounds to anyone for believing that the state was in collusion with evil men.

[1] ibid., col. 786.
[2] ibid., col. 789.

This defense of political censorship was to be generally accepted in the debates that followed in the Senate and the Dáil. There was of course the traditional double-think that espoused an open skies broadcasting and a reaffirmation of the need to control local output. There were some misgivings about a law which legislators were passing that in effect was telling people what they might not say if they did not wish to incur the displeasure of the government of the day, but no mention of the sanctions which might be taken if the law was not respected by the broadcasters. The Minister was in effect combining within his role the function of the Judiciary and the Executive. Again, there were others who feared that the words contained in the Bill, viz, 'Matter likely to promote or incite to crime, or lead to disorder' might just be acceptable in relations to the subversive, but to eliminate reporting of cases where disorders is always an attendant possibility, like strikes, processions, sit-ins, and other conventional forms of protest, would be to frustrate the whole purpose of reporting.

The Bill continued its way through the Senate and the Dáil. The Broadcasting Review Committee set up in June 1971 had reported to the Minister in April 1974. It omitted all reference to the dismissal of the Authority, to guidelines, to whether the Authority had actually discharged its statutory duty in implementing ministerial directives, in short all exploration of sensitive issues was carefully avoided. The elected members in discussing the Bill would therefore have had to draw on their own intellectual resources. Outside the legislature the President of the National Union of Journalists was reported as saying:

'Twelve months ago the Union warned the Minister that the section and the directive – constricting enough in themselves – would develop into an internal creeping censorship far more embracing than was the original intention.'[1]

The annual delegate meeting demanded action and refused the Minister the customary compliment of addressing them at a State dinner. O'Brien responded by reasserting his determination not to allow forms of reporting that could be interpreted as support for the IRA, and went on to declare that

Newspapers had to judge what to do within the law, but if implications of support for unlawful acts were to become prevalent in the State's broadcasting system, the tendency to legitimise the IRA would be greatly strengthened in the eyes of the Republic's citizens.[2]

In the Dáil the Opposition spokesman said:

Somebody must have the power to tell the RTÉ authority when to stop, and the only difference between the Minister and myself is about whether it is the Govern-

---

[1] John Bailey as reported in *The Irish Times*, 27th April, 1974, p. 8.
[2] *The Irish Times*, April 26th, 1974, p. 1.

ment who should tell the RTÉ Authority when they are overstepping or whether it is Dáil Eireann. That is the only difference between us.[1]

One Deputy protested that it was unjust to give the wild men of the extreme right a hearing and yet deny the same facility to the wild men of the left. Was there a fear that a minority view, given a fair share of time on the air and in the newspapers, would become the majority view? The *Irish Times* Editorial warned: 'A democratic Government must not set up itself as an agent of censorship: what it has to do is to strike the balance of moderate opinion. And no man is moderate when his prejudices are put to the question.[2] In the Senate the Minister was accused of paradoxically building up the IRA by the manner in which he exercised his powers of control and was even repudiated by his Coalition partners in the Dáil for his intemperate remarks on the futility of dialogue with the North, showing, it was alleged, the lack of restraint on the basis of which he had refused others permission to broadcast their views. The Minister was reminded that not everything advocated on television won automatic adherents, and least of all violence among a middle class who were not prepared to jeopardise their standards of living, with such a slender prospect of worthwhile returns. But Irish legislators on the whole were more concerned about the provision for a second channel than about keeping the existing one open to all political points of view. Questions of dilution of sovereignty by rebroadcasting British programmes with their impact on Irish moves were safer, better-known and more likely to catch the attention of the electorate than the abstract right of freedom of speech. *The Irish Times* in October of the same year devoted a leader of some 30 column inches, 'Now for the Real Questions' without even mentioning the controversial Section 31 of the 1960 Act, which had now become Section 16 of the 1976 Bill.

Probably the speech that put an end to the discussion on political censorship in the Dáil came from an Opposition deputy, Deputy de Valera. Son of the President, bearing a name identified with the national struggle for independence, he was a man of undoubted integrity, an experienced parliamentarian who had always retained the respect of all professional politicians; he was also Managing Director of one of the national dailies, *The Irish Press*. He was of the opinion, he said, that a television service was a community property of which the Government were the executors who must bear in mind the traditional duties attaching to that office. He felt that authority when delegated 'should be delegated thoroughly because a body or an individual cannot carry responsibility unless he has that inner certainty that comes from security to carry out that responsi-

[1] Deputy Ruairi Brugha, *Dáil Debates*, 30th May, 1974. vol. 273, col. 325.
[2] *The Irish Times*, February 18, 1975. p. 11.

ability.'[1] How the individual or authority was to come by that inner glow of confidence that he or it was doing a good job, given the history of the Broadcasting Authority and the minister's own public pronouncements upon limitations of freedom of expression, the Deputy did not say. Perhaps he experienced some misgivings for he went on to warn the minister of 'the collective force of a psychology that is generated by the administrative machine'[2] of civil servants who in the interests of protecting a minister were not known for encouraging public discussion. 'The only practical and fair form of censorship is the censorship of a mature mind,'[3] de Valera continued. Journalists are responsible people. There may have been a time in the past when there were attempts to infiltrate the media in order to demoralize an area of profound importance and to prostitute an honourable profession. That day was past and had never really amounted to a significant danger. Journalists' judgments of community values were just as likely to be as sound as the government's if only because there was a price tag on the objectivity they brought to the task of selling news. The minister, de Valera considered, was ill-advised to take the powers of Section 16 which would allow him to order the Authority to refrain from publishing an utterance that was 'likely to promote, or incite to, crime or would tend to undermine the authority of the State.'[4] What was crime in the context of broadcasting? Were not these powers more appropriate to a dictatorship than to a democracy? De Valera regretted that the minister had allowed his personal views on the political problem of Northern Ireland to intrude upon the rights of freedom to express alternative views and how these were to be reconciled with the general welfare. Censorship, he concluded, 'defeats itself but if proper standards are encouraged and there is a reasonable approach to these things, in my view there will not be a need for (it) in these matters.'[5]

This was the voice that reflected the balanced view. It represented quite honestly the traditional double-think that could accommodate the liberal distaste for prior restraint and an acceptance of an authoritarian definition of the limits to which it was just to use a public asset to influence political thinking. A spokesman for the political wing of the IRA commenting on the extent of his appearances on television pointed out:

Dr. O'Brien must feel very frightened and incapable of answering our arguments when even this ration of 5 minutes per year is now to be disallowed. In the Six Counties [Northern Ireland] where to use the Dublin Government's own words an 'armed conflict' exists, Republican spokesman appear frequently in both the

---

[1] Deputy De Valera, *Dáil Debates*. Vol. 285, Col. 870, November 4, 1975.
[2] ibid., col. 871.
[3] ibid., col. 875.
[4] ibid., col. 879.
[5] ibid., col. 884.

BBC and UTV. By Dr. O'Brien's own criteria, Sinn Féin is now the fourth largest political organisation in the State, with 26 local councillors elected in the last local elections. But even these elected representatives of the people are banned from RTÉ.[1]

By way of reply the minister issued to RTÉ the following directive which, with updating as more information became available on new subversive organizations, continues to this day, with the 1976 Act replacing that of 1960.

In exercising the powers conferred on me by Section 31 (1) of the Broadcasting Authority Act, 1960, I Conor Cruise O Brien, TD, Minister for Posts and Telegraphs, hereby direct you to refrain from broadcasting matter of the following class, i.e., interviews or reports of interviews with the spokesman for

(a) The Irish Republican Army (Provisional or Official).

(b) Organisations classed as unlawful in Northern Ireland.

(c) Provisional Sinn Féin.

This direction is to remain in force for 6 months from the date of issue, or until the passage of new legislation, whichever be the sooner.[2]

It was probably too much to ask serving politicians to canvass for an extension of the possibilities to solicit public approval when the beneficiaries would be in their view capable of endangering the institutions of state. Certainly there was no avalanche of protests on behalf of the right to communicate. Talisman words like 'public order,' 'civic responsibility,' 'stable government' worked their influence as the legislature processed the Bill through its different stages. And so while the theologians of the Catholic Church were thrusting before the consciousness of the faithful the obligation to use their individual judgment, the Oireachtas was discounting it by reducing its exercise to an area that would be defined by the political outlook of a particular minister. There were few who cared to remind members that media control leads inevitably to a loss of contact with, and awareness of, a reality that is represented by the views of charismatic individuals and enthusiastic minorities who do not fall silent just because one channel of communication is occluded. Opposition parties accepted too much as given. They were accustomed to differing within well-defined areas of contention. They were all too prone to believe the guilty-by-association label that from the McCarthy era had been attached to those who differed from an inchoate but official point of view which it was not profitable to challenge. That the IRA were murderers and thugs was a judgment that could rationally be held, but they were murderers and thugs in the Ireland of the seventies, and there had to be an explanation for that environmental and temporal attribute. Dáil Éireann decided that

---

[1] Seán Ó Bradaigh, reported in *The Irish Times*, October 1, 1976, p. 1.
[2] Deputy O'Brien, *Dáil Debates*, vol. 294, col. 162, 17 November 1976.

it would pass judgment on the IRA identity once and for all, thinking thereby to arrest its image at a point that would obviate the need to challenge the validity of its conclusions. The IRA represented the unknown experience as books imported from Britain and America had represented fifty years earlier the unknown experience to which it was felt it would not be prudent to introduce the Irish. Then as now, the awareness that might be engendered as a result would reflect unfavorably on the inadequacies and shortcomings of the current situation.

The Bill was passed into law and the broadcasters began to feel their way around the inside walls of a never acknowledged consensus which expanded and contracted depending on the Government, the British, the IRA and other socio-political factors. Semi-state bodies which are monopolies like RTÉ have no great incentive to take initiatives in territory which has been officially declared off-limits. There was a philosophic tolerance among media people about the vagaries of their political overlords which competed – at times, unsuccessfully – with their sense of professional outrage. As journalists they learned how to work within the parameters of policy. Guidelines were issued to staff obliging them to ascertain in advance whether the person they proposed to interview belonged to one of the proscribed organizations, not a requirement to be welcomed at the best of times and the best of times were of infrequent occurrence in Northern Ireland. There was, too, an inbuilt reason for not going out after the story that might be uncomfortable or even dangerous when there was little or no possibility of getting it accepted. When the NUJ investigated in 1977 how the prohibitions of the Act were affecting their members' work, the findings revealed unofficial discouragement to dig deep into 'Issues like allegations of RUC ill-treatment of suspects, British "accidental" killings, para-military racketeering, internal paramilitary feuds,' and on the other hand, 'a lop-sided prominence ... given to establishment thinking.'[1] The consequences were predictable. Who wanted to investigate stories whose message would be radically at odds with the Establishment point of view? What satisfaction was there to be derived in following up complaints from interned prisoners or from young girls harassed by British soldiers? Disinterest grew into insensitivity as the nerve ends atrophied in the midst of undercover army activities, kangaroo courts, arson, robbery and murder, all of which were to remain entombed in memory behind the veil of silence.

Censorship, it has been said, is self-defeating, and from the period of the Bards, the one great pacifist equalizer in Irish society was satire. The idiocies of the Censorship Board were now duly matched by decisions at RTÉ that were to make of news transmission an exercise in tragic absur-

[1] Reported in *The Sunday Tribune*. June 11, 1981, p. 17.

dities. A film of a parade outside a gaol was permitted provided there was no accompanying sound so that when a riot broke out, the result looked like a ballet in mayhem. An innocent director of traditional music was interviewed after an erroneous detention by British police with the proviso that no questions be asked that would turn him into a national hero. American activists were shunned, uncomfortable facts were buried, and when brutalization was so evident as to be undeniable, the story was passed on to an English network. This pusillanimity was not mirrored throughout the country. County Councils protested at the discriminatory treatment accorded to elected representatives. The junior section of the two main political parties condemned the double standards of reporting as practiced by RTÉ. Letters, articles, protests, deputations, all complained at the distortion brought about by the censorship that permitted a duly elected member of the British House of Parliament to appear on every screen in the English-speaking world, but not on an Irish screen. Local dignitaries were fined for refusing to pay their television license as a protest against the Act, pickets were mounted on national monuments, a television historical series was threatened, and the same air of bathos hung over RTÉ as had hung over the Censorship of Publications Board in the forties. All was to no avail. Each year regardless of which government was in power the guidelines were renewed.

In 1982 the prohibition was carried one step further. The RTÉ Authority had allocated two minutes on radio and two minutes on television to a political party, Provisional Sinn Féin, in accordance with electoral arrangements established as the potential of the medium came to supplement the traditional methods of appealing to the electorate. The minister on being apprised of the decision – RTÉ had no alternative – issued a directive excluding all broadcasts by the party. His statement was to the effect that 'Such prohibitions must remain in force until such time as Provisional Sinn Féin formally and publicly renounced violence and arranged for its terrorist wing to surrender its weapons, explosives and other instruments of murder and destruction.' The Provisional Sinn Féin Executive through one of its candidates for election thereupon engaged Seán MacBride to challenge the directive in the High Court on the grounds of its unconstitutionality. The Government as respondent was in consequence ordered to explain the imposition of the prohibition. The judge found in favor of the plaintiff on the grounds that the legislation which had excluded him from broadcasting did not appear to contain sufficient safeguards for the constitutional guarantee of the right of freedom of expression of opinion. The Government asked for a stay of execution and applied to the Supreme Court. *The Irish Times* carried an editorial the same day. As regards the judgment in favor of Provisional Sinn Féin candidates, it said 'there are few people so foolish as to vote for them: but it could do much for freedom of speech, which the Constitution guarantees but of which Governments seem so nervous.'[1] Five months later the Supreme Court handed down its decision upholding the appeal by the Government. The Chief Justice found that the Provisional Sinn Féin candidate had been deprived of a benefit lawfully accorded to him. He also noted thàt he was a member of an organization which aimed at undermining the authority of the state, a fact which he did not deny. 'Under the provisions of Article 40 of the Constitution the State is bound to ensure, inter alia, that radio or television shall not be used to undermine public order or morality or the authority of the State... A democratic State has a clear and bounden duty to protect its citizens and its institutions from those who seek to replace law and order by force and anarchy, and the democratic process by the dictates of the few.'[2] Accordingly the Court was of the opinion that the various grounds on which the exclusion of any order made by the minister had been assailed were not tenable in law, and therefore dismissed the appeal. The judgment is not rich in insights into the working of the constitutional right of freedom of expression within the conditions laid down to safeguard public order. However, it is important in the evolution of thinking about how the freedom of expression may be interfered with at peril to those who seek to curtail its benefits. First, the Supreme Court did not declare the particular sub-section of the Broadcasting Act to be unconstitutional, but neither did they declare its constitutionality, thereby leaving open the possibility of its being challenged. More important, however, as in the Irish Family Planning action, the first step had been taken in reviewing a ministerial order. Sufficient precedents already existed, e.g. the East Donegal Co-Operative case,[3] which made it mandatory for such orders to be issued in a manner that did not impair a citizen's rights or offend the principles of constitutional justice. The Court had made it quite clear that it was prepared to review the Censorship Board's decision. It was now serving notice again that no minister had unfettered powers in relation to the administration of an Act. In so doing it was reversing decisions it had taken itself in 1940 and 1957 when powers given to the minister under the Offenses Against the State (Amendment) Act, 1940, to detain a person were reviewed. Judicial orthodoxy hàd changed, and any decision taken by a minister must be factually sustainable and in accordance with reason. In short, the Minister for Posts and Telegraphs henceforward might be challenged in the courts if he prohibited a broadcast, and if he were unable to show that the authority of the state would be undermined by its transmission, his prohibition would be set aside.

[1] Editorial, *The Irish Times*, February 17, 1982, p. 13.
[2] *The State (Lynch)* v. *Cooney and the Attorney General.* (1982. No. 58 ss) I.R. 365.
[3] I.R. (1970) 317.

There appeared therefore to be some light at the end of the tunnel, but what did the broadcasters themselves think of the situation? The Annan Report had quoted with approval the BBC contention that its function was 'to ensure that every view likely to impinge upon public opinion was reflected at some time in BBC programmes. It was the responsibility of the public to realise 'when some of these voices are not valid voices, and were voices that indeed would undermine the very fabric of society'.'[1] Was this the view that was held by the policy-makers in RTÉ? Certainly the press they received throughout the decade left very little unrevealed about the constraints that were being imposed on their broadcast performance. Each year as the Minister duly laid on the table of the Dáil the directive that proscribed certain organisations, there was inevitably a review of the limitations that had been imposed on the functioning of a service that sought professionally to provide the public with what it needed to know in a democratic polity. 'DO NOT ADJUST YOUR SET – INTERFERENCE IS NORMAL'[2] is a typical headline of those that appeared in newspapers and periodicals during the period under review. Others were, 'Hear no evil, see no evil, speak no evil,'[3] 'RTÉ Ban on More Groups',[4] 'RTÉ ban violates rights of free speech – counsel'[5] and many more which came to light during research. Interference was manifest. Government interposition between the teller and the story was so well documented that it was understandable that certain reservations might be entertained as to how far RTÉ was discharging its responsibilities to the public as distinct from what it was doing to conform to the informal policy wishes on day-to-day events as made known by its political masters. Interviews were therefore sought with upper-level communication personnel in RTÉ and with their senior news reporter in Belfast (See Appendixes). The factual content on which general conclusions were based was subsequently validated with the participants.

In the views expressed, it was obvious that restraints imposed by law, by the restraints built into the Broadcasting Acts and by a sense of civic responsibility were accepted and recognised as necessary principles. At the same time, 'Is é dualgas an chraoltóra bheith ag iarraidh briseadh trí na teortha sin i gcónaí (It is the broadcaster's duty to try always to break

---

[1] *Report of the Committee on the Future of Broadcasting.* Chairman: Lord Annan. Cmnd 6753. HMSO 1977, p. 268.
[2] Jim Keady 'DO NOT ADJUST YOUR SET – INTERFERENCE IS NORMAL' *Hibernia*, Dec. 17th, 1976, p. 4.
[3] *The Sunday Tribune*, Feb 1, 1981, p. 9.
[4] *The Irish Press*, Oct 20th, 1976, p. 1.
[5] *The Irish Times*, Feb. 17th, p. 11.

through these limitations).''[1] Broadcasting, it was felt, was not just an obligation towards individuals, governments and the Opposition, or to any other sector in society, but rather to all the people whose communicative needs must be respected if the public service ideal is to have meaning. In providing this service, those responsible had to face, on the one hand limitations on what they might say and, on the other, compete with a much more powerfully resourced organisation which could say what it dared not. There had been a curious double-think on the part of legislators, urging 'open windows' to what came from abroad, and at the same time slamming doors to keep unseen and unheard what existed at home. Prior to the issuing of the directives the journalistic coverage of national affairs had been praised for its balance and independence. Now it was very obviously less than credible, and its deficiencies would be felt all the more keenly as interpretation of events in Northern Ireland continued to suffer the shortening of perspective and the distortion of incompleteness due to the obligation to broadcast by the guidelines (See Appendix 3). The necessity to get clearance from the Director-General himself before any programme is initiated in relation to the proscribed participants in Northern Ireland and the absolute exclusion of sound-recordings or sound on film might not be 'intended to put obstacles in the way of RTÉ staff professionally concerned with news and current affairs programmes', but their effects remained nonetheless inhibitive.

No one in these interviews attempted to strike an attitude of offended professionalism or injured integrity on the grounds that the information he wished to transmit had been subjected to this political screening. Neither was there any attempt to minimise the seriousness of censorship for a people in both parts of the island where the only possible means of mitigating the disastrous consequences of well-nurtured prejudices was the provision of news that sought to be impartial, objective and comprehensive. Violence that is depersonalised breeds apathy. The terrorist who has been banned from communicating in person cashes in on the public relations effectiveness of trained broadcasters who are limited to repeating his words but cannot discard their own innate skills in their presentation. Everyone was agreed that 'We must maintain a minimum consensus, about murder and a few other things, and allow nothing to weaken that consensus, or dilute people's natural abhorrence of cruelty by presenting its perpetrators as excusable,'[2] but was this attitude, it was pointed out, any more likely when the 'perpetrators' were never presented al all? During the course of these interviews there was no attempt

---

[1] Seán MacRéamoinn quoted in Mícheál Ó hUanacháin, 'The Broadcasting Dilemma', *Administration*, Vol. 28, No. 1 (1980), p. 62.
[2] John Kelly, 'Are our broadcasting structures out of date?', *Irish Broadcasting Review*, No. 2, (Summer 1978), p. 6.

to suggest that the IRA did not constitute a threat to Irish society. What was pointed out however was that the existence of this threat, far from evoking a determination to protect the liberties its presence endangered, in effect was being perversely capitalized upon to erode the power of the very institution that could reveal its menace. A former chairman of the RTÉ authority had written once about the safeguarding of institutions:

The preservation of the status quo is not necessarily always in the public interest: neither is the public interest always in complete harmony with every action or lack of action by government. A democratic society assumes that its broadcasting system should serve the public interest. It requires a great deal of freedom to discharge this responsibility.[1]

There was not much evidence from what was said that this freedom was forthcoming. No one in communications had any illusions about the absoluteness of its enjoyment for anyone but the owners and controllers of the media. They, as broadcasters, had a license from the government to broadcast, and licences by their very nature could be withdrawn or modified. They did not propose to claim access to information that would place Cabinet secrets on the same level of availability as results from sporting fixtures. They were conscious that there was a grave danger that they might end up worshipping their own image with all its omniscient and infallible aura of a priesthood bringing enlightenment to the ignorant. Yet when all these concessions to reality had been made, their duty as professional broadcasters working for a service funded by public money was to do their best to report events truthfully and intelligently. Their task would involve them in investigating where government policy would prefer they didn't and reporting their conclusions in a manner the government would consider not to be in the public interest. There should be tension not accommodation if the public and the government are going to be provided with real choices. The real danger was the part of the iceberg that wasn't seen. The truth that wasn't the whole truth provided misinformation because when people were told to look and listen they concluded that they had been given all they needed to know. Maybe everybody who told a tale was in fact a liar by virtue of what he left out. But if he told the truth as he knew it, at least he wasn't lying to himself. The knowledge he had that he was keeping faith with his audience was their best guarantee that the service was dependable.

The impression gained from these interviews is that a deep sense of professional frustration is shared at all levels of the Broadcasting Authority, if not by all its members. There is evidence in what was said in these interviews of an injured pride, an impatience with rumors of an infiltration that

---

[1] Dónall Ó Móráin, 'The Irish Experience', *Irish Broadcasting Review*, No. 10, (Spring 1981), p. 21.

was so pervasive as to be able to deflect the purpose of the organization, and a feeling of bafflement that so little was understood of the science and skill of communication. Irish politicians had made up their minds that television was a 'monster' that could only be tolerated as long as it was kept in captivity. The medium was a way of getting at an invisible public, and because they rightly contrasted their techniques with those of the professional broadcaster to the detriment of their own, they did not oppose the minister when he decided to restrict certain areas of public interest in which this expertise if given full play might drown out the sound of other messages. The theology of political censorship as has been seen was provided by journalists turned politicians. As late as 1981, one was writing of his belief that there was

at least room for an honest division of opinion among broadcasters about whether it is actually essential, in order for television journalists to tell the truth about terrorism, or about Northern Ireland, that terrorists or their spokesmen should be offered the kind of legitimation that direct access to the eleectronic media tends to confer.[1]

Whatever about the nature of this 'legitimation' which the medium would 'tend' to confer, whatever about playing Hamlet in the absence of the Prince, the political broadcasters in RTÉ found it hard to relish the academic exercise of arguing the best ways of telling 'the truth about terrorism' when the decision had already been anticipated. There was no evidence to show that anyone had actually been influenced in their political thinking by ideological communications from the air. If Britain were to serve as a useful yardstick of comparison, there would be grounds for assuming that the anxiety and fears of politicians were largely exaggerated. It would not be of course the function of the broadcasters to highlight this probability. The IRA was the evil exterior of a legitimate ideal that was as variegated as those who pursued it, but which in every case contained an unyielding demand for a justice that had been too long withheld. Its achievement portended trouble that would come from the streets where its denial was most keenly felt but should not be left there unresolved. The way forward was through politics from which no man could stand aside but it must be a politics for all vocabularies, if those who heretofore had preferred the sword to the pen were to be persuaded their present course was an exercise in futility. The current censorship gave a credibility to myth and rumor, was responsible for the suspended judgment of the uncommitted, fed the gnawing doubt of the student of comparative politics who has seen too many terrorists rehabilitated. Murphy

[1] John Horgan, 'Broadcasting and the Politicians' *Irish Broadcasting Review*. No. 11 (Summer 1981).

put one side of the case in urging that a trial modification of Section 31 should be considered.

It might be no harm to let the godfathers of violence be cross-examined on radio and television, to have their pseudo-historical mythology exposed, to hear them justify sectarian terrorism and have them tell us how the honour of Ireland is served by the murder of a civilian Protestant bus driver before the eyes of his young Catholic charges.[1]

Such apologetics, and whatever other insights are relevant, continued to be denied to Irish audiences. Cruise O'Brien, who had made the exclusion of the IRA from the communication scene an act of statesmanship in which other politicians might (and did) concur, wrote once of the troublesomeness of the Antigones of this world who do not respect the formulae in making their point.

We should be safer without the trouble-maker from Thebes. And that which would be lost, if she could be eliminated, is quite intangible: no more, perhaps, than a way of imagining and dramatising man's dignity. It is true that this way may express the essence of what man's dignity actually is. In losing it, man might gain peace at the price of his soul.[2]

It would be a reasonably safe prediction that the Irish people would consider the IRA's way is not 'this way', but in censoring the knowledge they needed to form their own judgment, the mute testimony of bodies in the dust would continue to subtract that amount of conviction from their verdict.

The printed media in Ireland represent a different story, a story that is replicated throughout the western world. A history of freedoms won down through time, a governing factor of economic viability, a lack of instantaneity that permits reflection and dialogue, a new conception of media complementarity, and a purposeful catering for a segmented audience would leave Irish newspapers going with mainstream development. The fact that they carry the highest value-added tax of papers in the West is a reason to expect their progress not to be other than sluggish. There has been over the period a tendency to blur dissimilarities, an unwillingness to be identified with any one institution or ideology, and a general convergence towards the middle ground of consensus that eschews a sustained radicalism found for example in the defunct periodical, *Hibernia*, and, equally, a toe-the-line conservatism that once kept an open connection to the religious, republican or ascendancy Establishment. As the capitalist press does not disregard socialist taste elsewhere, no Irish newspaper can, on the one hand, afford to ignore populist interest, nor can it,

---

[1] John A. Murphy, 'Tackling the Crisis', *Irish Broadcasting Review* no. 16 (Spring 1983), p. 26.

[2] Conor Cruise O'Brien 'Views' *The Listener* Oct 24th, 1968, p. 257.

on the other, fail to rise to the challenge to offer the in-depth treatment of particular topics, the expert assessment, the backgrounding and informal comment which the 'massness' of the electronic media might find inappropriate to supply.

Evidence of government attempts to censor newspapers in the Republic of Ireland is not available on a basis that could be supported in a court of law. Compared to the press in the United States or in most other European countries, or indeed to what it published a hundred years ago, the press in contemporary Ireland is traditionally very restrained in its treatment of politicians. There is a reluctance to intrude too much on personal inadequacies, though this self-denying ordinance has been broken more frequently in recent years as the vagaries of domestic politics stray more and more into the domain of the bizarre. As commercial ventures, the daily and provincial press are not immune from pressures from those with power in the community and from those who advertise. There are legal restraints to do with official secrets, emergency legislation, forcible entry, criminal law, sub-judice matters and the law of libel that can persuade the press to shelve a good story, to abandon a line of investigation, to leave out relevant details, to apologize in short when the instinct prompted further attack. One editor observed that his fear of libel cases in Ireland was not so much due to being wrong, or having to pay heavy damages, but to the obligation to be, with other members of his staff, more or less out of contact for months prior to going to trial.

The anti-terrorist legislation that has been on the statute books since the foundation of the state has resulted not in concrete acts of censorship, but in irritating confrontations with police officers or overzealous civil servants determined to seize upon infractions of statutory laws or regulations whether intended or otherwise. Thus a photographer was fined because his camera shot inadvertently took in a defense building. A journalist was abused because he accurately reported a Government Minister making a speech he would rather had been omitted from the record. *The Irish Times* was threatened with proceedings under the Official Secrets Act because it was intending to publish information that would reflect discredit on another minister's negotiating decisions. O'Brien revealed that he kept letters which had been published on the IRA in one of the national dailies.

When one turns next to litigation to find evidence of control of freedom of expression, the situation is not very different from that which would obtain in most countries. The *Sunday World* published an account of guardianship proceedings in which offensive comments were made on the treatment of such cases and carrying the implication that justice would not be available in Irish courts. Despite unqualified apologies both editor and journalist were fined. O'Higgins, C.J. in his findings stated that

The offense of contempt by scandalizing the court is committed, when, as here, a false publication is made which intentionally or recklessly imputes base or impro-per motives or conduct to the judge or judges in question.[1]

The right of free speech depended on the observance of an acceptable limit and did not extend to statements that would undermine public order or the authority of the State.

The next case involved *Hibernia*, the radical periodical which enjoyed considerable popularity among intellectuals. Following a sentence of death passed on a man and wife, it published two letters of condemnation of the sentencing court, the Special Criminal Court, one of which was written by a student and the other by the Public Relations Officer of a De-fense Committee organized on behalf of the couple. The first letter pro-tested at the manner in which the 'trial' (*sic*) was carried out and the other claimed that 'The only evidence against the Murrays (the guilty couple) were statements which they claim were extracted by the gardaí under physical and mental torture.'[2] The Court found that the proceedings in the trial court had been misrepresented and that in view of the fact that it had been reported at length in three Dublin newspapers, there was no mitigation of circumstance that would justify their not finding the Editor of *Hibernia* in contempt. The case is interesting in that it is marked by its punishment of the offender (a conditional order of sequestration against the company as well as a conditional order for attachment for contempt against the editor) which stands in great contrast with their decisions of fifty years earlier. The matter complained of was two unsolicited letters, published in a small magazine of limited circulation. There had been no mention of judges, the court case was a subject that had interested the public, and the forum of Letters to the Editor did not in the defense's opinion constitute evidence of an editorial intent to bring the Court into contempt. One last point, the High Court's earlier decision in favor of the defendant had been appealed by the Director of Public Prosecutions – a step that was without precedent.

The third case involved *The Irish Times*. It related to the same husband and wife who had been found guilty of the murder of a garda and had been sentenced to death. During the appeal that followed, the paper published under the heading 'Cabinet may urge easier sentence,' a news item which contained the paragraph below:

The Association of Legal Justice (Dublin Branch) said that it condemned the sen-tences unreservedly. It was particularly reprehensible because it was passed by the Special Criminal Court, a court composed of Government-appointed judges having no judicial independence which sat without a jury and which so abused the

---

[1] *In re Kennedy and McCann* (S.C. No. 142 of 1975) I.R. 1976, p. 387.

[2] Quoted in *In Re Hibernia National Review* (S.C. No. 121 of 1976) I.R. 390, 14 July 1976.

rules of evidence as to make the court akin to a sentencing tribunal. The imposition of the death penalty for the murder of the garda was illogical as it destroyed the principle that violence begot violence.

Henchy J. in his judgment said it was difficult to conceive of an allegation more likely to undermine the reputation of the Special Criminal Court as a source of justice since it implied that the judges concerned were unfit to hold judicial office of any kind. He found that 'In short, the facts adduced in this application to commit for contempt (to which facts no rebuttal has been offered) institute a classical example of the crime of contempt by scandalizing a court.'[1] In the circumstances it is difficult to imagine how he might have found otherwise. Certainly there was no suggestion subsequently of a deliberate and concerted attempt by the courts to muzzle the press. What newspaper editors were to object to was the uncertainty about how to report proceedings in future.

There were other cases during the period but these three are rightly considered to be the most significant. The Constitutional guarantee of 'the right of citizens to express freely their convictions and opinions' had been held to be subordinate to the dignity of the court, the impairment of which was equated with the undermining of public order or morality or authority of the State. It appears to be a somewhat forced conclusion to suggest that the effects of what had been published were quite as consequential as the Supreme Court claimed. All three, for reasons given, would certainly have not encouraged editorial staff to avail of their right to criticize the court, its procedures and findings. What was already been quoted earlier, 'Justice is not a cloistered virtue: she must be allowed to suffer the scrutiny and respectful, even though outspoken, comments of ordinary men,'[2] must have appeared to one of the editors held in contempt to be now devoid of meaningfulness. And yet the activist construction put on contempt of court, or on scandalizing of the court, could not by any means be interpreted as censorship. All the editors acknowledged their guilt, all bemoaned the particular stringency of the Irish libel laws that left the author, publisher and printer liable for damages, but the only protest that emerged was at the condignness of the punishment and the imponderability of how to couch further comment on judicial decisions.

Since there was no record of government censorship of the press and no one was so aggrieved by the operation of the law to claim that the courts were organized in a conspiracy to subvert the freedom of speech, another source of evidence that remained to be tapped was the national and provincial newspapers. Accordingly, interviews were conducted with the editors of the *Irish Independent*, *The Irish Times* and *The Irish Press*.

---

[1] *The State (D.P.P.)* v. *Walsh*. I.R. 442, 6 February 1891.
[2] See page 18.

With each the format was the same. A definition of censorship was agreed, viz. as that concept which is used to describe the processes whereby constraints are imposed upon the collection, diffusion and inter-change of information, views, opinions and ideas. Then the following seven statements were read, and each editor asked to comment in relation to himself and to his journalist staff. Where there was a significant discre-pancy in the reactions provoked, the collation of their answers bears wit-ness to the fact, but overall there was unanimity about censorship in the midst of a great divergence of views on other topics.

1. *Self-censorship in a newspaper occurs when an individual or the organi-zation, for conscious or unconscious motives, refrains from expressing in the appropriate form the contents of the communication.*

This form of self-censorship is pragmatic. Every editor has his antennae unconsciously attuned to libel, the Official Secrets Act, contempt of court, etc., so that he almost automatically cuts himself off when he wan-ders into any one of these minefields. He really is in trouble when he finds he has to go with his convictions, and print what he feels is appropriate. He knows he is committing himself not so much to the loss of money as to the loss of time. Libels are annoying because most of them are trivial and technical and are cheerfully settled out of court even though the extent of the damage for the 'victim' is minimal. As a result, when there is no great issue riding, the best plan when in doubt is to drop the whole matter and not to print. But the practice does tend to make editors a little too fearful for the paper's good. In addition, there is a certain amount of reserve, a disinclination to go into an account beyond the safe limits where, in fact, probably the public interest would really call for more investigation.

2. *Social censorship is when society or one or more of its sub-sets, groups, institutions or agencies declares out of bounds the expression of certain ideas and opinions as to content or to form, or to both. To the dissident newspaperman it may appear to be moral conscription, to the conformist it is no more than an act of social functionalism.*

Protests happen, with gratifying frequency, because it is good to know that somebody is out there reading, and thinking about what he or she has read. The reply is standard. The incident occurred, or the event took place, or the person said or did what is described in the newspaper. There is regret expressed if there is offense taken but the function of the news-paper organization is to report. There is no emotional overrider or politi-cal, philosophical or economic consideration that decides exclusively what goes in and what stays out. The duty that a journalist imposes upon himself in return for what John Citizen gives him for the news he sells is to tell honestly what has happened here in Ireland and outside in the world, not objectively for that claim would be pretentious, but as accurately as the reporter can make it and the collective brain of the editorial executive can organize it. Life is not pleasant, and its depiction can be criticized either for its presentation or omission. Most responsible Irish newspapers would prefer to sin against the first than be held guilty for crimes against the second.

3. *Legal censorship differs from social censorship in that sanctions are involved for those newspapers and their staff who transgress. These can be punitive to the extent that they constitute a form of prior restraint.*

There have been rumors, and indeed more than rumors, actual verbal menaces from ministers that proceedings would be taken against newspapers who failed to toe the line in relation to reporting the IRA. Among working journalists the imposition of Section 31 on RTÉ which is staffed by responsible and competent journalists appears as a ludicrous abuse of executive clout. One editor, speaking for all, indicated quite forcibly to a minister that there was no way that journalists in the print medium would ever be told what they could print. Apart from the politico-legal side which does not affect newspapers, however, precautions do have to be taken. An awful lot of trouble can be avoided by rewriting, rephrasing or resequencing ideas so that defamation, libel, or whatever can be turned into fair comment. There is always the day though when the embroidery will not work. Then the newspaper has to lay it on the line, or face internal disaffection that can eventually be more deleterious than an adverse court judgment. One editor was more Farragut in his approach. If the story was in the public interest, get the facts, publish them and face the fine later. Even paying it will be news.

4. *There may be censorship which is not legal but assumes legality because of the position of the person who wishes to impose his will. How does your newspaper cope with demands from Ministers, Police, Clergymen, and others of sufficient social stature, who wish to censor the contents of your paper?*

No editor had any experience of an intervention by an individual of eminence, political, civic or ecclesiastical, who had made personal overtures to have something censored. It would not however be true to suggest that any paper is immune from those influences with which its policy concurs. A paper with a strong Catholic conservative background is more likely to be nuanced to what is church thinking on any topic, just as another paper with a long republican tradition or a liberal newspaper would be exposed more easily to protagonists of ideas congruent with their own. Most papers are moving to the center, and the days of belief in the unique solution are gone. This movement has been more pronounced with a paper that was to the right of the political spectrum, and as it sought a new position and a new alignment of ideas, its susceptibility to any influence from any fixed source grew progressively less. The attitude of all editors is based on a mixture of survival and self-respect. What chance would they have as a commercial concern if there were a scintilla of suspicion that their contents were amenable to influences that lay outside the newspaper sphere? A national daily has a duty. That duty luckily happens to be a blueprint for its continued existence. It wasn't virtue, it was sheer pragmatism that made them print the news as they, and they alone, saw it.

5. *Voluntary censorship is when a free newspaper accepts the curtailment of its communications because of reasons that take precedence over its own purpose, e.g. during a war. There may be other occasions when the interests of image, associations, or professional codes cause your paper to exclude certain matters.*

Newspapers do not and should not refrain from attacking other newspapers. Each paper has its own conscience and anything printed which offends in another newspaper should be attended to without reservation. A scandal about people in high places should be covered by all newspapers, though each would need to be convinced it was news and not gossip. Being a national does not make one immune from small town tittle-tattle. There are limits, of course, but it would be impossible to lay down in anticipation any hard and fast rules. It is an editorial decision based on how the story breaks and each one must be decided on its merits. If that is censorship, so be it. That is the style of the newspapers, a symbiotic judgment of editor and staff that is articulated all right but about which no treatises get written. In short, one prints what one finds, but not everybody goes looking in the same places.

6. *Indirect censorship is when someone who is not a party to the transaction places a barrier on its completion, as for example when a bookseller refuses to carry an author's books or a newspaper refuses to run a particular story. Any comment?*

Every day, stories end up on the spike, for reasons that have been mentioned. Sometimes, it is a matter of choices, and if rejection means censorship, then every paper is guilty. There is however not enough room to carry all the stories, letters, features, articles, etc., that offer themselves for printing each time a paper is made up. There has to be selection, and the judgment is not always infallible. Oddly enough, levity, humor, and material that would make people relax, whether it is unavailability or censorship, the fact remains, not enough of it appears in newspapers. Any story that can be substantiated will appear in the newspaper.

7. *Is there censorship of newspapers in Ireland?*

Two editors said *no* categorically and the third qualified his negative. There were stories, documentaries, investigative reports, analyses and factual accounts that were not being written. It was censorship by anticipation. No one in Ireland was going to investigate alcoholism among the clergy, discrimination against homosexuals, the large family as a reason for lack of economic progress, the private fortunes made by ministers of government, and so on. They were difficult stories, and could often be judged not worth the trouble they would cause in putting them together. But their existence should be borne in mind every time there is too much talk about reporting all the news. One last point. Journalists are not above having recourse to the laws of libel because papers have published reports critical of, or have disavowed, their contributions. However much it may be pleaded that journalists who live by the words, should rely on them, they have the common tendency to want to censor out of existence that which displeases.

These three interviews were supplemented by an interview with the editor of *The Sunday Tribune* and the editor of the periodical, *Hibernia*. Both were more radical, but fundamentally their attitudes were similar to authority as represented by the Government or Church. No one interfered with what they wished to print, and it was unimaginable that any institution or corporate body would attempt to do so in the way control was exercised in RTÉ. They appreciated the fine quality of social reporting that went on in television, but its advantage in immediacy was compensated for by its loss in freedom. Given these findings about the daily newspapers, the next question was how about the provincials? Of these there are over fifty listed in the yearly *Administration Handbook*. Questionnaires (see Appendix 4) were sent to forty-two, that number being chosen because in some cases the same paper is printed under a different masthead, but with local news and advertisements the only variables, whereas others editorialize for different sectors of their sales area while retaining the same logo. Returns were obtained from 24 or 57%. Average circulation was 15,000, ranging from 5,000 to 35,000. The average number of years under current masthead is 81 years though with amalgamations of older papers that figure underestimates the measure of continuity. The range is from 2 years to 216. The range of staff, counting part-time correspondents, photographers and more or less permanent free-lance writers varies from 52 to one editor. Because permanent and non-permanent staff were not identified it is not possible to find any useful correlation between the personnel, size of paper (average 20–24 pages) and circulation.

In the questionnaire editors were asked had they ever refrained from printing as a result of pressure brought to hear by forces represented by individuals or institutions. Thirteen responded with a simple 'no' to all the suggested agencies that might have attempted to influence comments. One editor replied with some asperity that he considered it an insult to be asked such questions and was consequently refusing to answer them. The remaining ten made additional comments. One editor adverted to a threat of fire-bombing from the IRA which he had no option but to recognize. Another acceded to a request from a political party to postpone a report. There were also considerations of employment, mental health, subsequent information from local officials casting doubt on the authenticity of the paper's own proposed account, potential damage to a political career, and interventions from clergymen on behalf of families. In some cases there was reference to attempts to bring pressure, threats of withdrawal of advertising and, as might be expected, pleas from defendants found guilty in local court actions. The idea of a local newspaper which so distanced itself from its readers that no attempt at censorship would even be considered by its patrons would be unusual, particularly when the editors of the nationals accepted such attempts to change news content as one of the occupational hazards. Excluding the case concerning the IRA which occurred in a border county, and the one case concerning the politician, a unanimity of resistance to official, private or institutional pressure is manifest in these replies. Within the conditions, impediments and constraints attaching to selling any commercial product, it is quite clear the provincial editors in Ireland are not inhibited about what they publish in their papers.

If the consensus of opinion on the basis of the interviews and questionnaires is indicative of a freedom to print without let or hindrance what is considered of interest to a literate citizenry by national and local editors, what attitude did journalists adopt over the period? There is no rigid divide between electronic and media print journalists in Ireland, individuals passing between newspaper and television work with only minimal exposure to training for broadcasting.[1] The monopoly position of broadcasting, and the absence of a competing service, may have been responsible for a certain fossilization of attitudes, a continuation of restrictive attitudes and a narrowing of outlets for the individual, but it has on the other hand created a certain convergency of professional interests, an intimate awareness of one another's problems and a common reference point which their union, being an affiliate of the British based National Union of Journalists, is able to project on to a wider screen of comparison. In this situation the reaction of Irish journalists as a body to the dismissal of the RTÉ Authority in 1971 was predictable dismay and anger at the violation of a professional code. A deputation was refused a meeting by the Taoiseach and resentment continued to smoulder until the occasion presented itself at the NUJ Annual Delegate Congress held at Wexford in 1974 in which a motion was carried

to continue to press for repeal of section 31, the rescinding of the directive, and the restoration to RTÉ of a right and duty to provide the public of Ireland with a free, impartial and balanced news and current affairs service and to continue its defence of press freedom in Ireland.

---

[1] Peter B. Orlick, 'Systemic Limitations to Irish Broadcast Journalism' *Journal of Broadcasting* 20:4 (Fall 1976) pp. 471 ff.

This was the occasion when the Minister was denied an opportunity to address the Congress. In reply the Minister castigated his critics for being 'hooked on protest' and for an unwillingness to recognise the dangers inherent in the Provisional IRA. The journalists continued to lobby the elected members to Dáil Éireann throughout the remaining years of the period and claimed to have discovered support for changes in Section 31 of the Broadcasting Authority Act.[1] The Head of News criticised its operation to a sub-committee of the Oireachtas: the journalists kept pressure on the Authority itself by temporary withdrawals of labour; and there began to appear resolutions from County Councils and opinions from media experts that if only to spare the nation the embarassment brought about by the anomalies censorship causes, the much deplored Section 31 should be revised, put into temporary suspension or abolished completely.[2] The exclusion from the air of an eye-witness account of a fire in Donegal in which several people perished because the witness happened to be a member of a banned organisation signalled that a level of banality and ludicrousness had been reached so that some remedy seemed inevitable – seemed, but not proved inevitable.

Ireland, for internal and external reasons, is adapting slowly to the concept of a pluralist state. The necessary adjustments are being discussed and debated through the media whose nature and function are in turn being reviewed. The electronic media because of their access superiority to print media will continue to be subject to closer scrutiny as the meanings of the rights of information and rights to information are defined within the Irish polity. The enjoyment of these rights is made possible to the extent that freedoms, public and private, abound. It is the function of government to ensure that the protection of the State does not entail a dysfunctional reduction in the citizen's role of participation in its working. In no country of Europe is broadcasting wholly exempt from parliamentary control. Different powers of policy formation and development are granted to the regulatory bodies which interface with governments and production systems. All governments retain the right of intervention exercised through those appointed to represent the interests of the public. Retrospective supervision of programs guarantees conformity with legal obligations; administrative stipulations or guidelines ensure prior restraint. The extent of this supervision varies from the general in some countries to the detailed in others. Ireland in the European context, it is worth repeating, is not unique. Why then should Irish journalists continue to demand the abrogation of Section 31? Why should Irish governments not have the censorial powers available to other European govern-

---

[1] Report in *The Irish Times*, 31st August 1981, p. 6.
[2] Report in *The Irish Times*, 14th Dec. 1982, p. 11.

ments? Why do the Irish want and need to know more, and not less, of what is being done in their name?

There is a hierarchy of rights which corresponds with the fundamentality of man's needs. Without food or shelter, freedoms of religion or of expression become secondary. At the same time the mere satisfaction of these basic needs does not of itself offer more than the prospect of a biological existence. There is an inner drive to grow, to develop one's potential to renew society, in short to create a meaningful and personal experience out of existence. Such an activity necessitates the co-existence of others to verify and to extend one's own reality by exchanging meanings in a commonly understood form. Any curtailment in this communicative process is in effect an impairment of the personality which is thus deprived of information it needs to survive and evolve. Knowledge has always meant power and as such man has sought to conserve it often at peril to himself. When it was shared by others, civilization emerged which, usually by means of a cadre, ensured that the stock of information was maintained, enlarged and transmitted. As the mechanisms for dissemination improved, this power inhering in knowledge was more evenly distributed so that all might know enough to make their opinions matter. When these differed, additional information by way of guidance was sought from those who knew more either by their calling or by their expertise in collecting information and evaluating it in terms of what use it might provide. Since the use which such information served changed with time, circumstances and the motive of those who sought it, organizations came to recognize the importance of controlling its flow. The right to know and the right to communicate one's knowledge inevitably became a matter of tension as society balanced the individual freedom against the freedom of the collective.

Irish governments are therefore not unusual in seeking to determine the flow of information but neither too are its journalists in challenging the grounds on which limitations are placed on the communicative act. Britain, its neighbour, has shown evidence of an ability to accommodate within the framework of political discussion the presentation of programmes that would appear to many dispassionate observers to lie on the far side of tolerance, and yet, as has been seen, loud and rancorous have been the protests at media management and censorship on behalf of politicians. What has happened is that more information about more matters of concern is being received by more people. Public opinion is no longer a constant, predictable and inert, the birthright of the few. It is constantly being solicited, and just as wants create wants in information, so too does the need to have its results made known in order to gauge the difference between today and yesterday, and find out in consequence what is being said now that has never been said before. Public opinion made itself heard

during the Franco-Algerian War, the struggle in Vietnam, the banish-
ment of the Shah of Persia; it makes itself felt every time a political party
is rejected at the polls. Governments ignore it at their peril and therefore
must seek to côntrol it by the manipulation of data and the censorship of
views.

In full awareness of the importance of the free movement and exchange
of ideas, the Universal Declaration of Human Rights declared in 1948 in
Article 19, that

Everyone has the right to freedom of opinion and expression; this right includes
freedom to hold opinions without interference, and to seek receive and impart information and ideas through any medium and regardless of frontiers.

The European Convention for the Protection of Human Rights and Fundamental Freedoms (1950) states in Article 10

1. Everyone has the right to freedom of expression. This right shall include freedom to hold opinions and to receive and impart information and ideas without interference by authority and regardless of frontiers.

However it goes on to add

This Article shall not prevent States from requiring the licensing of broadcasting,
television or cinema.

And in the next section, it expands the idea:

2. The exercise of these freedoms, since it carries with it duties and responsibilities, may be subject to such formalities, conditions, restrictions or penalties
as are prescribed by law and are necessary in a democratic society, in the interests
of national security, territorial integrity or public safety,

This compares with the limitations imposed in Article 19.3 of the Universal Declaration, which states that the rights of freedom of communication
are subject to restrictions required

(b) For the protection of national security or of public order, or of public health or
morals.

Consider, however, the remainder of 10.2 of the European Convention,

for the prevention of disorder or crime, for the protection of health or morals, for
the protection of the reputation or rights of others, for preventing the disclosure
of information received in confidence, and for the authority and impartiality of
the judiciary.

all exceptions to the right to, and of, information which have been translated in Ireland into the negative statutory law of Censorship of Publications Acts, Offences against the State Acts, Prohibition of Forcible Entry
Act and others, not omitting the powers to issue directives that flow from
Section 31 and the apparent resolution of judges to make criticism of Irish
court procedure a very hazardous use of free speech.

When the European Convention article on freedom of expression is
contrasted with the Inter-American Convention on Human Rights
(finally ratified in 1979), the comprehensiveness of the limitations on free-

dom spelt out by the former document become more apparent. Article 13, paragraph 1, in the latter identifies the range of the freedom to receive and impart information, and then states:

2. The exercise of the right provided for in the foregoing paragraph shall not be subject to prior censorship but shall be subject to subsequent imposition of liability, which shall be expressly established by law and be necessary in order to ensure:

(a) respect for the rights or reputations of others; or

(b) the protection of national security, public order or public health or morals.

Human rights are either concessionary or fundamental, either based on law or on justice. Modern nations recognizing that freedom of expression is part of, and essential to, the human condition guarantee to their citizens its enjoyment by enshrining the right on which it relies in their basic law. In the Irish Constitution, this right, it will be remembered, is experienced as follows:

The State guarantees liberty for the exercise of the following rights, subject to public order and morality

1. The right of the citizens to express freely their convictions and opinions.[1]

There follows the assertion of the State's right of prior restraint in cases where it deems organs of public opinion are being used to undermine public order or morality or the authority of the State. It is obvious that the absoluteness of the right to inform or be informed is qualified since public order and morality have no standard and agreed connotation. For institutions, the disablement is more grievous since corporatively they are denied a right which their members possess as individuals. When contrasted with the rights outlined in the MacBride Commission's Final Report, the deficiencies stand out in bolder relief:

(a) The right to know: to be given, and to seek out in such ways as he may choose, the information that he desires...

(b) The right to impart: to give to others the truth as he sees it about his living conditions, his aspirations, his needs and grievances...[2]

Fisher cautions about the problems that arise from attempting to set down a normative definition of the right to communicate that is applicable to all forms of expression. Failure to differentiate the derivative freedoms, as for example, to publish a non-libellous statement, from the basic human right to communicate itself may result in the dilution of the latter. Better by far to state the right in absolute terms as the inviolable core and, separately, specify the freedoms it entails, the practical entitlements necessary for their exercise, the circumstances that may justify limiting such exercise, and the

[1] Constitution of Ireland, Article 40, 6, 1. i.
[2] *Many Voices, One World*. Seán MacBride, President, London, Kogan Page, 1980, p. 113.

extent of justifiable limitation.[1]

The limitations are justified before society by the need to protect superior or equal rights, for example, the communication of a government's point of view in a national emergency.

In Ireland, as in most western countries, the locus of human rights resides in the individual.

All powers of government, legislative, executive and judicial, derive, under God, from the people, whose right it is to designate the rulers of the State and, in final appear, to decide all questions of national policy, according to the requirements of the common good.[2]

From these powers flows 'the right to express freely convictions and opinions.' Other European countries have adopted a similar approach to the freedom of expression. The Austrian Constitution (Article 13) says that 'everyone has the right within the limits of the law freely to express his opinion...,' the Danish Constitution (Article 77) says that 'any person shall be at liberty to publish his ideas...,' the Constitution of the Federal German Republic (Article 5) says that 'Everybody shall have the right of freely expressing and disseminating his opinion by word of mouth ... and to inform himself without impediment from generally accessible sources,' the Italian Constitution (Article 21) says that 'All persons have the right freely to express their own opinions...' What these Constitutions have in common is the recognition of a right which the citizen possesses against the state and which cannot be abrogated unless it be shown to impinge on the right to another. Contrast this view with that which prevails in socialist countries where all freedoms are subordinated to the right of the state to determine their constituents in the light of what is conceived of as the national consensus and the common good. In view of the diverging views of human rights which these ideologies represent, the one limiting the power of the state, the other making it the guarantor and arbiter of freedoms; the first emphasizing the quasi-absolute right of the individual, the second identifying the state as charged with the responsibility of harmonizing freedoms with overall national purposes, it becomes impossible to conceive of a definition that would recognize the rights of both. MacBride does not try:

Our conclusions are founded on the firm conviction that communication is a basic individual right, as well as a collective one required by all communities and nations.[3]

While the Constitution of Ireland does affirm the individual's right, its enjoyment is conditional on 'organs of public opinion' not being used 'to un-

---

[1] Desmond Fisher in Harms, L.S. and Jim Richstad (eds.) *Evolving Perspectives on the Right to Communicate*. (Honolulu: East-West Communication Institute, 1977), p. 96.
[2] The Constitution of Ireland, Article 6.
[3] *Many Voices, One World* p. 253.

dermine public order or morality of the authority of the State.' This dilemma might be resolved by abandoning the conceptual extension that the same individual's right of necessity

exists in a community, a group of people, a nation or a region. Such groups may and do have a right to communicate. But their right is not the same – at least in degree – as that pertaining to the individual.[1]

As has been seen in Ireland, the responsible minister's power in the past to allocate broadcasting time, to direct the Authority to refrain from broadcasting designated matter, to dismiss the Authority over a conflict of views and finally to take decisions out of its hands, all underline the reality of the need for a differential definition if there is to be any coherency in who can say what in Ireland. Since the individual and society are meaningless abstractions without one another, as the progress of civilization demonstrates, a reconciliation of social constraints imposed in the interests of the individual with his emancipation from them as they prove detrimental to society at large is an ongoing problem which, without the right to communicate, is rarely solved this side of violence. While just such a solution is being sought, tension is inevitable as interests clash. Edmund Burke's words are still appropriate:

Liberty too must be limited in order to be possessed. The degree of restraint it is impossible in any case to settle precisely. But it ought to be the constant aim of every wise public council to find out, ... with how little – not how much – of this restraint the community can subsist. For liberty is a good to be improved and not an evil to be lessened. It is not only a private blessing of the first order, but the vital spring and energy of the state itself, which has just so much life and vigor as there is liberty in it.[2]

It is arguable from the imposition of censorship in Ireland that liberty has sustained the reverse process. The right to communicate would appear to derive less from justice and more from law, less from the absoluteness of the rights of the individual and more from the measure of freedom society is prepared to accord to their enjoyment. The right to read books and periodicals was absolute within the freedom of choice as defined by the state. If the two basic components of freedom are freedom to think and freedom to act, Irish law in general, in curtailing the civic rights of the latter, has violated the natural justice of the former. In declaring off-limits parts of the human experience, the law of the state not only denied its citizens access to them but also by withholding the evidence maimed their judgment as to the acceptability of the consequences. They were,

[1] Desmond Fisher, *The Right to Communicate: Towards a Definition*. Research Paper No. 37, International Commission for the Study of Communication Problems, Unesco monograph 94, p. 16.
[2] Edmund Burke, *Speeches and Letters on American Affairs* (London: Dent, 1961), p. 221.

therefore, to be denied the opportunity of bringing in their own verdict on the IRA.

CHAPTER 9

CONCLUSIONS

What had always been distinctive of the Irish struggle for independence was the interpenetration of Catholicism and nationalism. In the Anglo-Irish phase of the conflict, as young men with rosaries in their pockets ambushed and killed British Tommies, elderly bishops sought to reconcile the Christian principle of 'Thou shalt not kill' with the desire to show solidarity with their flock in the face of the foreign terror. The civil war that followed resolved their ambiguity. Brother pitted against brother in a war that was to cost many more lives than had the Rebellion and its aftermath was to leave an ever-expanding moral vacuum which they proceeded to fill to overflowing. The departure of the coloniser put an end to the pretensions to a holy war. The fratricidal strife that followed confirmed the Church's misgivings that the demoralization and dehumanization which were the by-products to be expected from guerrilla warfare were now possibly to remain on to infect the peace. This fear of anarchy and lawlessness, when the rights of property, the established order and social understandings no longer commanded respect among the people, was part of the heritage and folk-knowledge of a seminary which had originally been staffed by men fleeing the persecution of the French revolution. The way back to Catholic living was through obedience to the true teaching of the Church. No more foolish idealism of blood-sacrifices, no more dangerous notions of a social welfare state, no more of this imported secular radicalism that would disturb the relationships .that had always united Holy Mother Church to her erring flock.

What has characterized Irish Catholicism for churchmen was the conviction that emotions are malleable, even if the resulting configuration were not permanent. Human nature deviates from the Catholic norm, and the worst therefore must always be expected. If religion be nonintellectual and therefore based on ritual, devout practices and a willingness to accept a prescriptive ordering of even the minute details of everyday existence, the faithful would reap a fine crop of contentment. The immediate interest for the bishops was the restoration of law and order and the bringing back of all the people to a recognition of their duty to support the national government. A beginning would be made where they were most competent. They therefore proceeded to condemn immodest fashions in clothing, unhealthy and immoral cross-roads dancing, excessive drinking, strikes and picketing. But there were other evils about. Parental control was a thing of the past, self-denial and acceptance of suffering were neglected virtues, gambling and cinema films attracted the unwary, and of course the foreign press and the vile traffic in pernicious literature were in the vanguard in introducing an insidious immorality into every home in the land.

The Catholic Bishops of Ireland were therefore to be in a position of some strength in the first decade of independence. Their words might not be universally accepted but even those of the minority who chose not to listen were selective in their inattention. They had placed the government in debt by their pastoral support, and the government, by premeditation noninterventionist, was prepared to leave to them the drawing up of the moral charter. The bargain was advantageous to both. The Church was presented with an opportunity to graft into the national sentiment certain ultramontane principles without having to answer difficult questions from radicals and irregulars as to the legitimacy of their role in making up the new mind of Ireland. Again, it had the same interest as the Government in seeking the return to normality when family life and social responsibility might once more be invoked in carrying out God's plans. Finally, the Church in mounting a crusade against sexual immorality in particular was guaranteeing the permanent employment of its spiritual energies given the undependability of human virtue. The external enemy had retired across the seas. Now they could address their minds to tackling the internal foe. The government, for its part, in a country that had known terror, arson and murder, shared in the benefits of an increasing moral stability as the minds of citizens were directed to recreating a pure and simple Ireland that had been one of those enduring myths which attracted all Irishmen by their remoteness from a reality anyone had ever known.

The Catholic Church in Ireland from the Penal Days of the eighteenth century had been motivated, first, under the British 'to secure and retain the freedom to perform its duties, teach its doctrines, and insure the continuance of its faith among the Irish people: second, to discourage, to the best of its ability, the tendencies towards violence and social revolution.'[1] When the Civil War ended and the Government of the day, faced with a numerically increasing Opposition party, stood in need of whatever sup-

[1] Morley Ayearst, *The Republic of Ireland* (London: University of London Press, 1979), p. 213.

port and aids to credibility it could command, the time was right for that intervention which left, in O'Faoláin's words, the Church 'felt, feared and courted on all sides as the dominant power.' Not that the ecclesiastical authorities were likely to encounter much opposition from either side of the political divide to their crusade against sexual licentiousness. Post-Famine morality had been conditioned by demographic and economic factors, coupled with Victorian taboos, and marked by an innate puritanism that had characterized the Irish Church from its inception. While dissident Republicans might be excommunicated for their refusal to accept the conditions of the Treaty and for their efforts to continue their protest under arms, their leader made no bones about his determination to uphold the values of the Catholic majority. Later, when he assumed the reins of government he thought it quite appropriate to send his new Constitution to Pope Pius XI to ensure that as far as possible the Catholic moral code had been adequately enshrined in the basic law of the State. Another Taoiseach in the fifties was able to speak in the Dáil of the complete willingness of his Government to defer to the judgements of the hierarchy, even when one of the judgements in question was adverse to a proposal made by one of his cabinet colleagues who felt obliged to resign in consequence. The victory which this represented for the Church was not only the one instance of any Catholic hierarchy thinking it incumbent upon itself to go to such lengths to determine the provision of a country's medical services but also exemplified the powers it had garnered for itself in the thirty years since Independence.

At first glance this dominance by the clergy in the social and moral life of the Irish people would have appeared to continue unchallenged into the fifties. All dance halls, whether or not in the control of the clergy, were permitted to remain open only during specified hours. Statements on foreign affairs were aired with a simplistic superficiality that led one bishop to solemnly assure his flock that Senator McCarthy had been unjustly criticized. Catholic students were forbidden to attend Trinity College, Dublin, under the pain of mortal sin. One reason that the plans for a proposed non-university Agricultural Institute were abandoned was on the rather unlikely grounds that as education agriculture came within the legitimate sphere of interest of the bishops. Finally, as has been seen, one bishop announced that the bishops were to be the final arbiters of the rightness and wrongness of all legislation. These were the years that saw the frenetic activity of the Board of Censorship. It would seem as if Ireland were on the brink of becoming a theocracy.

A moment's reflection, however, reveals the preposterousness of the idea. Even when the bishops were in the ascendant, government ministers had not hesitated to express their criticism of some of their attempts to apply the irrelevant and outmoded teaching of the encyclicals to the

Irish situation. The apparent regime of clerical domination was now to face further resistance that would gradually reduce the role of the hierarchy to that of a pressure group which, since it obviously could draw support from a very numerous constituency, would never be ignored, if not always heeded. There were small incidents. The rejection of a request to cancel a football match against Yugoslavia has already been noted. An episcopally supported boycott was rebuked by the government. The Church's proposals for licensing hours were not adopted. But these were only disconnected manifestations of the government's wishing to be seen as the executive authority. They simply pointed out in each instance that the Church was wrong in its view. What was more important was the emergence of certain intellectual currents which were beginning to illuminate Irish thinking. Reference has already been made to the economic planning and to the consequent urbanization that began to gather momentum in the sixties. In 1957 John Kelleher writing in the American *Foreign Affairs* had considered seriously that the Irish were so beset by problems, which they had neither the talent nor the energy to resolve, that they might disappear from world view through 'an implosion upon a central vacuity.'[1] In complete contrast to such a nemesis, a few years later Thornley was able to write,

we are for the first time at the threshold of a delayed social revolution. It would be foolhardy to go on to predict its course. It seems certain that our island will become affected increasingly by the spread of European social and philosophical ideas.'[2]

The reasons have already been indicated. Economic buoyancy, Kennedy's New Frontier spirit, awareness of the possibility of entry to the EEC, the arrival of television, educational change following an OECD report,[3] and for the first time a declaration of an intercensal population increase rate of 3%, all were factors that engaged the minds of everyday people who found themselves co-opted into the debate about the material, rather than the spiritual, future as a result of their stake in its outcome.

The undoubted improvement in living standards that was to follow was not obtained without cost. As time went by, poor urban planning and inadequate housing either caused or were unable to abate a staggering increase in indictable crimes, prostitution, drug trafficking, which, coupled with the eventual political unrest arising from awakened interest in civil rights, were subsequently to leave the country requiring the highest ratio of police to population of all the countries of Europe. The transition to af-

[1] John V. Kelleher. 'Ireland ... and where does she stand?' *Foreign Affairs*, No. 3, 1957, p. 495.
[2] David Thornley, 'Ireland: The End of an Era'. *Tuairim Pamphlet*, 12 Jan., 1965, p. 12.
[3] *Investment in Education*. OECD, Dublin: The Stationery Office, 1962, p. 140.

fluence in the meantime while it still left a quarter of the population below the poverty line inculcated a new aggressiveness in society and a new ruthlessness in the determination of some to retain and add to what they had acquired. The easygoing egalitarianism of the forties and fifties that was a useful social lubricant when no one had anything was now to be exchanged for the ebullient, callous careerism of a competitive economy which looked upon poverty as a self-inflicted scar that identified those marked to fail as easy prey for those who were not. No wonder O'Doherty, a psychologist, would write:

One cannot radically change the material culture and hope to preserve all the rest intact. Yet this is our dilemma. We have set in train great and far-reaching processes within the material culture which inevitably will have great and far-reaching effects in other dimensions of the culture, which already have had such effects. But while we are anxious to achieve the desirable changes in the material culture, we are reluctant to accept the other changes they inevitably bring with them.[1]

Censorship had been part of the civil war measures. Statutory instruments banning certain films and books followed. Then came the war years when censorship became a patriotic duty. There ensued economic stagnation, the apogee of Church interference in politics and social affairs, low living standards and emigration that attained a figure of a half-million people out of a population of three in the decade of the fifties. No contraception, no divorce, no abortion, Ireland as a moral sanctuary was fast becoming a waste and sterile land where self-government seemed to some a poor return for helplessness, hopelessness and religious hubris. Finally came the eruption from the economic cocoon of national self-sufficiency. Ireland discovered it was part of the human race and began to ask the questions about the worth of the values that had remained after the first flush of puritanism had died. There were answers, only this time truth was no longer to arrive packaged and stamped with the seal of ecclesiastical or government approval. The social sciences had evolved methodologies characterized by realism rather than by revelation. Revisionist analyses challenged the concept of national redemption born in the necessary spilling of blood, rejected a moral awareness that was the unthinking by-product of confessional socialization, and distinguished true, analytical understanding from party political cant. There had always been Irish men and women dedicated to laying bare the theories of history, economics, theology and of general culture in a manner that would satisfy the rigorous standards of critical scholarship. The difficulty for Ireland lay in the fact that their truths had to coexist with the myths propagated by Church and State alike for such a long time before eventually they could hope to displace them.

[1] E.F. O'Doherty, 'Society, Identity and Change', *Studies*, Vol. 52 (1963), pp. 130–31.

In the debate that ensued on the validity of the principles which should guide the evolution of Irish society from the sixties onwards, the traditional Church found, as a result of internal forces and external pressures, that its views were growing more and more unacceptable as the discussion continued. Doubts about the consequences of its anti-intellectuality had always been present.

Too many people in Ireland today are trying to make do with a peasant religion when they are no longer peasants any more. We are a growing and developing middle-class nation, acquiring a middle-class culture and we must have a religion to fit our needs.[1]

This theme was to reoccur and to be elaborated, as the potential of the all-pervasive communication network of the sixties began to present ideas, cultural possibilities and theories of society for which the unintellectual approach of the average Irish churchmen was not always able to provide an answer. It was not only theologians who began to redefine the autonomy of the individual in relation to revealed truths. Sociologists also began to examine the role of religion in a society experiencing accelerated urbanization and modernization. The religious experience had for too long been taken for granted. Now the dishonesty of proposing judgments based on 'self-evident' truths and 'principles' enunciated by authoritative establishment figures was no longer to be tolerated. Gradually there seeped through the historic layers of defensiveness, dependency, orthodoxy and conservatism the realization 'that religion is both a constant, inasmuch as it is an aspect of habit, and a variable, inasmuch as it is responsive to changing social and intellectual circumstances.'[2] What had to be done was to create a new context for a culture that was relevant, based on identifiable and optimally verifiable premises, and willing to accept the conditions that its truths compete in open forum with other isms for the hearts and minds of men. Notice had been served on censorship in Ireland.

The nineteen-sixties witnessed a remarkable change in the relations between Church and State. The former no longer attempted to impose the 'integralist' doctrines of the encyclicals, no longer uttered dire warnings about the dangers of state encroachment, and no longer was disposed to summon the faithful to man the barricades when questions arose about areas in which it claimed to be the final arbiter. The State for its part consulted the Church when appropriate as the most important of many interest groups and continued to treat it with the same respect that had been

---

[1] John L. Kelly, 'Solid Virtue in Ireland', *Doctrine and Life*, 9:5 (1959), p. 120.
[2] David Thornley, 'Irish Identity', *Doctrine and Life*, 16:4, (April 1966), p. 181.

its custom. Within the next decade, Article 44 of the Constitution which acknowledged 'the special position of the Holy Catholic Apostolic and Roman Church' was to be removed by an overwhelming majority of those who took the trouble to vote for the relevant Amendment in the 1972 referendum. The hierarchy declared that it was well pleased with the result. What had happened to bring about the disposition? How was their silence on the tolerant Censorship Amendments Acts of the sixties to be explained? The answer was to be found elsewhere than in Ireland, and its import was to bring out into sharper relief the rights of citizens which hitherto had been sacrificed on the altar of a narrowly conceived morality.

It is an odd, but not exclusive, characteristic of the Irish people that there is no necessary correlation between their ritualistic commitment and their intellectual assent. The Catholic Church as teacher is listened to, and its decisions respected, until there is a situation which involves the individual in more than passive conformity. The Church, for example, as late as 1978 issued a statement drawing a bleak picture of the results of a failure to accept *Humanae Vitae*:

Societies in which contraceptives have become generally and widely used have experienced a lowering of standards in sexual morality. Marital infidelity has increased. The stability of the family has weakened. A whole new attitude towards sex has developed. Promiscuity has tended to increase. Legislation of abortion has usually followed.[1]

This amplification of deviancy is hardly borne out by the facts. Granted the illegitimacy rate had risen to 4.5% in 1977 which was the highest figure it was to reach, the fact remains that it had stood at 3.9% thirty-one years earlier. One rural deputy had expressed his conviction in 1974 that 'What is morally wrong cannot be made legally right.'[2] The Irish had however discovered new personal meanings to what was morally rational, and in the security of the reestablishment of the primacy of the private conscience had listened to their bishops and then decided that what was legally right was the end of the question as far as society should be concerned. Ever since the first outcry raised by the episcopal bench against immoral films and evil literature there had been no attempt to create an intelligent awareness of the problem of public morality. Instead, there had been the catalogue of social disasters that awaited society were precaution and prevention not immediately summoned to stand guard over an endangered purity of mind. Nothing had changed very much in the sixty years as far as the doomsayers were concerned. There was no dialogue, no reaching out to share the interpretation of the problem and its solution, only the tolling bell that announced decadence, degeneration and destruction of the so-

[1] Report in *The Irish Times* of 5 April, 1978, quoted in J. H. Whyte, *Church and State in Modern Ireland 1923–79* (Dublin: Gill and Macmillan, 1980), p. 413.
[2] Deputy Kitt, *Dáil Debates*, 4 July, 1974, Col. 359.

cial fabric. Neither the Irish people nor their Church had sought purchase on the ground separating the 'obey' and 'disobey' that still seemed the only options the authoritarian mind could bring itself to consider. But other rejections were being made as passive tolerance proved no longer a safe haven for unthinking indifference, and active assent or dissent became the only means of resolving the private dilemma. People were saying 'no' to other admonishments, councils of perfection, precepts of conduct and rules of behavior mainly because it was no longer comfortable or possible to keep on saying 'yes.'

The Irish are a church-going people. They are also nationalist-minded. They are conscious of the discrimination that their fellow-nationalists suffer in the north of the country. They had always known but it was not until 1969 that the plight of the latter began to affect them materially. Domestic legislation that was restrictive of basic freedoms was introduced. The cost of guarding an inland border came to escalate a hundred-fold. Murder, violence, robbery and kidnapping became endemic. There was a need obviously to review the situation, and the task should begin within its own territory with the question, was Catholic Nationalism Christian and democratic? A return to consideration of the Constitution in light of contemporary experience provided some indications. Its preamble begins,

In the Name of the Most Holy Trinity, from Whom is all authority and to Whom, as our final end, all actions both of men and States must be referred,

We, the people of Éire,

Humbly acknowledging all our obligations to our Divine Lord, Jesus Christ, Who sustained our fathers through centuries of trial, Gratefully remember their heroic and unremitting struggle to regain the rightful independence of our nation.

In its time, and for decades after, these sentiments reflected the political Irishman. He was for free speech, against arbitrary arrest, for universal franchise, the independence of the judiciary, right of assembly and against religious discrimination and interference with personal property. He was convinced of the truth of the Catholic faith and proud of his ancestors' struggle for independence – insofar as he informed itself about either. Then came the Civil Rights movement throughout the world, and with loud and particular emphasis on his front door. He slowly began to realize the truth in what Jefferson had said about the equal rights of the minority 'which equal law must protect and to violate would be oppressive,' in Tocqueville's fears of 'The tyranny of the majority' and Madison's warning that liberty was imperilled every time the majority decision impaired the minority's rights. How then could a constitution be acceptable whose preamble excluded Jews, agnostics and even sects within the Christian faith? How could there be serious talk of reconciliation when this Preamble in effect dissociated the one million Protestants in the North from the foundation of a state they were being asked to join? Were 'we, the people of Éire' to be restricted to those who were Catholic and nationalist in accordance with orthodox criteria? How could one support laws which reflected an attitude to divorce, contraception, abortion and censorship that was in accordance with one particular confessional morality? How should a bishop be answered who declared that the majority had the right to have its standards protected by the state? How to persuade all involved that the constitution was not intended just to serve the average Catholic Irishman but every citizen of the state? There was little to be expected from politicians by way of reply to those questions. As professionals they had always adopted the traditional stance of first finding in what direction the electorate was going and then assuming its leadership. No, the answer was to come from within the heart of the Church itself. For once, there was to be a dialectic between the two credos to which the Irish subscribed, their faith and their nationalism. A new sense of civic purpose would emerge.

The Declaration on Religious Freedom adopted by the Second Vatican Council proposes certain norms to Catholics by which they should evaluate and develop constitutional principles and instruments for all the citizens of a country. Its basic theme is the inviolable right of the human person – an affirmation that aligns it with Western constitutional thought in that guarantees are offered to individuals. In short the Declaration revealed that 'rights belong to persons because of their human dignity, not because of the validity of what they happen to believe ... just as a man who preaches outmoded or unworkable political theory may invoke his personal right of free speech, so also the right of religious freedom can be claimed by those who do not live up to their obligation of seeking the truth and adhering to it.'[1] This statement is in direct keeping with what Pope John XXIII had said in his encyclical, *Pacem in Terris*, 'One must never confuse error and the person who errs ... The person who errs is always and above all a human being, and in every case he retains his dignity as a human person.' What the Declaration was in effect saying for the first time to all Catholics was that man must not only not be forced to do what his belief prohibits, but also he must not be prevented from doing what his belief allows. Therefore what might appear good to the state could not therefore on that basis alone be imposed on the citizen. Christ was no political Messiah. He witnessed to the truth but did not seek to impose it. Conversion, not coercion, was the way of the Gospel. The Vatican Council was quite clear. Truth was its own best argument, in fact its only argument, if the citizen were to retain his rights in their plenitude. It was not to be identified with numbers. The hallmark of a majority Christian society

[1] Louis McRedmond, 'The Constitution of Ireland and the Declaration on Religious Freedom', *Law and Justice*, No. 70/71, Trinity/Michaelmas, 1981, p. 74.

was to be the amount and quality of protection that was to be extended to its dissenting minorities. Did this approach imply an absolute right to act on one's belief? Surely not. Restrictions are also found in civil law. The United States Supreme Court drew a distinction in examining religious freedom between the 'freedom to believe and the freedom to act. The first is absolute but in the nature of things, the second cannot be.'[1] Jefferson had talked about the need to intervene when 'overt acts against peace and good order' took place. The Irish Constitution in granting personal freedoms had introduced the proviso that their enjoyment should not 'undermine public order or morality or the authority of the State.' Enough has already been said as to the difficulty of defining the contents of such concepts. The Declaration did not offer objective public order, however, as a means whereby freedoms might be limited. The concept it proposed was 'a guideline on the methods of restriction to be employed. It restricts the restrictions. It does not justify them.'[2]

The impact of this new thinking on the rights of the individual had been like beating a cushion with a hammer, until the eruption of violence in the North forced its awareness upon people who realized that the basis of their society was being called into question in a manner they could no longer ignore. Irish theologians pointed out that the assertion of the dignity and freedom of the individual guaranteed in the Constitution suffered by its identification with the religion of the majority. O'Brien campaigned against a Constitution which intruded politico-national ideals where only the principles of the Irish social contract should find a place. Action groups complained that the Constitution coerced belief among its citizens, as, for example, the forbidding of divorce which disregarded the confessional convictions of the minority. With a momentum that continued to accelerate, the Irish people had now begun to question the premises on which the authority of their Church and nation were founded. Many were to discover the folly of resigning their right to question and challenge principles that far from reflecting their faith and patriotism impoverished them. Their confidence in the paternalistic benevolence of Church and State, so assiduously cultivated by both in the authoritarianism-personalism relationships mentioned earlier, had been found to have been misplaced. Censorship, now only a minor irritant, perhaps, and performing for the most part a useful scavenging function, remained as a symbol of their submission. However, the forces for review had been set in motion and were not to be halted.

In the early sixties there began to appear for the first time a readiness to interpret the role of the Constitution in relation to equity and common

---

[1] *Cantwell* v. *Connecticut*, 310 US 296, 60 s.ct. 980, (1940).
[2] McRedmond, ibid., p. 78.

law, the results of which, taken in conjunction with the new declarations of the Vatican Council, were to change the definition of the individual in relation to his institutions in a manner that was out of all recognition with what had gone before. The Irish Supreme Court is not a specialized constitutional court. Its jurisdiction is wide and its functions diverse. While this absence of concentration may have its drawbacks, it has meant for the last twenty years that there has been in every field of litigation a sense of the relevance of the Constitution. The law is now being administered at all levels in awareness of this supervisory function of a higher tribunal, a situation that was very different in an Ireland of a generation earlier. Evidence of its willingness to intervene in the censorship of publications and in Orders made under Section 31 of the Broadcasting Authority Act has already been described.

The most significant of the Supreme Court's decisions were, however, to fall in the area of human freedoms. What was being affirmed now was the constructionist role which had been previously rejected. The judiciary were determined to play their part in asserting their power to determine the enjoyment of the fundamental rights of the Constitution. Whether it was the common law which was invoked or the Christian ethic or the democratic nature of the State, 'the way was opened to a series of decisions ... establishing a number of 'unspecified' personal rights entitled to constitutional protection.'[1] These were to include the right to earn a livelihood, to recover damages against a wrongdoer, to privacy in marital relations, to a passport, to free movement within the State, the right to use the Irish language in all dealings with the State, and the right to communicate. In this latter case, Costello J. stated: 'It seems to me that as an act of communication is the exercise of such a basic human faculty that a right to communicate must inhere in the citizen by virtue of his human personality and must be guaranteed by the Constitution.'[2] Further, it is significant that over the period the courts have taken the opportunity to emphasize that the beliefs or dogmas of the majority faith are to be subordinated where appropriate to Christian principles and whatever secular construction of the common good seemed suitable. At the same time, and paradoxically, when two professors were removed from their posts upon being laicised, the Courts found in favor of the Seminary when an action was taken against it for alleged discrimination on the grounds of religious status. The reasons given were that the prohibition of discrimination applied only to the State, that by this limitation the Constitution intended 'to give vitality, independence and freedom to religion' and that 'Far from

[1] C.K. Boyle and D.S. Greer, *New Ireland Forum: The Legal Systems*, North and South. Unpublished Study, 1984.
[2] *The Attorney General* v. *Paperlink Ltd.* The High Court, 13th July, 1983, Unreported, p. 20.

eschewing the internal disabilities and discrimination which flow from the
tenets of a particular religion, the State must on occasion recognize them
and buttress them."[1] In short in order that the State maintain a rigid separation from the Church, it was ready to support it to do what it did not
permit itself. There are other cases and other interpretations of the Constitution. Measured against the Declaration on Religious Freedom, they
be-
tray the limitations of a constitution made when Ireland reflected the
dominance of papal social teaching. What has preserved its libertarianism
so far has been the scrupulosity of the judicial review, the new insights
into man in society and the resolve to interpret the Constitution in the
light of that canon of justice which appeared to be indicated, regardless of
its provenance. This attitude of the Supreme Court has resulted in substantive law which has reasserted the dignity of the individual in the face
of the dominant orthodoxy.

Much remains to be achieved before Ireland can claim to be a pluralist
state in the sense that the term is used in the anglophone world. The Declaration on Religious Freedom as a document is more generous in determining the rights of conscience for the individual as absolutes than many
national Catholic Churches are prepared to concede. Much is heard of
Humanae Vitae, little or nothing of the former. In spite of this comparative lack of emphasis the mind of the Irish would appear to be functioning
in an environment where the proponents of the liberties of Vatican II, as
representing the affirmation of the inviolability of the individual's vision
and of his personal truth, however distorted or erroneous either may be,
still continue the fight for these liberties. There is for a conservative
people, in addition, an impressive body of constitutional precedents all
asserting the citizen's powers which have been granted by the Constitution and which the Courts are determined to uphold. Finally, there is the
movement within, if not of, the Catholic Church which rejects the concept of acting as the conscience of the state and instead affirms that it is a
matter for the individual to decide whether to use contraceptives, get divorced, read banned books or look at pornographic films. There will still
be many occasions when a bishop will declare that the so-called 'tyranny
of the majority' is in fact the blessings of the democratic process, and yet
would be horrified to be accused of preaching the morality of numbers.
There will, on the other hand, be a few occasions when a bishop will go
out of his way to say nothing that will make the minority feel alienated or
of second-class status. Now and again, however, and progressively more
and more, as the Church wishes to avoid exacerbating the growing impatience the Irish are showing with religious formulae and confessional

[1] Unreported judgment of Supreme Court, Nov. 1979, quoted in J.M. Kelly, *The Irish Constitution* (Dublin: Jurist Publishing Co., 1980).

stereotypes, there will be recourse to the theologians cited in these pages who seek to reconcile religious freedom as a civil right and the requirements of social performance imposed by a common regard for human dignity.

The question may legitimately be asked, Why not dispose with the censorship of publications completely? Or put another way, in a pluralist society in Ireland, Would censorship be retained? The speculativeness en tailed in attempting a response to this problem is pertinent not for any conclusions that might be arrived at but for the light that might be shed on current Irish attitudes. Pre-Famine Ireland could be bawdy in its conjugal fidelity, reverent in its pleasure-seeking. A place was found for the clergyman in society, but symbolically enough he was still addressed as Mister, the paternalism/filialism of 'Father' being a later phenomenon. With Pius IX there came ultramontanism, tighter and more rigid ecclesiastical control from the center and, as has been seen in Ireland, a sexual morality that attempted to cope with a problem created by a population of around eight million, a laissez-faire distribution of national resources in a backward, rural economy and the emergence of a scheme of tenure for the land-hungry Irish. Abroad, Victorianism and Comstockery were to gather momentum in the second half of the nineteenth century. Across the western world there were great waves of people moving in search of alternative lifestyles. There was for the Irish at home, in Britain and in the USA much poverty and degradation. This condition was not permanent. In Ireland a middle class emerged that had a vested interest in a stability and order that would protect property and possessions. One contribution everybody could make was to live according to rules on which material success had been built: hard work, thrift and puritanism. This conclusion was not confined to Ireland. What made the Irish version unique however was a combination of two factors. The pursuit of material possessions was confined to those who could enter the race or believed that the prize was worth running for: there was too much poverty and too little opportunity in Ireland to persuade the majority that hard work and thrift would significantly alter their prospects. The second factor was a sense of other-worldliness, a conviction that the Church sedulously fostered that this earthly sojourn was temporary and that real 'living' began after death. A million dead takes its time to work its way out of the national consciousness, and socio-economic conditions, relieved partially by the departure of the emigrants, were never so favorable as to allow a peasantry that made up three-quarters of the population before independence to forget that death and preparation for death were the few certainties upon which it might rely.

The puritanism that came therefore to dominate Irish society after the famine responded at the very least to motives that transcended where they did not eclipse the capitalist ethic. Its propagators were a clergy whose standing in society rested firmly then, and remains securely fixed, even today, on the heroism of their celibacy. Given, then, the proponents of a sexual morality whose standpoint of necessity reflected their personal commitment, given a climate of Victorian puritanism that was reinforced for the socio-economic reasons described among a rural, conservative majority, and given that the rules and taboos of this morality were represented as the good life in preparation for a good death to a literate but uneducated population, it is arguable that, even were a wider version of spiritual self-responsibility accepted and understood, there would remain a desire to be protected from being disgusted or shocked. Acts can affront public decency without undermining moral conduct. There is a submerged equation between sex and morals which defies rationalization, and not only among the Irish. The protagonists of Irish censorship today while admitting that there is no proven causality between evil literature and personal corruption still would argue that just as necrophily, cannibalism, cruelty to animals, copulation *coram populo* and other manifestations of behaviors that outrage current notions of decency, should not be permitted, so too, censorship should be retained totally apart from any considerations of a sectional morality. The damage, they would argue, for Christians, Jews and all others, lies not in the possible stimulation to vicious practices but in deadening the sense by which public decency is measured.

Among media people in Ireland who obviously believe that words and images do have influence directly or indirectly there is another function censorship performs. Information, they point out, is being purveyed in one form or another to more and more people by fewer and fewer people who are determining the criteria for its dissemination on the grounds that it give the largest amount of satisfaction to the largest number of customers. Writers and television producers are expected to create for an imputed taste. The people who decide that taste will be the new censors, for they alone may one day stand at the gate to decide what currency will pass inspection. In opposition to this imposition of the profit-motive as a criterion stand paradoxically the Irish Supreme Court and the Irish theologians. Their numbers are few, but they are read by some thousands of Irish up and down the country who still are quite effective opinion leaders. Their argument about censorship in a truly pluralist Ireland remains unchanged. What is to be examined is not the impact of the book on the reader, but the intention and purpose of the author in writing it. Whatever guilt will lie, criminal or moral, will be determined not by the putative harm done, but by the discovered reasons of the doer in doing, so that the deliberate corrupter without saving merit stands revealed as an enemy of society. It is still a matter for comment in Ireland how communications have not only been amplified but accelerated. There is little conviction today of the short-term benefits, at least, of Milton's grappling between truth and falsehood. Truth and decency are always the first if not the permanent casualities at the hands of both good and evil when they contend. Yet now that censorship as a security service to the majority Church is no longer a matter of public scandal, there is still a need for some agency, not as a protector of morals, not as a public prosecutor of the criminal corrupter, but as the preserver of social decency, rather like the Roman aedile who in Lord Radcliffe's words was concerned with 'keeping the roads clean and the air sweet.'[1]

So much for moral censorship: what of political censorship? An examination of the educational level attained by sitting members of Dáil Éireann in 1977 (the fluctuation in membership has rarely been more than 10% from one election to the next) reveals that 35% have a degree or degree-level qualification, 58% have had an unspecified number of years of second level education and at the very least 7% have only first level education. One analysis over a period of time of 64 secretaries of government departments (in the Anglo-Irish context the top permanent civil service advisors to the government of the day) showed in 1972 that 97% were Catholic, 82% had come from urban areas and 26% had a university degree.[2] An earlier study had found in 1963 that 8 of the 15 heads of de partments had entered the civil service at the lowest rank of clerical officer, that is, with the schools' terminal certificate. Further investigation of these civil servants' educational backgrounds shows that they have been recruited mostly from a narrow, examination-intensive environment. There were obvious advantages in this classless bureaucracy, specifically in the in-group mutual understanding the uppermost and lowest echelons had of one another's position. There are also disadvantages. Chubb was of the opinion that

Higher civil servants generally perhaps tend to be intellectually able and hard-working, but rather narrowly practical in their support and inclined to be concerned with the short-term objective. They are little prone to speculate broadly or to reflect on long-term end or cultural values. With rather narrow secondary education in the case of so many ... they may well have restricted horizons.[3]

There is no reason for thinking that this profile has changed significantly.

As has been pointed out, the State since 1958 has been committed to planned development. Accordingly therefore as it took a more active part in economic and social organization, the complexity and volume of its business increased and the bureaucracy with its strongly developed links

[1] Lord Radcliffe, *Censors*. The Rede Lecture, 1961 (Cambridge University Press), p. 7.
[2] A. Cohen, *The Irish Political Elite* (Dublin: Gill and Macmillan, 1972), pp. 25–29.
[3] Basil Chubb, *The Government and Politics of Ireland* (London: Oxford University Press, 1971).

of 'upward' responsibility was presented with more scope to play a decisory role. 'The civil service is now expected to be an active and creative agency in policy matters, submitting policy recommendations to ministers.'[1] There are two other factors in assessing the political culture of the Irish civil service, both of which have been mentioned. Any bureaucracy is conservative; in Ireland it is, in addition, authoritarian, in the sense that administration is seen as exercising controls, and it is personalist in that action is effected through personalities so that often the urgent is confused with the important. One last strand in weaving the texture of the political process is the doctrine of ministerial responsibility which the Irish inherited from British parliamentary practice. According to this theory, the Minister is responsible for everything and knows everything. The deputy who is promoted to ministerial rank must therefore not only be an expert in what is politically acceptable to the public in terms of legislation, but is also now expected to master every brief his experts present to him, to anticipate all the difficulties he will encounter in the Dáil and Seanad, to prepare fallback positions, and reconcile what he is proposing with all other parliamentary business being conducted by his fellow-ministers if he is not to be exposed to attacks for being inconsistent or heterodox. When one considers, therefore, a civil service whose code entails protection for one's ministers at every possible interface with the public for which he can be called to account, whether it be a letter of inquiry from a private citizen, a parliamentary question, a debate, or the drawing up of legislation; whose functions have included over the last three decades the taking of decisions, certainly, but decisions in the making of which the political repercussions always constitute an element; and finally, whose education and formation leave them disposed to an approach that is pragmatic and precedent-bound; when one considers these these attributes belong to advisors proposing to their Minister to put solutions to a Dáil whose speculative experience of the working of a democracy may well be as limited as their own, then the decision to shut out the IRA from the dialogue of the public broadcasting system can be understood. At all costs the area of exposure of policy must not be made available to those who do not play by parliamentary rules. The analogy of the (unproven) effects of violence on the viewer provided the necessary rationale.

The various conventions on human rights that have been cited concur in guaranteeing freedom of expression. They differ as to the conditions which limit its exercise. The right is independent of the state in the sense that unlike education it can be enjoyed by the individual drawing on his

---

[1] Peter Pyne, 'The Bureaucracy in the Irish Republic: Its political role and the factors influencing it', *Political Studies*, Vol. 22, (March 1974), p. 20.

own resources. The state 'has no constitutional duty to provide any of the means which the citizen might wish to employ in order to express himself. It must allow him to speak. It does not have to build him a platform.'[1] The Irish Constitution goes further. Twice in the section dealing with freedom of expression it enjoins on those who control organs of opinion that nothing can be uttered that will impair the common good or public order. Such reserved powers are commonplaces of constitutional law throughout the world. No Irish government could be faulted for its refusal to provide a license for the apologists for IRA assassinations to air and defend views that it is claimed, would result in the overthrow of the state, provided ... provided that it is acting in accordance with the principles of constitutional justice in each case that it denies access.

A country that came into existence as the result of an armed struggle, that experienced immediately afterwards a much bloodier civil war, that steered a difficult and dangerous course in maintaining its neutrality, and that all the years of its existence experienced, inside and outside its borders, the effects and consequences of armed dissent would be unusual if, as has been seen, it had not introduced legislation that derogated from the rights and freedoms proposed in its Constitution. Special Criminal Courts, military custody, restrictive legislation, abrogation of safeguards and documented violence by the forces of law and order have usually, but not always, affected none but the marginals of society. Civil liberty organizations in Ireland, on the other hand, have had neither the strength in membership nor proven credibility to impress on successive governments, or on the public throughout the period, that rights belonging to the generality were in danger of being eroded. Injustices have been committed which have remained uncorrected. A few have been vindicated in the European Court of Justice. More important, it has been established that the Supreme Court in Ireland will require of the State to justify the use of its powers in each case that come, before it. On the one hand, it has said, as befits the Supreme Court of a conservative people, that

an Act of the Oireachtas, or provision thereof, will not be declared invalid where it is possible to construe it in accordance with the Constitution, and it is only a question of preferring a constitutional construction to one which would be unconstitutional, where they both may appear to be open but it also means that an interpretation favouring the validity of an Act should be given in cases of doubt.[2]

In short, it would appear that whatever is done in accordance with the provisions of an Act must get the benefit of the doubt as to its constitutionality. But the benefit of such doubt is not to be taken as implying an

[1] Louis McRedmond, 'Irish Radio Controversy', *Irish Broadcasting Review*, Autumn/Winter, 1978, p. 63.
[2] *East Donegal Co-Operative Livestock Mart* v. *Attorney-General*. Irish Reports, 1970, p. 341.

absolute guarantee. Government action must be performed in such a way as to respect the Constitution since the Oireachtas must be presumed to pass only legislation that is constitutionally sustainable in all its working. The Supreme Court went on to state in the same judgment:

At the same time ... the presumption of constitutionality carries with it not only the presumption that the constitutional interpretation or construction is the one intended by the Oireachtas but also that the Oireachtas intended that proceedings, procedures, discretions and adjudications which are permitted, provided for or prescribed by an Act of the Oireachtas are to be conducted in accordance with the principles of constitutional justice. In such a case any departure from those principles would be restrained and corrected by the Courts.[1]

The intention of the Court to look for constitutional validity in the operation of the Act is therefore to be paralleled with its commitment to judicially review any alleged abuse. As has been seen, the Supreme Court refused to set aside a Minister's decision not to permit a political party to broadcase its election address, but it did scrutinize his executive action in a manner that did not preclude further decisions. What will happen in the future is problematical. The social responsibility theory that is shared by all European governments will not be lightly abandoned. Broadcasters in seeking to present the excess of power and failures of government have experienced tension, hostility, and the ultimate affront, dismissal. One must assume that for every threat about which the public learns, there are many that remain undocumented, given the authoritarianism of the central government. Irish broadcasting has never established for itself the legitimacy of autonomy that accrues to other members of the fourth estate.

This skirmishing between governments and public service broadcasting has of late been seen to possess paradoxically one redeeming characteristic – its futility. Already, the remote towns of Ireland are beginning to gain access through cable to British broadcasting, and the further enlargement of their information sources only awaits the arrival of satellite broadcasting. Governments cannot continue to accept the reduced credibility of the national station. Political censorship is no longer effective when what is denied transmission is available to the Irish viewer at the turn of a dial. The only hope for a solution – 'The education of public opinion being, however, a matter of such grave impact to the common good' (Article 40.6.1.i) – lies in the politicians realizing, as they have in the past, that the nature of the communications medium determines the message. Already the electronic media have changed the nature of Irish political rhetoric. Ministers are challenged, statements are analyzed, and

---

[1] *East Donegal Co-Operative* v. *Attorney General*, Supreme Court judgment quoted in Kelly, ibid., p. 234.

despite efforts to the contrary public awareness is enlarged. In the prevailing circumstances, it is the unanimous opinion of broadcasters that the information which treats of Northern Ireland subversives, since it will enter the State anyway, should be allowed the freedom of the air if only to ensure that it is subjected to that critical appraisal the Irish have a right to expect from their public service.

These pages have attempted to chronicle the growth and development of censorship as a social institution that was intended to reflect the response of Irish society to changes in their moral and political values. The principal agents in making it a purposeful instrument to shape attitudes and beliefs have been, first the Catholic Church in its approach to the prohibition of evil literature, and second, successive governments in the limitations they imposed upon broadcasting of, and about, named subversive organizations. Censorship in its first manifestation has been shown to have been self-defeating. In its later progress, whatever socially useful function it might possibly have served was brought into disrepute by an exaggerated fearfulness that betrayed a dangerous reluctance to recognize the individual's self-responsibility. Initiated as part of that endemic puritanism that accompanies all successful patriotic revolts, tolerated during World War II as an expression of solidarity, moral censorship in the forties and fifties exemplified the old adage that those whom the gods would destroy are first driven mad. Certainly the negativism of their decisions mirrored the hopelessness and loss of sense of direction that characterized governments and people in those decades. Emancipated in the sixties concurrently with the new thinking on man's responsibility to and for himself, the Irish citizen was next confronted with the denial of information about the evolution in another part of his island. In this situation as in the previous, censorship was to prevent him from reaching a full understanding of himself and of his political environment. While the story is not complete, aberrations that inhere inevitably in the exclusion of information are beginning to parallel the experiences of moral censorship. However, the rate of change of technology has been so marked in the electronic media that the earlier prohibition is not likely to be emulated. Knowledge is accessible from sources outside the state and is transported within, by means that are not possible to control. Irish governments are not considered by media experts to be facing in the right direction. The problem, these latter believe, does not arise from the terrorists' access but from the access of multinational information industries whose messages would be infinitely more insidious and therefore more perilous than any propaganda a subversive organization might transmit. In their view, rights are valuable only so long as they can be exercised, even if exercised at risk. Rights which atrophy through confinement and disuse are least valuable in recognizing those less obvious dangers to the democratic institutions that have made the struggle to exist as an independent nation worthwhile.

APPENDIX 1

BOOKS BANNED BY THE CENSORSHIP BOARD

Year	Number of books prohibited	Number of books prohibited which were referred by Office of Revenue Commissioners	Number of books prohibited which were formal complaints	Number of books examined
1969	131	127	4	227
1970	160	160	0	314
1971	291	288	3	367
1972	300	295	5	340
1973	255	249	6	302
1974	199	191	8	266
1975	158	146	12	217
1976	138	126	12	233
1977	58	53	5	149
1978	000	000	0	000
1979	111	111	0	139
1980	74	70	4	139
1981	108	93	15	152
1982	39	31	8	48
1983	26*	18	3	33

*figures include 5 books examined on Board's own initiative

APPENDIX 2

PRESSURES ON PUBLIC LIBRARIES

Dear Librarian/Acting Librarian,

I am investigating the censorship of books, 1969–83 and wish to establish the extent to which this constitutes a problem in public libraries. It is appreciated that books banned by the Censorship Board do not pose a problem, but there may be other considerations which determine whether you can offer a book for loan to your patrons. I am interested in establishing what these considerations are and the extent to which they are effective in modifying your selection procedures. I wish to assure you that all replies will be treated in confidence and nothing other than global statistics will appear in any publication of these findings without your written permission. I append a short autobiography and have secured permission from the gentlemen mentioned below in proof of my *bona fides*.

I am, in grateful anticipation,

Yours sincerely,

Kieran Woodman

Mr. Alf MacLochlainn, Mr. T. Sharkey,
University College, Courthouse,
Galway. Galway.

(1) Name of county/city Library

(2) No. of branches (if appropriate)

(3) Size of population served (approx.)

(4) No. of books, records, maps, pictures etc. for loan of consultation (approx.)

(5) No. of all staff (in whatever capacity, responsible to the Librarian)

(6) System of selecting books (please tick)

Personal (P.)   Personal and Approved List (P. & A.)

(7) Have you withdrawn a book/periodical from distribution any time in the period as a result of pressure brought to bear on you, officially or unofficially, by (a) a minister of religion, (b) a political party, (c) A local Government representative or employee, (d) The police or other civil authority, (e) An institution, society, association, etc. (f) a private citizen; *Yes, No*
No. of times: 1–10, 11–20, 21–30, 31 plus; Reasons given by complainant: Immoral, Subversive, Advocating abortion, Other (Please specify)

[Summary of returns:
    minister of religion: 2 by 10 times; reasons: immoral 2, subversive 1;
    local government representative/employee: 2 by 10 times;
    institution, etc.: 2 by 10 times;
    private citizen: 12 by 10 times; 1 by 20 times; 5 by 30 times; 1 by 50 times.]

Data per Library Returns

	No. of Branches*	No. of Staff	Mode of Selection**	Size of Population	No. of Books	Ratio ***
Carlow	n.a.	n.a.	n.a.	n.a.	n.a.	n.a.
Cavan	12	20	P. & A.	53,855	85,086	1.58
Clare	13	40	P. & A.	86,000	155,000	1.80
Cork City	5	54	P. & A.	135,000	250,000	1.84
Cork County	35	80	P.	257,000	1,107,588	4.31
Donegal	17	23	P. & A.	125,112	90,000	0.72
Dún Laoghaire	4	21	P.	60,000	190,000	3.17
Galway	27	66	P.	171,836	293,759	1.71
Kerry	10	41	P. & A.	120,000	400,000	3.33
Kildare	18	29	P. & A.	112,000	350,000	3.13
Kilkenny	5	20	P.	70,000	130,000	1.86
Laois	7	6	P. & A.	50,000	117,000	2.34
Leitrim	9	6	P.	28,000	5,000	1.79

	No. of Bran- ches*	No. of Staff	Mode of Selec- tion**	Size of Popula- tion	No. of Books	Ratio ***
Limerick City	2	12	P. & A.	60,000	120,000	2.00
Limerick County	24	36	P.	96,000	300,000	3.13
Louth	4	20	P.	88,514	128,000	1.45
Meath	n.a.	n.a.	n.a.	n.a.	n.a.	n.a.
Mayo	12	20	P.	114,000	190,000	1.67
Monaghan	7	17	P.	51,000	112,000	2.20
Offaly	9	18	P.	58,000	150,000	2.59
Roscommon	7	15	P. & A.	54,189	·150,000	2.77
Sligo	4	14	P. & A.	55,500	125,000	2.25
Tipperary	17	35	P.	135,000	220,000	1.63
Waterford	9	19	P.	50,118	110,689	2.21
Longford-Westmeath	17	50	P. & A.	91,000	270,000	2.97
Wexford	6	18	P. & A.	99,016	280,266	2.83
Wicklow	15	9	P. & A.	64,596	163,615	2.53

*   Branches: Part-time Branches and Mobiles counted as Branch.
**   Selection: Personal and Approved List.
***   Ratio: No. of books divided by size of population.

APPENDIX 3

Guidelines

in relation to

Broadcasting Authority Act, 1960 (Section 31) order, 1978

1. On 20th January 1978, the Minister for Posts & Telegraphs made a Statutory Order (S.I. No. 10 of 1978) in the following terms:

Terms of Statutory Order of 20 January 1978

'I, Pádraig Faulkner, Minister for Posts and Telegraphs, being of the opinion that the broadcasting of any matter which is a matter of a class hereinafter specified would be likely to promote, or incite to, crime or would tend to undermine the authority of the State, in exercise of the powers conferred on me by Section 31(1) of the Broadcasting Authority Act, 1960 (No. 10 of 1960), inserted by Section 16 of the Broadcasting Authority (Amendment) Act, 1976 (No. 37 of 1976), hereby order as follows:

(i) This Order may be cited as the Broadcasting Authority Act, 1960 (Section 31) Order, 1978.

(ii) Radio Telefís Éireann is hereby directed to refrain from broadcasting any matter which is an interview, or report of an interview, with a spokesman or with spokesmen for any one or more of the following organisations, namely,

    (a) the organisation styling itself the Irish Republican Army (also the I.R.A. and Óglaigh na hÉireann),

(b) the organisation styling itself Provisional Sinn Féin,

(c) the organisation styling itself the Ulster Defence Association,

(d) any organisation which in Northern Ireland is a proscribed organisation within the meaning of Section 28 of the Act of the British Parliament entitled the Northern Ireland (Emergency Provisions) Act, 1973.

(iii) This Order shall come into force on the 20th day of January, 1978, and shall remain in force until the 19th of January, 1979.

Signed: Pádraig Faulkner'

2. Reference should be made as required to Divisional Heads for up-to-date information on organisations described in Paragraph (ii) (d) of the Statutory Order. (At the time of the issue of the Statutory Order, the organisations proscribed within the meaning of Section 28 of the Northern Ireland (Emergency Provisions) Act, 1973, were: The Irish Republican Army (Provisional and Official); Cumann na mBan, Fianna na hÉireann; Saor Éire; Ulster Volunteer Force; Ulster Freedom Fighters; Red Hand Commandoes). *Organisations proscribed in Northern Ireland*

3. RTÉ recognises that in cases where observance of the Statutory Order would involve a conflict with normal broadcasting practice, the Order will have precedence. It has, therefore, approved the following procedures for compliance with the Statutory Order. *Procedures for compliance with Statutory Order*

4. In news bulletins, the broadcasting of matter consisting of factual reportage relating to organisations de- in the Statutory Order is not prohibited by the Statutory Order. Statements from these organisations, or from a spokesman or spokesmen for them, on significant developments, including the acceptance or denial of responsibility for violence or other unlawful activity, may be reported. Appropriate use of mute films or stills to illustrate such reportage is permitted at the discretion of the Head of News, but sound recording or sound-on-film of a spokesman or spokesmen for any one or more of such organisations, or interviews or reports of interviews *Effect on news bulletins*

with such persons, is not permitted. In all matters concerning news treatment of the organisations described
in the Statutory Order, the Head of News will, where appropriate, consult with the Director-General.

5. In cases where developments are considered to necessitate the treatment in news features or current/public
affairs programmes of matter connected with any one or
more of the organisations described in the Statutory
Order, the following procedures will apply:

Matter connected with organisations described in the Statutory Order in programmes other than News bulletins

(i) before any positive step is taken in the matter, the
Divisional Head concerned must first obtain the approval of the Director-General for the proposed programme treatment, including any approach to the organisations in question, or to a spokesman or spokesmen
for such organisations, which is considered to be required by the circumstances;
(ii) The Divisional Head concerned will satisfy himself
that the matter proposed to be broadcast will not conflict
with the Statutory Order. In no circumstances will sound
recording or sound-on-film of spokesmen for organisations described in the Statutory Order, including interviews or reports of interviews with such spokesmen, be
permitted;
(iii) the approval of the Director-General must be obtained before the matter is broadcast.

6. In all cases where the above procedures entail consultation with the Director-General, his nominated representative will, in his absence, act on his behalf.

Director-General's representative

7. The above guidelines are not intended to put obstacles
in the way of RTÉ staff professionally concerned with
news and current affairs programmes maintaining normal professional contacts.

Maintenance of profes- sional news contacts

8. These guidelines are intended to assist RTÉ staff in
complying with the Statutory Order. In cases of doubt
about their particular responsibilities in the matter,
RTÉ staff must seek instructions at the appropriate level
of responsibility and comply with such instructions. The
strictest care must be taken in these matters and action
will be called for where individuals are deemed to have

Staff to seek instruction in case of doubt

disregarded the guidelines or to have been careless in observing them.

Radio Telefís Éireann

APPENDIX 4

PRESSURES ON NEWSPAPERS

Dear Editor/Acting Editor,

I am investigating the extent by which our constitutional right to freedom of expression may be curtailed. I appreciate that in the composition of the newspaper, it is necessary to bear in mind the legitimate interest of various constituencies. I also appreciate that a newspaper is a commodity that is for sale. Where attempts to interfere with the flow of news, however, fall outside the limits of commercial considerations, then the function and duty of a paper to provide for an informed citizenry is endangered. I would be grateful for your help in my attempt to establish the extent of the problem for the period 1968–1983. To that end I am enclosing a short questionnaire and an additional page for any comments you might care to make. All replies will be treated in confidence. The following editors have allowed me to use their names as guarantors of the *bona fides* of the research.

I also attach a brief curriculum vitae.

I am, in grateful anticipation,

Yours sincerely,

Kieran Woodman

Mr. Liam D. Bergin,
The Nationalist
and Leinster Times Ltd.,
Carlow.

Mr. S.V. Fahy,
The Connacht Tribune,
Market Street,
Galway.

(1) Name of Paper

_____

(2) Circulation figures available (if approximate)

_____

(3) Years in existence under current masthead

_____

(4) No. of all journalist staff (part-time and whole-time)

_____

(5) Average no. of pages per issue

_____

(6) In deciding not to print a report or feature, have you at any time in the period done so as a result of pressures brought to bear on you by (a) an individual member of the Oireachtas *or* by an official representative of a political party? (b) an elected member of, *or* an official of a local authority? (c) the police or other form of civil authority? (d) a minister of religion? (e) an institution, society, association, club, etc.? (f) a private citizen?; No. of times; Reasons given by complainant: Indecent; Subversive; Other (Please specify);
[Summary of returns:
    (a) individual member of Oireachtas *or* official party representative: 1 paper;
     1 paper; 10 times; political reasons
    (b) elected member/official of local authority: 3 papers; 10 each;
    (c) police/other civil authority: 1 paper; 10 each; criminal proceedings;
    (d) minister of religion: 1 paper; 10 times;
    (e) institution etc.: 2 papers; 10 times; quality of information both times;
    (f) private citizen: 4 papers; 10 times; court appearances.]

Name of paper	Circulation	Year of Establishment	Staff*	Average no. of Pages	Comment**
The Argus	8,000	1950	4	24	Yes
Clare Champion	n.a.				
Connacht Tribune	30,000	1909	13	24–28	Yes
Connacht Telegraph	13,000	1828	9	20	No
Donegal Democrat	18,300	1919	27	20	No
Donegal Pupils Press	n.a.				
Drogheda Independent	n.a.				
Dundalk Democrat	n.a.				
Dungarvan Leader	9,750	1938	9	8	Yes
Dungarvan Observer	n.a.				
D. Cork News	n.a.				
The Echo and S. Leinster	18,600	1902	5	24	No
Herald and W. Advertiser	n.a.				
The Kerryman	n.a.				
Kerry's Eye	8,000	1974	1	20	No
Kilkenny People	18,690	1892	8	24	Yes
Leinster Express	12,500	1831	7	40	No
Leinster Leader	12,000	1881	10	20	No
Leitrim Observer	8,000	1898	22	16	Yes
Limerick Chronicle	8,000	1766	4	20	No
Limerick Echo	14,300	1981	10	24	Yes
Longford Leader	21,000	1936	5	24	No
Mayo News	11,500	1894	24	10	Yes
Mayo Post	14,000	1971	2	10	Yes
Meath Chronicle	17,000	1897	10	20	No
Midland Tribune	n.a.				
Munster Express	n.a.				

Name of paper	Circulation	Year of Establish-ment	Staff*	Average no. of Pages	Comment**
Nationalist and Leinster Times	17,000	1883	52	32	Yes
Nationalist and Munster Adver-tiser	n.a.				
Nenagh Guardian					
Northern Stan-dard	n.a.				
People Series	35,200	1853	75	56	Yes
Roscommon Champion	n.a.				
Roscommon Herald	n.a.				
Sligo Champion	16,500	1836	10	26	No
Tipperary Star	11,500	1909	36	20	Yes
The Tullamore Tribune	5,000	1978	2	16	No
Waterford News	n.a.				
The Western People	n.a.				
The Westmeath Examiner	12,800	1882	3	16	No
Westmeath-Offaly Independent	12,500	1968	6	16	Yes

*   Staff includes part-time, correspondents, regular free-lancers.
**   Refers to interpretation of the word pressure and/or a reinforcement of the rejection of the idea of censorship which respondent thought appropriate to add.

INDEX

Asterisked references imply bibliographical details